YANKEE JACK
SAILS AGAIN

Dedicated to the ancient mariners of the Southwest
and those who have followed in their wake

Tony James

YANKEE JACK SAILS AGAIN

A sentimental journey
to the forgotten ports
of the Southwest

SEAFARER BOOKS

© Tony James 2006
Foreword © Martin Hesp 2006

Published in the UK by
Seafarer Books · 102 Redwald Road · Rendlesham · Suffolk IP12 2TE · England
www.seafarerbooks.com
ISBN-10 0-9550243-2-3
ISBN-13 978-0-9550243-2-0

A CIP record for this book is available from the British Library

Photographs as credited, otherwise © Tony James
Every effort has been made to identify copyright holders and to obtain permission for the reproduction
of all images subject to copyright, but in some cases the identity of the photographer is not known.
Any relevant and reliable information will be given due consideration by the publisher.

Project co-ordination and picture research: Vivienne Merson

Copy-editing: Hugh Brazier

Design and typesetting: Louis Mackay
Text set digitally in Proforma

Printed in China, on behalf of Compass Press Ltd,
via MBC Print Consultancy

Contents

Foreword

Like Tony James, I also once made a comprehensive tour of the West Country's harbours. Each week for an entire year I visited some port or quay to write a series of articles for my newspaper, the *Western Morning News*. And what an adventure it was – 52 havens explored, experienced and written about in a single year. However, unlike Tony, I did the landlubber thing and approached by road or footpath. The only port I ever sailed into was St Mary's in the Scillies. Exploring the rest usually meant finding space in a car-park rather than hooking onto a buoy.

For me, harbours were about the human element. They were living, breathing working places that had pasts, presents and futures. They were places with stories to tell. Tony also focuses on the human element and this book is packed full of the same sort of people I met – the harbourmasters, pilots, boatmen, trawlermen, long-liners, lobster- and crab-potters, fish dealers, filleters, fish smokers, pub landlords, café owners, museum assistants, local historians ... I sat in their wheel-houses, filleting rooms, smoke-houses and bars, and now I can meet them again in the pages of this wonderful new book.

Tony's approach is perhaps more straightforward than mine was. He experiences the West Country harbours as a sailor. He ties up to their ancient quays (and alongside their not-so-ancient supermarket car-parks), he worries about their tides and winds, he understands their whims and ways. The old havens weren't built for the future amusement of visiting journalists, they were designed for – and largely by – unromantic and hard-working mariners. To really get under the skin of a harbour, you must come to it by sea. And what a way to make a journey – in a boat he built himself, reviving the almost-forgotten tradition of the Bristol Channel flatner, named in honour of a man who knew the harbours of the Southwest when they were all busy working ports.

Tony has an instinct for identifying the key features of each place and the knack of describing them and their inhabitants succinctly and memorably. Meanwhile, his companion Wilberforce lurks in the background, always ready to remind us of more down-to-earth matters. The voyage of *Yankee Jack* is a real voyage of discovery. This is history brought to life, enhanced by the delightful photographs that accompany the text.

The difference in our methodologies has led to some interesting differences of opinion. For example, Tony often laments the passing of the good old days when these places hummed with life. I too observed that sepulchral, place-that-time-forgot side of things time and again, but I also noticed a sense of optimism cropping up on harbour-sides around the region. It had something to do with the government's intention of reducing carbon-based fuel usage by getting some of the traffic off our roads. Many people I met believed that the smaller coastal ports might yet see something of a renaissance – you can get an awful lot of lorry-loads into the hold of a ship.

Of course, the clatter of commerce will never echo again in many of the more picturesque jewels in our crown. Villages like Porlock and Polperro and lovely rivers like the Tamar and the Dart are unlikely to witness industrial shipping again. Their quay and jetties are now merely bits of interesting, but rotting, archaeology. With Tony, I share a great love of these places and would happily return to any of them again, and again. After my series on harbours I moved on to market towns, and then to Dartmoor and Exmoor – but I still miss my old salty rovings. Now, at least, I have this absorbing and remarkable book to remind me of the magical places that were once such vibrant junctions 'twixt land and sea.

Martin Hesp
Writer and broadcaster

I
Yankee Jack – the man

To see him walking along the quay
was something I'll never forget

I never met the man who inspired this book and who sent me on an unexpected voyage to a forgotten world. He was John Short, a Victorian seaman better known as Yankee Jack, who died two years before I was born. Today, in the town of his birth, the small Somerset port of Watchet, few people even know his name.

There is no memorial to our hero in the town, apart from a small plaque on his cottage and another which got his date of birth wrong and has been taken out of public view. Even his grave remains unmarked. But once John Short was the closest Watchet had to a folk legend and when he died in April 1933, at the age of 94, he was hailed as the last and most famous of all shanty-men, responsible for saving dozens of long-forgotten sea-songs from extinction. He became the first able seaman to have an obituary in *The Times*.

John 'Yankee Jack' Short outside his Watchet cottage, 1914.
© *English Folk Dance & Song Society*

Watchet is a drying harbour on the Bristol Channel six miles east of the holiday resort of Minehead. There has been a port there since Saxon times despite the sea's strenuous efforts to get rid of it. In 1724, Daniel Defoe described it as 'a place without protection from violent wind and tide', and little has changed since then. Jack's nearest rival as a Watchet legend is probably St Decuman, a Celtic monk who was supposed to have sailed across the Bristol Channel from Wales on a hurdle accompanied by a cow. On arrival he was promptly stoned and decapitated. Being a saint, he was able to replace his head after rinsing it in a nearby well. There is no record of what happened to the cow.

They called him Yankee Jack in Watchet, where everyone has a nickname, for hadn't he sailed a Yankee clipper during the American Civil War? But John Short's undoubted skill as a seaman, particularly on ketches and schooners sailing the Southwest Peninsula, was largely eclipsed by his singing. Today's standard versions of such classic sea-songs as *Rio Grande, A-Rovin, Spanish Ladies, Stormalong John* and *Shenandoa* are those which were first sung and notated in Jack's parlour over ninety years ago when the old sailor, in his mid-seventies, had come ashore for good, but still had a true voice and an uncanny memory for the songs of a fast-vanishing maritime world.

Now town crier and captain of the fire brigade, he was a still-active 75 when, in the summer of 1914, his past caught up with him in a fairy-tale manner. Two visitors called at the harbour-side cottage where Yankee Jack nursed his invalid

Cecil Sharp in 1922.
© *English Folk Dance & Song Society*

wife Annie Marie. He knew one, the parson of the nearby village of Carhampton, the Reverend Dr Allen Brockington, who told him, 'I've brought a friend who would like to hear you sing.'

The companion was Cecil Sharp, distinguished musician, friend of Vaughan Williams, Percy Grainger and Gustav Holst, and at 55, despite gout and asthma, the world's most celebrated folk-song collector, an occupation he had pursued with missionary zeal for nearly twenty years. After his first collection – of Somerset songs – he had founded the English Folk Dance and Song Society, dedicated to recording for posterity songs hitherto passed on only by word of mouth.

An appointment was made for the following week. Then, on a dozen occasions over the next five months, Yankee Jack sang over 100 shanties, patiently repeating some half-a-dozen times for the benefit of Cecil Sharp's secretary, Maud Karpeles, who painstakingly transcribed the words and music, in those distant days before tape-recording. A total of 42 subsequently appeared in Sharp's volume *English Folk-Chanteys*, including 13 never previously recorded. It was an unlikely culmination of fifty years in sailing ships, many of them as shanty-man, singing the solo parts of the work-songs which were an essential part of seamanship under sail.

Sharp, an academic intent on 'rescuing' English folk music by seeking singers 'untouched by the onrush of education', was thrilled by the old man's tenacious memory, musical ability and rich powerful voice. He was not surprised to learn that as town crier, Yankee Jack could be heard two miles across the cliffs from Watchet in the next village of Doniford on a calm day.

In her biography of Sharp, Maud Karpeles remembered the days spent in Watchet:

> John Short liked to be near the sea and so he and Cecil Sharp would sit side by side on the quay and Mr Short would sing happily through the noise of the wind and waves while Cecil smoked his pipe and jotted down the tunes. I particularly remember one song he sang was called *General Taylor* and we wrote it down as Mr Short sang it, with complicated improvisations known as melisma by folk-song collectors. Mr Short said sailors called them 'hitches' after the way ropes were tied to objects aboard ship.

The Reverend Brockington was present on the second day John Short sang for

Cecil Sharp and remembered a small but touching incident:

> We were in the parlour of the cottage and when John had finished one song, Cecil asked him about the health of his wife. The sailor led us to a bedroom where lay a sweet-faced smiling old lady, crippled and twisted with rheumatism. Cecil questioned her and she told him that John did everything for her, cleaning the house, cooking the food, carrying her downstairs from her bed, and that he was her sole attendant. I could see Cecil was moved, and when we were once more out of the lady's presence and preparing to resume singing, he said: 'Mr Short, you are a very fine singer, but your greatest achievement is in the next room.'

Yankee Jack with the Reverend Dr Allen Brockington, 1914.
© English Folk Dance & Song Society

Amid the rural sweep of Exmoor and the gentrified villages set deep in the soft plump hills, Watchet had seemed a starkly urban community when I first moved there in the mid-1980s. The streets had a gritty northern feel. It was on the sea and was reputed to be the setting for Coleridge's *Rime of the Ancient Mariner*, but it was not a holiday town.

For a thousand years, Watchet life had centred around its nine-acre drying harbour, which by the 1980s was silting up and in decline as a commercial port.

In any event it was a strange place to have a commercial harbour: coasters could only enter two hours either side of high water of the second-highest tide in the world (the highest is in the Bay of Fundy), and spent the rest of their time aground on mud-banks the consistency and colour of chocolate mousse.

Watchet was without doubt the muddiest of all Bristol Channel ports – yet once it was so clean that cricket could be played on the harbour bed. The problems started after the western pier was rebuilt of solid stone after a disastrous storm in 1900 had destroyed ten coastal ketches sheltering from the weather, and from then on the harbour became a sump for Severn mud.

Watchet harbour in the late nineteenth century.
Valentines / Somerset Studies Library

I first heard about Yankee Jack from Ben Norman, a noted figure in the town, author and publisher of the definitive *Tales of Watchet Harbour* and curator of the town museum. An avuncular figure then in his late sixties, Ben was born into a family long established in the coasting trade. He had sailed with his father, Captain Frank Norman, on his ketch *Charlotte*, and also with Captain Reuben Chichester on the sailing coasters *Bonita* and *Democrat*. In later years Ben ran a fishing boat from Watchet harbour and was a member of the Watchet Hobblers' Association, who berthed and moored ships in the harbour. He remembered, as a small boy, hearing Yankee Jack, then frail and in his nineties, singing at a local Baptist church concert, brushing aside well-meaning ladies who attempted to help him onto the stage and singing several sea-shanties in a surprisingly powerful voice.

The hobblers' watch-tower – now a holiday cottage.

I tried to find out all I could about Yankee Jack, but he seemed to have had no surviving relatives and information was sparse. From yellowed cuttings in the local newspaper library and from the archives of the National Centre for Traditional Folk Music, Dance and Song at nearby Halsway Manor, it seemed that he was born in Watchet in 1839 in a cottage a few yards from the harbour, and was fascinated by ships from childhood. His father was skipper of a coastal smack, *Richard*, and John joined him as a teenager, mainly on coal runs to and from Welsh ports. But he soon became restive with the life of a Bristol Channel 'down-homer' and yearned for blue-water adventure. The term down-homer originally meant trading in the Bristol Channel as far west as Bideford Bar. To continue further west was 'down and along', and then 'round the land' into the English Channel. It seemed that this no longer appealed to the young sailor. In 1857, at the age of eighteen, John and two other Watchet youngsters signed as deckhands on the Bristol brig *Promise*, bound for Quebec, via Cadiz.

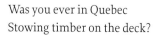

> Was you ever in Quebec
> Stowing timber on the deck?

Yankee Jack's cottage today.

Ben Norman could remember hearing the old sailor sing these lines from *Stormalong John*, recalling the tough days of the Canadian timber trade. It was the start of a deep-sea career which took John Short to every major port in the world from the South Seas to Arctic Russia.

One of his earliest ships was an old East Indiaman, the *Earl Balcarres*, running to Bombay and Karachi, but he preferred little barques and brigs like the 230-ton *Hugh Block* in which he sailed to Valparaiso, taking six weeks to beat around Cape Horn in a near-hurricane. He disliked steamships, saying they didn't produce 'real sailors', and served in only one, the *Queen of the South*, which in fact was a fully rigged three-master with a tiny steam auxiliary.

In the 1860s he earned his lasting soubriquet by serving on American ships running the Civil War blockade. One square-rigger, the *Levant*, chased by the US cruiser *Alabama*, had by some means managed to transfer to British registry by the

Some of the shanties collected from Yankee Jack by Cecil Sharp

Amsterdam

A-Roving

Banks of Sweet Dundee

Billy Riley

The Black Ball Line

Blow Away the Morning Dew

Blow Boys Come Blow Together

Blow Ye Winds of Morning

Bonny was a Warrior

The Bully Boat is Coming

Bully in the Alley

Carry him to the Burying Ground

Cheerly Man

The Dead Horse

Do Let Me Go Gels

Fire Fire!

General Taylor

Good Morning Ladies All

Handy My Girls

Hanging Johnny

Haul on the Bowline

Haul Way Joe

Heave Away My Johnny

He Back She Back

The Hog-eyed Man

Homeward Bound

Huckleberry Hunting

A Hundred Years on the Eastern Shore

I Wish I was with Nancy

Johnny Bowker

Knock a Man Down

Leave Her Johnny Leave Her

Let the Bulgine Run

Liza Lee

Lowlands

Lucy Long

Mr Tapscott

Old Stormy

One More Day

Paddy Doyle

Paddy Works on the Railway

Poor Old Man

Poor Old Reuben Ranzo

Rio Grande

Roll and Go

Roller Boller

Rosabella

Round the Corner Sally

The Sailor Likes His Bottle, Oh!

Santy Anna

Shallow Brown

Shenandoa

Sing Fare You Well

So Early in the Morning

So Handy

Spanish Ladies

Stormalong John

Sweet Nightingale

The Times are Hard and the Wages Low

Tom is Gone to Hilo

Tommy's Gone Away

Walk Him Along

The Watchet Sailor

Whip Jamboree

Whisky is My Johnnie

Won't You Go My Way

Cecil Sharp favoured the American 'chantey' spelling, but 'shanty' is more common elsewhere.

time she was eventually apprehended, but Yankee Jack, never one to become involved in international politics, remarked only that he enjoyed his time on American ships because, compared with their British counterparts, the food was so much better.

He assiduously learned new shanties from each new ship and his American service yielded such classics as *The Black Ball Line, A Hundred Years on the Eastern Shore, Huckleberry Hunting, Liza Lee* and *A Sailor Likes His Bottle, Oh!* Friends would remember that he never wrote down the words of any of the shanties he sang, relying on his total recall of songs for making sail, walking the capstan, heaving braces and laying-in halyards. He took his job seriously, once remarking that sailors coordinated by the right shanty could often do a job in half the time.

John Short had married 26-year-old Annie Marie, daughter of Captain George Wedlake, at Taunton in July 1873. They had two children, George and Alice, and eventually Annie persuaded her husband, then 51, to return to the home trade so that his growing family could see more of him. For a while he sailed with Captain Henry Pulsford of Porlock on what he derisively called 'shopping trips' from Somerset ports to Bristol, and sailed as mate on several coastal ketches and schooners for the next 20 years, serving West Country ports, complaining that it wasn't 'real sailoring' and that he missed the deep-water life.

But his skill and experience were appreciated by the 'down-homers'. Isaac Allen, master and owner of the ketch *Annie Christian* of Liverpool, in which Yankee Jack sailed as mate for two years, provided a glowing, if idiosyncratic, reference which read:

> This is to certify that John Short of Watchet, as serve as Mate on bord thee Annie Christian of Liverpool for to yeares in a honest and faithfull SeamanLike manner, one cold be trusted.

Isaac Allen's grandson, John, remembered: 'John Short was the last of the old salts to wear earrings and we were all familiar with his wonderful voice. He was a fine man, and to see him walking along the quay was something I'll never forget.'

One of his last trips on the *Annie Christian* was a winter voyage from Padstow, round Land's End to Charlestown for china clay. Gales and blizzards drove the ship off course and she narrowly escaped being driven ashore on the Lizard rocks. John Short, aged over 60, conned the ship through blinding snow and rarely left the deck.

The ketch *Annie Christian,* in a painting by marine artist Thomas Chidgey.
Watchet Market House Museum

Ashore for good at 65 after taking his discharge in 1904, Yankee Jack kept himself busy as town crier and fire brigade captain, and as one of the crew of Watchet 'hobblers'. As Watchet flourished as a commercial port, accommodating up to seventeen ships at a time, mainly handling iron ore from the nearby Brendon Hills, Yankee Jack was usually to be found in the little watch-tower on the west quay where hobblers waited for ships. It's now part of a holiday cottage.

Hobblers had for centuries been responsible for the movement and berthing of ships in Watchet Harbour. In the days of sail they rowed out to meet vessels and towed or warped them in. The boats were owned by different families and fiercely competed against each other to be first aboard and to negotiate the handling charge, known as a hobble. Sometimes there were fights between competing crews, resulting in the formation of the Hobblers' Association, which co-owned the hobble-boats and regulated fees, usually around five shillings a ship.

The job was highly sought-after, and prospective hobblers were voted on by members throwing black and white beans into a bucket. Those with the most white beans got the job. When Yankee Jack returned to Watchet and took up his hobbling duties, no one threw a black bean into his bucket. He remained a regular crewman in one of Watchet's three hobble-boats until he was almost 80. He also used his skills in decorative ropework to make sennit (flat braided cordage) doormats, and the exquisite ropework handle of his seaman's chest is today in Watchet's Market House Museum.

He was now a celebrity in the district and in great demand as a singer. Of his deep baritone voice, Cecil Sharp wrote:

> It is rich and resonant, and yet so flexible that he can execute trills, turns and graces with the delicacy and finish which would excite the envy of many a professional vocalist.
>
> Mr Short is 75 but so far as physical activity and mental alertness go he is still in the prime of life. He has the folk-singer's tenacious memory and although I am sure he does not know it, a very great musical ability of the uncultivated unconscious order. It would be difficult, I imagine, to find a more experienced exponent of the art of chantey singing and I count myself particularly fortunate in having made his acquaintance.

In 1920, Yankee Jack agreed to collaborate with folk-song authority Sir Richard Terry on a three-volume shanty collection, which included Yankee Jack's particular favourite *The Sweet Nightingale*. ' 'Tis not a sea-song, but I used to sing it aboard ship,' he told Terry. He said it reminded him of the birds which sang in the hills above his home town. It was one of the last songs he sang, a few months before his death, at 94, from what were described as 'senile changes'. In the *Times* obituary, the Reverend Brockington wrote:

St Decuman's Church, immortalised in Coleridge's *Rime of the Ancient Mariner.*

> He was a very remarkable natural musician. He always spoke with affection of Cecil Sharp, to whom he owed his reputation as a singer, though he himself thought little of reputation, and much of homely things.

Jack Hurley, editor of the local newspaper *The West Somerset Free Press*, later contributed his own eulogy in the purple prose fashionable at the time:

> The last song must be sung. On April 9 1933, he drew his last breath which filled the sails of an eternal barque which carried the prince of chanteymen over the horizon of time. They buried him at the kirk upon the hill of Coleridge's *Ancient Mariner.*

To a reading from Tennyson's *Crossing the Bar*, the man described as 'a very fine old Watchet character' was buried in the town's churchyard with a red ensign on the coffin. Exactly where still remains a mystery and there are no clues in the church register or the public records. Some seven decades later, while the 42 songs in *English Folk-Chanteys* might remain his true and lasting epitaph, another reminder of Yankee Jack was created in his home town: a little boat in Watchet harbour which bore his name.

2

Yankee Jack – the boat

No offence my boy, but I think you'd be better on the bus

In the spring of 1996, with no boat for the first time for twenty years – I had demolished my previous craft against a very large red Bristol Channel buoy a few months earlier – I decided to build a boat and name it after Yankee Jack. I had already made what seemed to be an appropriate choice: for centuries, Watchet apparently had a fleet of 19-foot double-ended flat-bottomed fishing boats known as Bristol Channel flatners, used for spratting, tending the foreshore stake-nets and even bringing small quantities of coal from Wales. They remained in the harbour until the end of the nineteenth century when, like the Ancient Mariner's albatross, they suddenly disappeared, and no flattie had been built or sailed in Watchet for nearly a hundred years.

I had only seen flatners in books and in Ben Norman's faded photographs, but that was fortuitously remedied shortly afterwards when the only remaining sailing flatner still in existence arrived in Watchet on loan from Somerset County Museum as part of a publicity campaign for a possible community-run marina in the town.

The boat was hardly what I expected. It looked like something more suited to the Nile or a north African beach. It had no keel and the hull, with its piratical sheer, was shaped like a slice of melon. It was painted duck-egg blue with red thwarts and gunwales. The inside was custard-coloured and the bottom-boards black. The square-sided oars were used with thole-pins. The rudder was six feet long and only a foot wide and the enormously long tiller reached almost amidships. I had never seen a less English-looking craft.

Built by some unknown craftsmen for use in the lower reaches of the River Parrett and in Bridgwater Bay, the flatner was discovered and restored in the 1960s by Harold Kimber, a well-known local boat-builder in the small port of Highbridge. He had sailed it to Bristol and presented it to the city museum, which off-loaded it to the Somerset County Museum, which in turn put it in store next to a horse-drawn hearse and a replica Roman sewer-pipe. They were delighted to get rid of it, albeit temporarily, as they needed the space.

Looking at the boat on its trailer, everything about it seemed deliberately perverse. The rig was a rectangular mainsail set on a sprit and an unstayed mast.

The tiny jib was set flying on a pitchfork-shaped spar tied to a ring-bolt on the stem and the mainsheet led to a horse under the helmsman's knees so that when going about the helmsman would need to lift his knees high over the mainsheet while passing the hinged tiller over his head. The Bristol Channel osteopaths must have been kept busy.

What we were looking at was basically an over-engineered dory. The bottom was dished rather than flat and made of nine-inch-wide two-inch-thick oak planks secured to the sides by massive grown-oak knees. A faded note accompanying the boat said it originally had elm sides but these had rotted and Harold Kimber replaced them with marine ply. Flatties, according to our unknown informant, might have been the ancestors of the North American dory, possibly taken as flat-pack deck cargo on Cabot's *Matthew* in 1497 to establish the Newfoundland inshore fisheries.

Shipwright Harold Kimber with his rebuilt flatner, c.1960.
Ben Norman collection

Flatners, it seemed, came in several categories. There were *river boats*, 16-foot rowing craft used largely on the muddy creeks of the Parrett to dip-net for salmon and spear eels, *withy boats*, pulled along the ditches of the Somerset levels to carry bundled willow-shoots for basket-work, *turf boats*, again used on the drainage ditches or rhynes, and *gore and bay boats*, like Harold Kimber's, which were 19-foot daggerboard sailing craft, venturing over the shoaling Gore Bank of Bridgwater Bay and racing against the competition back to the markets of Bridgwater and Burnham-on-Sea with sprats and mackerel. There were also larger Clevedon and Weston-super-Mare boats, used for fishing and trips round the bay.

We put the flatner under cover in a derelict cargo shed. She was, in museum parlance, 'stuffed and mounted', far beyond her useful life and of value only as a fishing-net-draped exhibit. She was thick with dirt and the years ashore had shrunk the timbers until there was daylight along the chine where the sides met the bottom. She was a sad old thing, but there was a jaunty elegance which interested and impressed me. The more I looked at her the more I wondered whether it was feasible to build an exact replica – the first fully operational Bristol Channel sailing flatner to be launched in Watchet for a hundred years.

As a private feasibility study I made a small model out of a cardboard box and found to my surprise that it came together almost magically as though following some unknown geometric rules: first a teardrop-shaped bottom, then matchsticks glued on both pointed ends at 35 degrees to form stem and stern posts. The top edges of the sides were straight, but as they were bent from bow to stern to fit the line of the bottom they automatically curved to form the rakish sheer of the original and fitted snugly to the stem and stern. The cardboard frames and gunwale stringers were fitted later. It was an exact reversal of normal boat-building practice,

Tony James with *Yankee Jack's* Somerset oak stem post.
© *Bruce Scott*

in which keel, frames and bulkheads came first and the outer planking came last. Building a flatner, I decided, would be more like building a wardrobe – and that was a strangely comforting thought.

I had owned and maintained several old wooden boats in the past but I was realistic enough to know that building a boat from scratch would be beyond my capabilities, never mind trying to bring an extinct species back from the dead. There were no plans, no complete specifications, and there was no one still alive who knew how to build or handle a sailing flatner. So I sat next to what was now known as Kim's boat and once more waited for serendipity to dictate what happened next. Sure enough, someone told me about Derek Vivian, a retired Rolls Royce engineer and flat-bottomed boat devotee. When I asked if he would like to become technical director of the Watchet flatner construction project, he said he would be delighted.

Derek's plans were an amalgam of the lines of Kim's boat and the detailed measurements of a derelict sailing flatner found up the River Parrett and annotated by some long-dead enthusiast. Freeboard and sail area were slightly increased but the major change was in weight. Traditional flatners were around a ton – weight was traditionally regarded as essential for bad-weather fishing in the estuary's short vicious seas – but Derek took a calculated gamble to reduce the replica to under half a ton for trailer-sailing.

The biggest weight-saver was making the sides of 9 mm exterior ply: two 10-foot × 5-foot sheets were cut in half and scarfed to make two 20-foot lengths. And instead of fitting heavy oak knees to support sides and bottom, twelve knees were laminated from 3-inch × 3/4-inch pine strips sandwiched between 9 mm ply. Trimming and fitting them to the hull was the last major construction job.

Fitting the gunwale stringers, with Derek Vivian (centre) and Graham Coggins (right).
© *Bruce Scott*

When we started work, Kim's boat, standing nearby, was an invaluable guide and reference, and a comforting reminder that what we were trying to do was actually achievable. But sometimes we began to wonder. With no sailing flatner builders around to consult, the problem of how to bend five 14-foot 1-inch × 9-inch Scandinavian red pine planks to form the dished bottom was a major headache.

Everyone told us something different, from building it in a low shed and bending the planks with props from the roof, to putting them in a cowshed and allowing the cows to lie on them, to weighting the planks with forty gallons of water and leaving them for a year. Yet another alternative was heating one side of the wood and dousing the other with cold water. Eventually we dismissed all the folk tales and made a scaffolding frame 20 feet long and 3 feet high, and built the boat on top of it, pulling down the bottom planks to the required bend with lengths of threaded ³/₈-inch studding. The flatner remained in tension on the frame until all major building was complete, although the strain was so great that it twisted the scaffolding several inches and we were frequently adjusting the studding to keep the correct bend.

Next, the floors – 3¹/₄-inch × 2-inch cross-members – were secured to the bottom timbers

Tony and Derek Vivian fit the flatner's plywood sides.
© Bruce Scott

with galvanised coach bolts hidden under wooden dowels. The shape of the bottom was marked out and roughly cut and Somerset oak stem and stern posts bolted on at 35 degrees. The two 20-foot 3-inch × 1-inch gunwale stringers, which form the top edge of the boat and provide its bold highly distinctive sheer, were carefully bent around from bow to stern with a Spanish windlass, guided by a series of plywood shadows tacked to the floors.

Fitting the port-side stringer was the most tiresome operation of the build: expensive kiln-dried lengths of Columbian pine broke three times during fitting despite being immersed for a week in a nearby stream, and made a hole in the roof. Eventually they were replaced by a piece of cheap white pine, scarfed in the middle, which bent perfectly.

Further shadows were necessary to hold the gunwale stringers in an exact curve when the plywood sides were fitted, glued and fastened with stainless

1³/₄-inch screws and bronze gripfasts. The twelve knees were then fitted, screwed and glued to the hull and attached to the sides of the floors with galvanised nails. Only when the daggerboard case, thwarts, aft bulkhead and mast step were in place were the restraining bolts removed from the jig. It was feared there would be some terrible woodworking version of brewer's droop, but in fact nothing moved when the tension came off.

Derek did most of the serious carpentry, while I did the tedious sawing and planing. The boat left its jig in spring 1997 and after sanding and finishing, both the interior and exterior were treated with high-penetration WEST System epoxy resin. The thick timber absorbed coat after coat but eventually the entire boat was encapsulated in a resin film making it impervious to water. It was then treated with an ultraviolet inhibitor and the topsides painted dark blue, with a red rubbing strake emphasising the attractive sheer.

We agreed that if we were doing the job again we would pre-bend the bottom planks by soaking and heating. The boat was under tremendous strain throughout the build and it made things a lot more difficult. We would also use cheaper timber – ordinary Scots pine protected by resin would do the job perfectly well.

The launch of *Yankee Jack*, in July 1997, was meant to be a modest affair but quickly got out of control as the shed became crowded with noisy well-wishers and passers-by attracted by the free drinks. Songs and toasts continued until the booze ran out and eventually, hours behind schedule, led by the Watchet town crier and a platoon of sea scouts, the flag-decked flatner moved erratically down the main street to the harbour. Musicians and singers had climbed into the boat, which was now being pulled by anyone who could stand up. Walking soberly behind, I wondered how long the launching trolley would bear all that weight.

As it happened, the flatner was launched uneventfully on the slipway after a blessing, inexplicably in Celtic, by the local vicar and I had my first sail later that day to discover how the boat performed in a light offshore breeze. There were no leaks and most of the rigging was in the right place, but it was a curious sensation to sail a boat you had built yourself, particularly as it behaved in an unexpected manner, sliding along the surface of the water with almost no bow-wave or wake. Close-hauled, it was hard to make it heel. A total of 54 square feet of sail may sound a bit meagre but it fitted the traditional equation of 100 square feet per

Yankee Jack's completed hull.
© *John Nash*

ton and drove the boat well. I had never sailed a boat which needed so little wind to move it.

But it still needed some, and when the wind dropped completely it soon became obvious that trying to row a half-ton boat against the world's second-highest tide was a pretty pointless exercise and that another power source would be necessary, despite any considerations of authenticity. In fact it only took a few day-trips in anything more than a force three to make me realise that in her present form the flatner was basically unsafe for serious sailing in the Bristol Channel. For a start there was no way of reefing the mainsail or even hauling it down. It was permanently lashed to the mast like an enormous flag and the only way to stop sailing was to pull the mast out of its hole in the thwart and throw it, and the sails, into the bottom of the boat. I manfully resisted fitting an outboard engine for months but finally capitulated when, after helping me row fifteen miles in a glassy calm, my partner Vivienne threatened never to set foot in the boat again unless I brought it into the twentieth century.

Both Derek and I had hoped to keep *Yankee Jack* as a virtual replica of Kim's boat but for safety's sake this was clearly unwise, and after that first season it was back to the shed for some drastic modifications, including a 3 hp Mariner outboard

Yankee Jack heads for the harbour on launch day, pushed by the Sea Scouts and led by the Town Crier.
© *Brian South*

fitted to a stainless-steel bracket on the port side of the stern. A brailing-line was fitted, as on a Thames barge, which allowed the mainsail to be furled by hauling the sprit parallel to the mast. This was simple and worked well. A vang – a line fitted to the top of the sprit – also allowed the sail to be sheeted in when close-hauled, thus stopping the head of the sail sagging to leeward.

A traditional rolling hitch on the snotter – the rope which held the sprit against the mast – tended to slip under pressure and was replaced by a line running through a small block spliced around the mast and held in place by a small wooden chock. The snotter, and other halyards, were made fast on a cleated spider-band on the mast a foot up from the thwart.

When it was found that the original solid mast had already badly cracked, a 13-foot hollow wooden mast was fitted, with stropped blocks, held by chocks, for jib and staysail halyards. Two rope running-backstays were fitted, made fast to cleats on the gunwale, mainly for psychological security but also to support the mast when on a reach in a blow.

The small jib, patterned on the original, had been found to be grossly inefficient, producing lee helm and putting the boat in irons when going about in any sea. This was replaced by a 25-square-foot jib and, in appropriate conditions, a 25-square-foot staysail, set flying from the stem-head. These would transform the flatner's performance, particularly off the wind in light airs. The jib was fitted with furling gear.

Jib and staysail sheets, which originally ran through holes in the knees and often jammed, were diverted through wooden blocks to clam-cleats in reach of the helmsman. The bowsprit-boathook was replaced by a 10-foot bowsprit running through a gammon-iron on the stem and bowsed down with a running bobstay. This was found to keep the luff of the jib much tighter and to improve windward performance. We fitted a lanyard round the tiller, attached to two cleats, so holding the tiller straight when the single-hander needed to leave the helm – thus preventing sailing round in ever-decreasing circles, a sight much enjoyed by other yachtsmen.

The mainsheet arrangement, authentic but ridiculous, was finally changed, dispensing with the horse running on the edge of the helmsman's seat and replacing it with two blocks on the central frames. These held the sail down more efficiently, and avoided the need to lift your legs over the sheet when going about. A trial sail in a brisk northerly soon showed that the changes had certainly been worth making: trimmed properly, the flatner would now sail some ten degrees higher to windward and was at least a knot faster off the wind.

On the slip, watched by well-wishers and holiday-makers.

Over the years the boat also acquired a portable VHF radio, flares, two anchors, compass and medical kit. There was general relief in the harbour that I had at last apparently come to my senses, but there was in fact another and less laudable motive for finally kitting out the boat in a seamanlike manner: why shouldn't Yankee Jack sail again? The little boat that bore his name could rediscover the Southwest Peninsula's largely forgotten commercial ports. Using chart, lead-line and compass we could recreate John Short's coasting journeys 'round the land' from the Bristol Channel to the River Exe, based on the records of the vessels in which he sailed and his few remaining personal papers. It seemed to me, from the security of my armchair, to have all the makings of a jolly good adventure.

The plan, finally formulated in the early days of 2002, was to start at Bridgwater, a port often visited by John Short, and gradually work westward down the Iron Coast of north Cornwall, where only lunatics would consider putting a port, let alone sailing into it without an engine. My companion would be Wilberforce, an enigmatic figure with whom I could share experiences and whom I could blame when things went wrong. Like popes and hounds, Wilberforce's identity might change but his name remained the same. The idea was to sail the entire way to our destinations and to visit the ports in the sequence chronicled in this book but, as events would prove, this was not always possible. As the journeys grew longer and the coasts more inhospitable we found it more sensible

Co-builder Derek Vivian supervises early sea-trials.
© Apex / Tim Cuff

to take the flatner by road at least part of the way, particularly when duplicating passages we had made before. I also didn't want to frighten myself any more than necessary and it was pretty easy to do that in an open 19-foot boat in the Bristol Channel. I thought I already knew all about that from years of sailing the estuary in small boats, but as the next few months would show, I didn't actually know the half of it.

Maybe it's worth mentioning that the Bristol Channel is one of Britain's nastiest

Tony helms while his friend Bruce Scott inspects the sails.
© Apex / Tim Cuff

Somewhat over-pressed, *Yankee Jack* passes Watchet Lighthouse.
© *Apex / Tim Cuff*

stretches of water. It lies fully exposed to every gale from west to northwest, making it a lee shore with a 3,000-mile unimpeded fetch from America. Its mouth is 50 miles wide, from Hartland Point in the south to St Ann's Head in the north, and the shores of the channel run eastwards for about 100 miles until they meet the waters of the River Severn, gathered over a length of nearly 200 miles. Not surprisingly, the convergence of sea and river can kick up vicious seas, but it is the tides up to 48 feet high which make the Bristol Channel such a challenge to sailors and which made the skippers and crews of engineless coasters such heroes.

Tides rule your life in the Severn Sea: no yacht can sail against them. You have to plan your passages in legs rather than in absolute mileage. When you are running out of a favourable stream it's time to look for a friendly harbour or for some sheltered nook in which to lay out a couple of anchors and a good scope of chain. Remember that the speed of tidal current can vary quite dramatically from that shown on a chart or in a tidal atlas. For instance, a wind that has been blowing up or down the Bristol Channel for a day or so can create a current about two per cent of the wind speed. So a 25-knot wind can generate a half-knot current, which, if parallel to a one-and-half-knot current, will cause it to run at two knots.

Bristol Channel down-homers knew all this. They also knew that inshore streams often turn around headlands some time before the main tide so you can gain an advantage by standing inshore at the end of a foul tide and offshore at the end of a fair tide. If conditions were suitable, a sailing vessel could also use the tides to its advantage by passing headlands with a fair tide and bays with a foul one. Tides also speed up in the vicinity of Bristol Channel races like Hartland, the Foreland and Trevose Head, and the wind often becomes noticeably stronger when entering a tide race, usually due to the opposition of wind and tide, which creates an increase in apparent wind.

It could take skippers years to learn the intricacies of the north coast tides. 'In fog, my dad could tell exactly where he was by the movement and smell of the sea,' said Stan Rawle, a sprightly man in his early eighties, who had coasted under sail for seven years. I visited his Minehead cottage to ask his advice about the proposed trip.

Leaving the Navy after the war, Stan had sailed with his father and uncle on the coasting ketch *Emma Louise* until she was laid up near Barnstaple in 1953, where she remains as a hulk to this day. He said he had more scares on the *Emma Louise* than during five years on the Arctic convoys. 'My dad would sail in any weather because he couldn't afford not to, and also because he knew every nook and cranny which would give him a lee and where he could anchor to ride out a storm.'

Stan said that with a few exceptions like Portishead and Ilfracombe, all Somerset, Devon and Cornwall north coast ports and harbours dried out at low water and it was essential to have a boat which would safely take the ground. He said that most of the smaller Bristol Channel smacks and ketches were specially strengthened to sit high and dry among the rocky ridges of the Somerset and north Devon coasts and discharge limestone for beach-side agricultural lime-kilns. 'The boats got knocked about something cruel and my dad would never handle limestone if he could help it,' Stan said. 'Coal was dirtier but it was easier to handle and paid better.'

'When sailing into those little rocky creeks you would drop a kedge as you went in so that you had a chance of hauling the boat out if the wind turned foul and blew up. There were about fifty places on the Somerset coast alone where you had to take the bottom to unload limestone. No one in his right mind would take a boat into any of them if he didn't need the money.'

I showed Stan a photograph of the flatner, told him how far we hoped to sail and asked him what he thought. There was a long pause while Stan stirred his tea. 'No offence, my boy,' he said finally, 'but I think you'd be better on the bus.'

———◆———

But Yankee Jack did sail again, on a sentimental journey around the forgotten and not-so-forgotten ports of the Southwest Peninsula – a series of adventures under sail that were always fascinating and occasionally alarming. This book is the record of those journeys.

3
Watchet – home port

Remains of ships were offered free
to anyone who would cart them away

When John Short was born in a cottage at the top of the slipway in March 1839 Watchet harbour was going through a period of prosperity. At one time the town had ten pubs, including one called The Sailor's Delight, and according to a contemporary report, 'The streets rang with the revelry and violence of sailors and miners when in drink.'

Watchet became a minor Klondike. It had a small but vigorous shipbuilding industry and its busy wharves saw over 500 arrivals and sailings that year. Main imports were grain, coal and timber, totalling over 10,000 tons. Exploratory work was already being done on the possibility of shipping iron ore from the nearby Brendon Hills through Watchet harbour to the ironworks of south Wales, a trade which would eventually exceed 40,000 tons a year in the 1860s, with up to 11 ships a week loading ore.

Sadly the boom didn't last. The ore was found to be of poor quality and the trade gradually died out, but Watchet remained a busy port with shipwrights,

A brig awaits the tide in Watchet harbour, 1860.
Ben Norman collection

sailmakers, ropemakers and iron and brass foundries. My office, overlooking the harbour, was once a sail-loft.

When young John joined his father's 70-ton smack *Richard* in 1852, Watchet was home port to 37 smacks, ketches and schooners, many owned by the Stoate family who owned rapidly expanding flour mills, subsequently burned down in 1911. Coasting under sail at £1 a month, which often included shovelling 50 tons of coal from the hold at the end of a voyage, soon lost its charm for young John. In 1857, soon after his eighteenth birthday, he travelled to Bristol with two friends, William Smith and Edward Chidgey, to sign as deckhands on the *Promise*. He wouldn't sail into Watchet again for another thirty years.

He was stormbound in Falmouth in the *Annie Christian* on the night of 29 December 1900, when Watchet's harbour and town were changed for ever. In the early hours of the morning, a force 10 storm and a massive spring tide over-whelmed the wooden western breakwater and ten ketches and smacks were smashed to pieces in front of hundreds of horrified onlookers.

Ben Norman describes the scene in his book *Tales of Watchet Harbour*:

Mature and tough seamen could be seen on the quay openly weeping as they helplessly watched and heard their beloved ships grinding and groaning in agony as they ripped and

A schooner dries her sails beside the wooden breakwater, *c.*1890.
Ben Norman collection

The brig *Emma Ernest* (nearest camera) in a busy harbour scene, *c.*1880.
Ben Norman collection

tore each other to pieces. These tormented vessels represented the entire life savings of the seamen and their families and were their only means of livelihood.

Of the 13 craft in port, only three, *Electric*, *Forest Deer* and *Commodore*, escaped destruction. The remnants of the once-proud fleet were put up for auction. The *Hermatite*, a once-smart 100-tonner, was sold for a mere £5 and other remains of ships were offered free to anyone who would cart them away.

Two years later work started on rebuilding the west pier of solid masonry at a cost of £16,000. No longer sluiced out twice a day, Watchet harbour became a repository for forty tons of mud a tide, and still is. Even as a modern marina the harbour has never fully solved its massive silting problems.

A steamship unloads at high tide on the east pier, *c.*1890.
Herbert Henry Hole / Ben Norman collection

Harbour trade boomed during the First World War. Welsh coal was shipped through Watchet to relieve pressure on the Severn railway tunnel and pit-props cut from Exmoor forests were carried as return cargo. Afterwards, business slumped and in 1920 the local council leased the west pier to a ship-breaker as a means of increasing revenue. The arrival of the first ship was something of a shock. At 7,000 tons the obsolete battle-cruiser HMS *Fox* was by far the biggest vessel ever to enter Watchet and could only be floated in on the largest tide of the year. It took three years to turn her into scrap-iron and the ship-breakers went out of business shortly afterwards.

One of their last victims was Ben Norman's father's ketch *Charlotte*. Her spars, keelson and deck-beams were used to build a shed for a bus company. Her stern post, left in the mud, was discovered some sixty years later during marina excavations and today is bolted to the wall of the Watchet Boat Museum.

Gradually Watchet's fortunes revived and by the early 1980s, when I arrived in the town, the docks were busier than for decades. Two or three small freighters could usually be seen unloading timber and fertiliser or taking on scrap-metal or bales of newsprint. The current prosperity was mainly due to the fact that as one of the smallest commercial ports in the country it came outside the Dock Labour Scheme regulations and so could work almost unlimited hours to turn vessels round in record time. Later the regulations would change, and that was the beginning of the port's slow but eventual demise.

Indeed, by the early 1990s, Watchet docks had become a fossil of an extinct species and they finally closed in 1993. Efforts to encourage other shipping lines to use the port came to nothing: no one carried scrap-iron, esparto-grass, bicycles, waste-paper, hen-food and skirting-boards by sea in small coasters any more.

By the mid-1990s Watchet was a ghost port. Weeds grew on the empty quays and vandals were busy dismantling the warehouse. Only a few local yachts and small fishing boats used the harbour. All dredging and

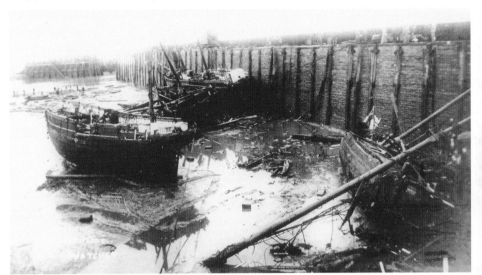

Aftermath of the great storm of 1900. A total of 10 vessels were destroyed.
Ben Norman collection

pilotage had long ceased, but until Watchet was officially stripped of its port status by Act of Parliament the harbour was required to be manned by qualified staff. The radio was silent, the phone rarely rang, and ships sailed past to other destinations.

For the next seven years controversy raged over what best to do with the harbour and its three quays. A succession of unlikely schemes, including a whelk-boiling factory and a hovercraft service to Wales, came to nothing, as did a plan to build a hotel on the quayside in the shape of a huge concrete liner. In 1994, plans for a retained-water marina with waterside housing were first suggested, followed by two years of virtual civil war in the town orchestrated by SWAMP – Stop Watchet's Appalling Marina Project – which urged that the dockland should be used for community purposes.

A public inquiry costing an estimated £300,000 finally sanctioned a £5.1 million 240-berth marina, which was opened by Sir Robin Knox-Johnston in July 2001. It was jammed with visiting boats rafted three or four deep and cheerful with flags and bunting. Watchet harbour was finally back in business. That night every pub in the town ran out of beer and fireworks made daylight of the sky.

Since then, the marina has prospered and so has Watchet. House prices have more than doubled in the past five years. Visitors come to look at the boats and the town has evolved to accommodate them. There are two museums, a fine art gallery, four restaurants and a delicatessen.

Coleridge is said to have sketched out his epic poem in the bar of Watchet's Bell Inn, and now a life-size statue of his Ancient Mariner, with crossbow and albatross, looks out over the harbour at Somerset's first marina. The Bristol Channel still delivers forty tons of mud per tide, but with the retained water no one can see it.

———◆———

Yankee Jack sailed eastwards in the spring of 2002 to investigate the derelict harbours of Highbridge and Bridgwater, the first leg of a journey which was meant to last a few months but which in the end extended to more than two years and some 250 miles. We never intended to go so far and take so long. Certainly not without a kettle or having somewhere to lie down.

Watchet marina, opened in 2001 and now a major tourist attraction.

We finally left Watchet on a grey April morning, with my friend Wilberforce as crew. He had brought his own sturdy vacuum flasks containing hot water, soup, warm Ribena and something which looked like regurgitated spinach about which I didn't inquire too closely. Wilberforce had also brought several airtight boxes of sandwiches which he made clear he had no intention of sharing. I had a Co-op carrier bag containing two tins of Coca Cola and several Mars bars, on the assumption that when and where ever we eventually arrived in civilisation there would be a café still open. This is in no way to disparage Wilberforce, who would be the first to admit that food was never far from his mind. He also sang from time to time in a loud tenor which could be distracting in difficult circumstances, but he would soon prove to be a good man in a tight corner. The sentimental journeys of *Yankee Jack* would not have been the same without him.

4
Looking for Highbridge

It was politics rather than mud that finally put an end to Highbridge Wharf

Anyone needing a sharp reminder of just how ephemeral life can be, should take a trip up the muddy River Brue in the bottom right-hand corner of Somerset's Bridgwater Bay, in search of the port of Highbridge. It simply isn't there. Or if it is I'm damned if we could find it.

Yet little more than fifty years ago a bustling maritime community built around impressive granite quays was berthing up to six ships on a tide and dispatching up to 2,000 tons of steel, coal and timber a day from its own railhead. Highbridge wharf was the main employer of the Somerset Levels town and 80 per cent of families had someone working there.

Today, the grandiose dream of a major Bristol Channel terminal for coastal and foreign trade lies beneath 20 feet of brown blancmange-like mud, or under a wasteland of weedy infill and 1960s social housing. A visitor to Highbridge, a busy little town on the A38 between Bridgwater and Bristol, would see no signs of nautical heritage. There's not even a pub called The Ship.

An unidentified schooner at Highbridge Wharf, *c.*1890.
David B Clement collection

It was, on the face of it, a funny place to have a port. The narrow deep-water Brue channel, navigable only after half-tide, contorts through 180 degrees in the mile from where it joins the River Parrett at Burnham-on-Sea, and up to Highbridge Pill. With a tidal range of 14 metres and up to a five-knot tide at springs, strandings were frequent and wrecks dotted the steep mud-banks.

Wilberforce and I saw no other shipping on our three-hour journey from Watchet, which was hardly surprising: nowadays, the wastes of Bridgwater Bay, where unmarked drying banks of sand and mud reach out five miles from low featureless shores, are something of a maritime no man's land, used little by commercial traffic and avoided by pleasure sailors in anything of an onshore blow.

A buoyed channel from the west is maintained for a few sand-boats plying the Parrett and a leading mark onto Burnham seafront is provided by a wooden lighthouse on the beach, standing on stilts like a huge white henhouse. Before that was built, in 1832, a fisherman put a candle in his window. A green starboard buoy marks the beginning of a channel which runs the full length of Burnham beach and turns sharply to port at the end of the Victorian seafront into the Brue at Pillsmouth, where *Yankee Jack* found the highly hospitable members of Burnham Yacht Club having a pig roast in the boatyard. Predictably, Wilberforce concealed two portions of pork and several sausages about his person and took them back to the laid-up cabin-cruiser on which we had been allowed to stay the night. We ate them for breakfast the next morning.

There was a metre of brackish water when we entered the Brue on the noon flood and the slimy mud rose steeply 30 feet high on either side. To add to the surreal scene, yachts and fishing boats on moorings laid in the mud-banks hung at 45 degrees above our heads. An occasional marker post or withy gave a rough indication of the channel but, with no buoyage or leading marks, bringing a laden 100-foot engineless ketch up what was, in effect, a large airless ditch must have had its interesting moments.

After navigating two shallow legs of a bend marked on nineteenth-century charts as Little Hope Reach and Great Hope Reach, we assumed we had arrived at Highbridge when the river was abruptly blocked off by two large steel doors keeping the sea out of freshwater drainage ditches. On the port side of the river from seaward, a few yachts and fishing boats lay against dried-out pontoons. A few yards of crumbling jetty, still hung with tyres, disappeared into a bramble thicket. A small mountain of mud completely blocked off any access to what had been the docks.

The ketch *Galley* in front of the Severn trow *Norah*, c.1900.
Rod Fitzhugh collection

This, it seemed, was all that remained of the port which once hoped to dominate the Bristol Channel coasting trade.

Highbridge, home of a busy brick and tile industry, had been chosen by the Somerset and Dorset (S&D) Railway for development as a maritime railhead and ferry terminal in 1854 on a dredged stretch of river leading to the sea-lock of the 14-mile Glastonbury Canal, and five years later it was a thriving port. A

The ketch *Fanny Jane* waits for the tide.
Watchet Boat Museum / Colin Wilkins collection

600-foot stone quay containing tracks for steam cranes could accommodate five or six ships and was extended in 1862, backed by sidings and two acres of goods yards. By 1880, ten companies were renting wharf space. Coal and railway lines were shipped from south Wales, and timber from the Baltic. Six ketches did little else but export fruit and vegetables to Welsh mining areas, along with cured bacon and cheese. Much of the Caerphilly cheese sold in Wales in the 1880s was made of Somerset milk shipped from Highbridge.

Despite the constant problem of silting, which exceeded twenty feet a year, Highbridge prospered. Over 20,000 tons of railway lines were imported each year from Welsh foundries by S&D ships including the ketches *Julia*, *Railway* and *Richard and Emily*. But the Bristol Channel exacted a high price: within six months the *Richard and Emily* sank during a storm off the Nash light on passage to Swansea, and the *Railway* was wrecked off Cardiff.

By the turn of the century ships were entering and leaving Highbridge on every tide. One archive photograph, shown to us by a local historian, Alan Francis, was of three white Scandinavian timber brigs and barques and half-a-dozen local colliers moored on New Wharf, discharging cargoes ranging from culm (anthracite coal-dust used for firing lime kilns) to grain, flour, timber and stone-chippings for roads and railway lines.

Trade peaked in the years up to the First World War and Highbridge never saw such permanent prosperity again. The coasting trade had been hit badly by the opening of the Severn Tunnel and cheaper road and rail traffic, while another problem was that coal was giving way to fuel-oil. Highbridge was not equipped to handle this cargo and S&D, sensing fatal decline, were unwilling to make further capital investment in a port that had little relevance to future plans.

'S&D wanted Highbridge Wharf to die,' Alan Francis said, 'but they wanted it to happen as quickly and cheaply as possible.' But, contrary to all expectations, Highbridge hung on and the Second World War saw a dramatic revival of coaster trade to relieve the hard-pressed roads and railways. Sidings were reopened and more cranes brought in to cope with a massive coal trade sometimes exceeding 1,500 tons a day.

The brigantine *Livonia* among five vessels at Highbridge, 1910.
William Sharman / David B Clement collection

The elderly workforce – Highbridge's young men were away at war – worked whenever the tides served. One night, while unloading a collier, driver Ernie Pitcher narrowly missed being drowned when his steam crane overbalanced and tumbled into the dock. Shocked but uninjured, he went home to recover – until a foreman arrived to insist that he returned to finish his shift. 'There's a ship full of coal and a war on,' he said.

But in the months after the war, when shipping declined dramatically to perhaps one coaster a week, and as the mud relentlessly encroached on the channels and wharves, Highbridge became literally high and dry. 'It was the mud that put an end to Highbridge Wharf,' Albert Buncombe, master of the harbour tug *Rexford* remembered. 'We hadn't the equipment to move it and it was too expensive to bring in dredgers now there was so little trade. It was only a matter of time, really.'

In fact it was politics rather than mud that finally put an end to Highbridge Wharf. The S&D was nationalised as British Rail and all commercial shipping was suspended in 1948 after the trading situation was assessed as hopeless. In June 1948 the Dutch timber ship *Jola* brought in Highbridge's last commercial

The steam coaster *Elemore* unloading coal, c.1910.
Rod Fitzhugh collection

Highbridge today: (above) all that remains of Highbridge Wharf, and (left) a derelict hulk among the flowers.

Yankee Jack taking a breather at the pontoon, Highbridge.

cargo. A handful of dockers stayed on for a few months, under harbourmaster Fred Wiltshire, until the wharf saw its final ship movement – Albert Buncombe's faithful tug *Rexford* was towed away for scrap.

Fred Wiltshire was 71 when he retired, having served fifty years at the wharf. In his young days he ran a team of three shunting horses. 'I stayed long after my retirement age owing to the muddle after the war and people used to say "Isn't it time you called it a day?" When I did finally go, they closed the place down a month later.'

Rail traffic from Highbridge was finally discontinued in 1964 and the entire S&D system closed in 1966. From then on disintegration was unstoppable. By the late 1980s warehouses had been demolished, wharves filled in and Highbridge Wharf had vanished under houses and roads. Arch-nostalgist Sir John Betjeman said in a TV documentary on lost railways that Highbridge Wharf had died and drifted out to sea, but more accurately, and more prosaically, it had drowned in its own mud.

It was raining when *Yankee Jack* left Highbridge and caught the first of the ebb down the Brue, on passage up the Parrett to another lost port at Bridgwater. We left nothing behind. Indeed it would not have been hard to convince ourselves that there had never been anything there at all.

5
Rough ride to Bridgwater

Hobblers, a rough and ready crew,
would fight each other for jobs

'Keep to the middle of the river but tend towards the outside of the bends,' advised the writer of the *Bristol Channel and Severn Pilot*, but goodness knows what boat he was in.

Wilberforce and I had left Burnham-on-Sea in *Yankee Jack* at half-tide for the 14-mile run up the River Parrett to Bridgwater and soon found that rudder and tiller were purely ornamental once we were in the grip of a six-knot tidal bore which carried us sideways through the flat bleak fields. We were on passage to a port that we knew wouldn't let us in. It seemed, on the face of it, a rather pointless enterprise.

With a spring tidal range of 35 feet, the 40-mile Parrett is one of Brtain's most dangerous rivers, and certainly the muddiest – it officially carries more natural silt than any other watercourse. It has drowned over a hundred people in the last century, and having claimed a victim it tends to wash the body up and down the river for weeks or even months before its final surrender.

The trow *Emma* is moored on the right in this early river scene.
David B Clement collection

Five miles up-river, off the village of Combwich, a gull perched on a weathered pole sticking at 45 degrees from the starboard-side mud. This was the topmast of the 80-ton ketch *Trio*, taking the ebb from Bridgwater in 1939 when she grounded on a mud-bank known as Pursey's Mare, capsized and was a total loss. The skipper was later blamed for hurrying seaward too late on the tide.

Some four miles on, steerage-way returned with the slackening tide as we passed the lonely quay at Dunball Wharf, destination of the occasional sand-boat. From then on we were the first technically commercial vessel on passage up the Parrett for nearly twenty years. There is no recognised buoyage. A former Bridgwater pilot, Captain Chris Muller, recalled that many skippers couldn't bear to watch their craft being piloted through the narrow mud-glistening channels, which changed with every tide. 'They usually went below to make a cup of tea and left the job to me.'

On the outskirts of Bridgwater, the river, now the colour of Mulligatawny soup, straggled through streets of drab terraces reminiscent of Burnley on a wet Wednesday. Overhead, a monolithic chimney decanted the sort of fumes one would expect from a fire in a wellington-boot factory. It soon became apparent that Bridgwater, once the major Bristol Channel port on the English shore after Bristol, servicing 4,000 ships a year, is simply not interested in boats any more.

Low tide on the river, c.1890.
Blake Museum

The Victorian docks, with its two locks, floating harbour and elegant cast-iron bascule bridge, once handling 300,000 tons of shipping a year, is now a trendy housing estate, irrevocably cut off from tidal water by a concrete wall. Mooring is prohibited on the town's riverside waterfronts, two fixed bridges prevent the passage of boats with masts, and all the town slipways have been blocked off as part of flood-prevention schemes.

We tied up where we could – to the remains of a precarious staging, part of a long-forgotten shipyard – and scrambled ashore into a supermarket car-park. As the tide flows into the town for two hours, stands for half an hour and then runs out for the next ten, our stay in Bridgwater would necessarily be brief.

Thankfully, first impressions were deceptive: surprises were all around. On the west side of the river, the eighteenth-century waterfront is largely as it was when you could take a ship from Bridgwater to Australia. The *Emanuel* left West Quay in 1578 to sail with Frobisher in his search for the Northwest Passage to China. By the eighteenth century, Bridgwater ships were trading with the United States, Canada, South America, Spain, Norway, Russia, the Baltic and the West Indies. Nine countries had vice-consuls on the West Quay.

By the 1830s, the tidal river simply couldn't cope with the volume of shipping. Bridgwater was now Somerset's leading industrial town, with five shipbuilding yards, textile factories, brickworks, glass factories and foundries. In the river's heyday as many as twelve vessels would be moored along each quay. The last sailing craft to use West Quay was probably the ill-fated *Trio* in 1934.

Over 200 ships were registered in the town, mainly smacks and schooners built for coastal traffic. Bridgwater smacks were built with full and deep lines, straight stems and square sterns. The last boat launched from a riverside shipyard was the ketch *Irene* in May 1907 from Carver's yard. A newspaper of the time reported:

> Precisely at 12 o'clock the graceful *Irene* glided into the water amid the deafening cheers of the surrounding thousands. We never saw a finer launch and not the slightest accident occurred.

Pilots and hobblers were legendary figures on the river quays. Twenty pilots, including such Bridgwater folk heroes as Warpy May and Jibo Searle, serviced the port, bringing ships from Burnham to Bridgwater for a five-shilling fee, while over 100 hobblers hauled ships with tackle from riverside bollards into vacant berths. When work was scarce, hobblers, a rough and ready crew, would fight each other for jobs.

In 1837, when the river wharves finally couldn't cope, work started on the construction of Bridgwater Docks, surrounded by stately warehouses and designed to handle ten ships at a time. At first it was feared that the five-acre dock was too big, but trade soon grew so dramatically that up to thirty vessels crammed the docks and it was often possible to walk across the decks of ships from one side of the docks to the other.

Dock trade was already declining when this photograph was taken in 1900.
Somerset Studies Library

The port was the home of nearly two dozen classic ketches, usually Bridgwater-built and sailed by local men. One, *Fanny Jane*, built by Gough in 1858, was the last vessel to sail from Bridgwater without power. She was hulked as a lighter in 1958 and burned two years later. Her fierce rival was the 76-ton *Sunshine*, built 1900 and owned for over twenty years by Captain Lewis Nurse of Bridgwater, who reportedly paid a hundred pounds for her finely carved figurehead. After being laid up during the war, *Sunshine* was sold away in 1946 and was arrested in Malta for alleged smuggling. She was last seen in Genoa in 1951 but her ultimate fate is unknown.

Sadly, the prosperity of Bridgwater docks didn't last. Having peaked at 300,000 tons in 1861, dock trade had halved by 1900, mainly due to the opening of the Severn rail tunnel, which almost overnight destroyed Bridgwater's lucrative coal trade. The docks finally closed in 1971 after Courtaulds, owners of the landmark chimney, changed from coal to fuel-oil, and dockside buildings were converted into flats. A council-funded marina scheme was launched in the late 1980s but achieved only limited success. Today, however, although the locks giving access to the river are shut, the dock flourishes as a narrow-boat haven for the Taunton–Bridgwater canal.

You must walk along West Quay and turn up from the river into Castle Street for

Muddying the waters

Mud was always a problem in Bridgwater – a spring tide could bring an inch of silt into the town's docks and river berths – and numerous methods were tried over the years to control and remove it. In 1844, Isambard Kingdom Brunel was asked to design a steam dredger for use in Bridgwater docks and produced the 45-foot *Bertha* (right), now probably the oldest operational steam-powered vessel in the world.

As *Bertha* pulled herself backwards and forwards on chains attached to the quayside, a large blade beneath the boat scraped and stirred the mud, which was then sluiced from the basin into the river. As much as half a ton of coal was consumed by *Bertha* during a working day. She was retired in 1968 when the docks closed and has since been an exhibit in several maritime museums.

Out in the River Parrett, where silting was even more severe, the Somerset Rivers Catchment Board experimented with a variety of steam dredgers, but with little success until the 50-foot *Pioneer* was hired in 1893 and worked on the Parrett for the next 23 years, despite complaints from farmers on the Somerset Levels that the steam whistle frightened their cattle.

Pioneer was followed by the dredgers and weed-cutters *Eroder*, *King Alfred* and *St Dunstan*, none of

Douglas Allen / Blake Museum

which seemed up to the job, sending the river board to look for something more revolutionary. The result was *Persevere* (below), a 47-foot hydraulic erosion dredger commissioned in 1932 at a cost of £5,550 and fitted with six high-velocity water-jets to blast away the silt on the river beds and banks. *Persevere* was always sure of an audience for her spectacular water displays.

After twenty years on the river *Persevere* was considered too expensive to run and increasingly difficult to manage in the Parrett's fast currents and narrow channels without the skilled watermen who no longer seemed available. She was sold in 1952 for £615 and eventually ended up in the port of Watchet, where she cleared silt from the freighter berths until being broken up in the 1970s. Watchet harbourmaster Vernon Stone, who worked the dredger with a colleague, Preston Ley, remembered the problems of starting the two massive Petter three-cylinder 'Atomic' diesel engines by hand. 'Operating that high-pressure hose was a really tiring job. The only good thing in the winter was that when you had a break you could sit next to those big engines and keep really warm.'

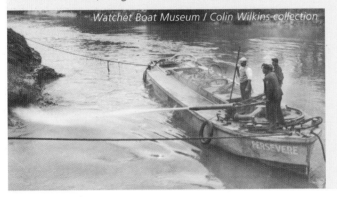
Watchet Boat Museum / Colin Wilkins collection

perhaps the richest reward for visiting Bridgwater – a tiny and totally unexpected wonderland of exquisite Georgian and Regency architecture regarded by English Heritage as perhaps the finest in the West Country. Standing guard at the top of nearby Cornhill is a statue of Bridgwater's most famous son, Robert Blake, Cromwell's favourite Admiral, who won more naval battles than Nelson. Not bad for someone who was originally in the army and scorned port and starboard in favour of left and right.

There's no memorial in Bridgwater for the town's other famous sailor, Bridgwater businessman and Liberal candidate Donald Crowhurst, who left Plymouth in his catamaran *Teignmouth Electron* in the first *Sunday Times* round-the-world

(Upper) Bridgwater Town Bridge was opened in 1795 and later replaced. *Blake Museum*

(Lower) The Town Bridge today.

race in 1969. Unable to keep up with his competitors, he spent three months aimlessly sailing the south Atlantic, sending false reports of his position. Finally, unable to accept the ignominy of discovery, he is thought to have committed suicide. The boat was later found drifting in the Sargasso Sea. 'Most people in Bridgwater felt very sorry for Donald,' said a local historian, Charles Cooper, who went to school with Crowhurst. 'We are still a sort of seagoing community.'

But not so you'd notice. Back at the car-park, *Yankee Jack* was being examined by a council official and, bizarrely, a lady traffic warden, who pointed out the remains of a Victorian 'No Mooring By Order Of The Harbour Commissioners' sign among the rusting supermarket trolleys.

It was still raining when we left soon afterwards on the first of the ebb, with a written warning about unauthorised mooring, a copy of the River Parrett bylaws, and a pretty good idea of just why the unfortunate skipper of the *Trio* had been so anxious to get away.

Up the creek at Combwich

Five miles up-river from Burnham-on-Sea, the village of Combwich (pronounced Cummidge) was a major port long before Bridgwater existed and had the only low-tide crossing on the Parrett, used by pilgrims en route to Glastonbury. The

The ketch *Woodcock* at Combwich on a calm high tide, *c.*1910. *Rod Fitzhugh collection*

causeway or 'cassy' was still being crossed by horse-drawn wagons in the early twentieth century but is now under ten feet of mud.

Today only a few moored yachts and motor-cruisers hang at about 45 degrees down the sides of a narrow steep-sided creek and Combwich Pill has a somewhat desolate air as a port of call. But for *Yankee Jack* it was a place of pilgrimage: a century earlier Combwich was the Bristol Channel's flatner stronghold. It had a fleet of 16- and 19-footers and those built on the quayside by Henry Wilkins and his sons were regarded as classics of the flatner-builder's art.

Combwich Pill was at its busiest in the 1880s. Vessels could offload coal between tides. This was faster than sailing another nine miles to Bridgwater and you could evade the harbour dues. Trade was mainly with Ireland and Wales and some thirty ketches, schooners and Severn trows regularly berthed on the long stone quay. The nearby Anchor Inn did a brisk trade, providing 'Luncheons, Teas and all classes of Refreshments.'

Regular visitors, discharging coal and loading Combwich-made bricks, included the Bridgwater-built schooner *Princess of Thule* and the ketches

Seen here at Combwich Pill, the ketch *Emily* was lost in the Bristol Channel in 1934.
Rod Fitzhugh collection

Squirrel, Woodcock, Fanny Jane, Irene, Sunshine, Sarah Jane and *Emily*. The last two came to a sad end: *Emily* capsized while bringing coal to Bridgwater, drowning the mate, and *Sarah Jane* was wrecked off Ilfracombe.

Other fine ships died more slowly and painfully in the Combwich mud. The ketch *New Design* was laid up in the Pill for years and ended her days as a hulk in Bristol, while the Bridgwater-built trow *Severn* gradually disintegrated and was finally broken up and burned.

As the shipping declined, Combwich turned to salmon-fishing, which for a while proved profitable, but eventually the fish also drifted away and by 1910 eight or ten fish was the catch for the entire season. Luckily the village's fields and hedgerows had other wild bounties: in August and September wives could earn more mushrooming and blackberrying than their husbands earned on the quay or in the brickyard. There were occasional excitements: a porpoise swam into the pill, was shot and put on show at twopence a time for the benefit of the village cricket club funds.

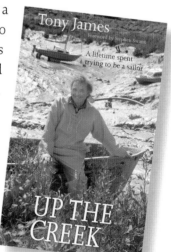

Gradually the dock silted up, warehouses were replaced by housing, and by the 1960s ships no longer came to Combwich. Twenty years later the wharf was refurbished in order to land equipment for the nearby Hinkley Point nuclear power station but now that, too, stands empty. I last visited Combwich to pose on the edge of the pill for the cover photograph of my sailing autobiography *Up The Creek*, my smile growing more fixed as I sank steadily into the mud. When the photographer finally dragged me out, it had reached my knees.

6

Bridgwater Bay – men from another age

If you fell in, nobody would find you

On the way down the Parrett and westward across Bridgwater Bay we paused to talk to men who made a living from the sea in ways which dated from medieval times, the last survivors of hard trades which were at the mercy of wind and tide. As Wilberforce observed, they must be gluttons for punishment.

Three miles from the mouth of the Parrett, on a gaunt promontory known as Black Rock, two flatners, slightly smaller than *Yankee Jack*, lay on the river bank next to a black windowless shed. They were rowing boats made of wood and adapted to carry outboard motors. They were used to dip-net for salmon and they belonged to an elderly man with a long white beard who could have been a minor prophet in the Old Testament. His name was Bob Thorne, and he was nearing eighty. Apart from war service he had worked on the river all his life.

Bob said he still occasionally used the flatners for dip-netting if he could find anyone to go with him. You needed one person to row and the other to sit in the

A salmon-butt in Bob Thorne's flatner.
© Gerald Ambler

bow with a six-foot-wide dip-net shaped like a huge catapult. Salmon were chased up-river and caught as they surfaced when their gills became blocked by mud. In the old days Bob would use both boats to do what was called pitching. This involved lashing the flatners side by side, anchoring them broadside in the river and streaming 30-foot-wide salmon nets. It could be a dangerous occupation when a big tide was running and it was wise to carry an axe to cut the anchor warps should the boats

Bob with his impressive wall of salmon-butts.
© Gerald Ambler

get into trouble. 'I'm too old for all that now,' Bob said.

Black Rock had changed dramatically since I was there a few years earlier and so had Bob Thorne's life. Then he was the last Parrett fisherman to use traditionally made salmon-butts or putchers – six-foot-long cones made of local withies and built into barriers stretching nearly halfway across the river. The banks of putchers were anchored into the rock by wooden stakes and enmeshed fish swimming down-river on the ebb in spring and summer.

Bob had taken over the butts from his father and his uncle Cecil, and when I previously saw him he was maintaining walls of 200, half his legal allowance, visiting them twice a day regardless of time and weather and complaining that there were now so few fish in the Parrett that the job was hardly worth doing. 'I can go a week without catching a salmon,' he said. 'For every one that swims up the river there were a thousand in my dad's day.'

At that time Bob was still making seventy or eighty new butts a year from withies he grew himself with such resounding names as Black Smock, Levantine, and Prince Albert. I had visited him in his cottage over the fields in the village of Pawlett which Bob had inherited from two aunts and in which he lived alone. Visitors were usually unwelcome. The house, below river level, flooded so regularly that Bob no longer bothered to furnish the ground floor, using the flag-stoned living room as a workshop in which he made his salmon-butts.

On my previous visit Bob was busy making a butt – a minor masterpiece resembling a huge wicker ice-cream cone, its main ribs held at intervals by bands of woven willow. 'A proper butt must have a shackle.' He pointed to the closely

43

woven bracelet of pencil-thin withies which formed the mouth of the trap. 'The opening of the shackle is as wide as your fist and the space between the main ribs is two fingers wide at first and three fingers further up.'

'You've got twenty withies in a butt. The ribs are two year old and all your weaving stuff is one year old. All the specifications have been passed down for centuries. When I'm finished, no one will know how to do it.' He seemed neither pleased nor saddened by the prospect. He said he had been able to make a butt for as long as he could remember. 'When I was a young boy I would see the old men doing it. They would let me have a few withies and I'd make a butt as best as I could. Before I left school I could make one as good as any man. Fifty years ago there were seven families butt-fishing for salmon on the Parrett but there's only me doing it the proper way now. If a youngster came along and wanted to learn, I wouldn't teach him. There's no future in butt-fishing for anyone.'

Bob drives in a stake with a traditional mauler. The boy, Peter Lee, is now Bridgwater's harbourmaster.
© Gerald Ambler

Now, six years later, as we stood by the river with Bob Thorne, things were different. Black Rock was bare of salmon butts and the water swirled unimpeded towards the sea. It began to rain. 'I burned them all,' Bob said. 'I took up the stakes, brought the butts ashore and burned all 200 of them on the river bank. It made a good blaze, I can tell you.'

He said that when he first took over the butts from his father, a licence for 200 had been £2. It had steadily increased over the years to £200. 'Sometimes I didn't get a fish for a month and it seemed so unfair to charge that much. I was so angry I burned them all as a protest. When they heard what I'd done, the river authority backed down and said we could have come to an arrangement, but it was too late then. I'll never make another butt and I've cut most of my willow trees down. They destroyed something which went back centuries just by being greedy.'

Bob was sitting by his flatners as we left, like a figure in a Victorian tableau, his arm slightly raised, his eyes towards the sea. A few minutes later, man and boats had faded in the rain. Like the lost port of Highbridge, it would not have been hard to believe they had never been there at all.

━━━◆━━━

A few miles westward along the coast, beyond the uninhabited sandy hump of Steart Island and in the shadow of the monolithic Hinkley Point nuclear power station, we saw another man from another age, alone on the mud-flats half a mile from the shore. He was pushing a wooden contraption somewhere between a sledge and an upturned kitchen table. He was wearing a blue woollen hat, blue shorts, a yellow raincoat and what appeared to be women's stockings cut off at the knee. His name was Brendon Sellick and he was, at that time, the world's last surviving mud-horse fisherman.

Twice a day he pushed his sledge, evolved in the Middle Ages, across the vast expanse of mud to the fishing nets, known technically as 'fixed engines', which had given his family in the tiny village of Stolford a living for over 400 years. The half-mile of nets hung like tattered banners of past victories from gaunt stakes – Brendon had been out to these nets, twice a day, for the past forty years.

He had seen the fishing decline at a heartbreaking rate. 'In my dad's day it was nothing to come back with 200 pounds of shrimps and some lovely big fish.' Brendon's day's catch was 40 pounds of fish and half a bucket of shrimps. The fish included a hake, which Brendon said was lovely cooked in the oven with a drop of vinegar and eaten with a nice bit of bread and butter.

'I've brought up seven children through the fishing. Years ago we didn't need a quarter of the nets we put out now. At one time there were eight families making a good living on the mud. Now sometimes when you go out there's nothing worth bringing home. It's so unpredictable.' He blamed the

Brendon Sellick with his mud-horse (above) and nets (left).
© *Bruce Scott*

nearby power station for sucking in millions of gallons of water every day to cool the nuclear reactors, killing marine life. 'They say the entire volume of the Bristol Channel goes through those things every seven years. I can't see anyone taking on this job after me,' he said.

The mud, capped by a sinister greenish crust, appeared completely featureless but Brendon picked his way unerringly along the hidden paths he trod daily. 'Keep behind me,' he called 'It's fifteen feet deep away from the path. If you fell in nobody would find you.' A couple of times on the forty-minute trek we paused for a breather. 'I'm the last mud-horseman in the world,' Brendon said. 'There's no better way of doing it. We bought a snow-sledge from Sweden once. Beautiful little thing, like a motorbike. It only lasted six weeks before the mud got in and ruined it. We had to go back to the sledges.'

Over the years the desolate mud-flats north of Stolford have become Brendon Sellick's natural habitat. His legs moved with the methodical rhythm of someone climbing a long staircase. He leaned over the sledge, making it skid away across the mud leaving a trail of tumbling slime which splashed him continuously at waist level, an inconvenience which seemed to go unnoticed.

Did he enjoy his work? It seemed to be a question he had never previously considered. 'It's hard and it gets harder as you get older. In the winter you can be covered in icicles but I've never done anything else since I was fourteen. I'm still fascinated by fish after all these years. I think my favourite is silver eel, done in the oven with a little drop of milk.

'We caught a seven-foot sturgeon once. The Queen's fish. We had to offer it to Buckingham Palace but they said they didn't want it. I suppose we live a primitive kind of life, but we've always managed. I think anyone taking the job would get demoralised before he became established. Most of my fish goes to regular local customers. In my dad's day it went on the train to London in trucks. How things change, eh?'

Had he ever thought of doing anything else? Once again there was a look of near-incomprehension. 'Never crossed my mind,' Brendon Sellick said. 'When you've been on the mud as long as I have, it gets in your blood.' It's nice to report a story with a happy ending. Since our visit Brendon's son and grandson have joined him in the mud. The mud-horseman of Stolford have, it seems, a future after all.

A cover-up at Lilstock

For over 50 years there was a small but busy harbour at Lilstock in a sheltered cove two miles west of Hinkley Point power station in Bridgwater Bay. Then four days after Christmas 1900, it literally vanished overnight. The force 10 storm that laid waste Watchet harbour also threw up a 30-foot-high bank of sand and stone across the entrance of Lilstock harbour, and no ship ever entered or left again. Today there is absolutely nothing on that desolate shore to suggest that there was ever

Lilstock in Victorian times.
Somerset Studies Library

maritime activity at Lilstock. Over the years the sea has rolled millions of tons of shingle over the harbour and smothered it to death.

In the 1850s a local landowner, Sir Peregrine Acland, built a road to the sea and excavated a 100-foot-long harbour on the landward side of the shingle beach, accessed by a dredged channel. There was a massive stone quay, a small warehouse, a pub, three lime-kilns and cellars cut into the cliff. The harbour could take up to five small ketches, bringing in limestone and coal and taking out cargoes of grain. Later Sir Peregrine built a stone pier to accommodate pleasure-steamers from Ilfracombe and Wales.

It was said he spent nearly £100,000 on creating Lilstock harbour, but it wasn't just trade he had in mind. When his daughter and heiress became ill and was advised to live near the sea, Sir Peregrine built her a wooden pavilion overlooking the harbour with its own drive down to the beach. The open-air life suited Felicity Acland. She recovered completely and married a local baronet. Sir Peregrine built a school in a neighbouring village as a thanks-offering, recording the event in an inscription over the door.

After his death there was a half-hearted attempt to dredge out the harbour entrance but the decline in small coastal shipping made it uneconomic and Lilstock was left to the wind and waves. In a recent book on the Somerset coast a writer observed, 'Today Lilstock is not worth finding. At the end of everything there is nothing there.' Maybe – but once, as the photograph above shows, that was not the case at all.

7

Last voyage from Minehead

My dad never went to sea again

The *Bristol Channel and Severn Pilot* didn't like Minehead much. It described it snootily as 'a rather hectic resort' containing 'a rough and tumble of rather dubious delights, over-populated during the summer and swamped periodically by nearby Butlins campers'. But it couldn't fault the harbour, cosily protected from everywhere but the northeast by high walls and wooded cliffs, and drying to clean firm sand.

Yankee Jack had scuttled down from Watchet on the ebb in little more than an hour on a sunny spring morning and was soon high and dry on a mooring we had borrowed from a friend on the inside of the western quay. Minehead has been a port since the fifteenth century and by and large it has always given satisfaction. A French traveller, calling in en route for Ireland in 1544, described the quay on which we were moored as 'the most beautiful in the channel, resisting the waves of the sea and protecting vessels against the wind'. In 1724, Daniel Defoe, on one

Included in this 1883 scene is the *Harriet Ann* of Bridgwater. The man in the centre is believed to be a customs official.
Herbert Henry Hole / David B Clement collection

of his peregrinations, also gave it unqualified approval: 'No ship is so big that it may not come in and no weather so bad but the ships are safe when they come in.'

Minehead still had a fleet of some thirty smacks, ketches and schooners when John Short returned to the coasting trade in the 1880s. The last one sailed away almost fifty years to the day before *Yankee Jack* arrived in the harbour. Indeed that was the main reason we had come.

It was in the spring of 1953 that Stan Rawle, just 30, and a survivor of the wartime Murmansk convoys, made a journey into history he would never forget. With his father and uncle, he sailed their 66-ton trading ketch *Emma Louise* out of Minehead on a journey from which the ship would never return. After twenty-five years earning her living under sail in the Bristol Channel, the postwar slump had finally succeeded in doing what wind and tide could never do: breaking *Emma Louise's* heart.

The relentless grind of the coal run – three trips a week from the Severn port of Lydney to Minehead gasworks, and back with pit-props for the Forest of Dean mines, at a parsimonious £3 a ton – had taken a heavy toll of hull and gear which paint and loving care could no longer hide.

The ketches *Destiny* and *Telegraph* unloading coal at Minehead.
Graham Haw collection

For years she had only paid her way because the crew accepted £2 a week wages and a living hard almost beyond belief. There was no money for major repairs and now a massive refit would cost thousands. Without it, the *Emma Louise* could no longer work. Her days as the last Bristol Channel sailing coaster were finally over.

Fifty years later, Stan Rawle, a sprightly 80, leaned on the sea-wall of Minehead harbour and remembered the day that he, with his father Philip and his uncle Tom, sailed *Emma Louise* out of Minehead for the last time, and the years had not lessened his regret.

'We prettied her up and everything was painted and polished, but she was seventy years old and we knew we couldn't afford the work that needed doing. The sun was out and we had a nice northeasterly, but that last run over the bar and into Appledore was the most miserable I remember. Trade had been going down since they nationalised the mines and the railways and we were the only sailing coaster still working. We brought coal from Lydney to Minehead gasworks. Then they started sending it in by rail and by lorry and at the end we were lucky to get one trip a week.

'There was just no money put by for a big refit. When he saw the survey, my father just shook his head and told us that was it. He sold her for a pittance to

Former harbourmaster Stan Rawle.

Local seamen admire the schooner *Perriton* and the smacks *John & William* and *Bessie Clarke*, 1892.
David B Clement collection

The ketch *Argo* and the smack *John & William* alongside Minehead Customs House, 1892.
Herbert Henry Hole / John Gilman collection

Captain Peter Herbert of Bude and we went home on the train. I know my father felt the loss – she had given us a living for a long time – but he never spoke of it. He was nearly 60 and it was a hard life. I think he'd had enough. He became full-time harbourmaster in Minehead and never went to sea again. He wanted to remember how it was in the old days.'

The old days had indeed been very different. Philip Rawle would recall that after the First War it was not uncommon to see up to twenty schooners and ketches windbound in Minehead harbour and the quays piled high with grain, malt, bark, timber and flour, and coal, culm and limestone from Wales. The Rawles had sailed Bristol Channel down-homers for generations. Stan's grandfather, the redoubtable Captain Tommy 'Hammer' Rawle, skippered the 50-ton ketch *Orestes*, built by David Banks in Plymouth in 1885 and owned by Minehead businessman Thomas Kent Ridler, known as 'TK'. After the *Orestes* ran ashore off Porlock and was nearly lost when she failed to rise with the tide, Hammer decided to call it a day and handed over to his twenty-year-old son Philip.

'I thought this was pretty good going, considering the reputation of this channel with its currents and big tides,' Philip would remember. 'It was still the heyday of commercial sail – smacks of 30 and 40 tons were doing local runs. Schooners and ketches of up to 100 tons were coasting everywhere, and the *Orestes* was never short of work.

'We took local bricks to Ilfracombe, Padstow and over the bar to Barnstaple and Bideford, and if we had nothing better to do in the summer we took culm to Saundersfoot and limestone from Aberthaw and built big dumps by the kilns for firing in the winter.

'When the coal trade was slack, Tom Ridler would take a holiday with us and we'd take a cargo of coal or bricks to Ireland and pick up what cargo we could for Cornwall or the Isle of Man – anywhere so that we could be away for a month or so. It made a change from the usual routine. By then lorries had killed the market runs and we were almost always carrying coal.'

In 1928, T K Ridler sold *Orestes* to an entrepreneur who fitted her out for an expedition to the Cocos Islands in the Indian Ocean in a vain search for treasure said to be buried there in the sixteenth century. She met her end in 1955 when she sank after a collision in Tanga harbour, Mombassa.

Philip Rawle, now 30, was looking for his own ship – and found her in Minehead harbour. The *Emma Louise*, a pretty 75-foot × 19-foot ketch, was the last wooden ship built by Westcott of Barnstaple in 1883. Originally a topsail schooner, she was reduced to ketch rig when an engine was installed in 1926 but still carried a topmast and jib-boom, although these were dispensed with when a more powerful Dutch engine was fitted in 1944.

'Father had been everywhere looking for a trading ketch but nothing took his fancy,' Stan Rawle said. 'Then he saw *Emma Louise* when she came into Minehead and after a lot of haggling he bought her from Alfie Watts of Braunton for £100. That was a lot of money and his brothers Tom and Bill came in as partners. When Bill went back to the deep-sea trade, Hammer Rawle, who was now herring-fishing from Minehead, bought his share, but never even came on board so far as I know. He'd had enough of coasting.'

The Rawle family's ketch *Emma Louise,* moored at the quay.
Ben Norman collection

When Stan left the Navy in 1946, he was invited to join his father and uncle on the *Emma Louise*. 'I'd had a pretty tough time. I was on Admiralty trawlers on the Murmansk convoys and later in the Middle East and North Africa. I was at the invasion of Italy. But the next seven years in the Bristol Channel were as hard as anything I experienced in the war! I was 22. Father was skipper, Tom was mate and engineer and I was everything else, including cook. Trade was beginning to fall off and soon we were doing nothing but coal and pit-props. We brought coal to Minehead and Porlock from Lydney, Sharpness, Newport, Port Talbot, Swansea and the Eley River, but eventually it dwindled down to Lydney – no one else wanted to go there because you could get five-knot tides at springs, which were faster than the boat!

'My father would sail in any weather. He knew that if we missed a load, someone else would get it and there wouldn't be any money. We would leave Minehead when she floated on the flood and would be off Lydney by the next tide. We sailed whenever we could to save fuel and it could take us ten hours to get home against a westerly. Many times we would be in sight of Minehead and be pushed back up-channel in a westerly blow, even with the engine going full throttle, and have to anchor in Barry roads until things calmed down a bit.

'As soon as we got into Minehead or Porlock we would unload the coal. She carried 102 tons and four of us shovelled her out in about seven hours. Then, if the tide served, we would be back to sea again. And all for £2 a week! But it was the natural thing to go to sea when you came from a family like ours. We were always working on the boat. If we anchored to wait for the tide, the old man would get the paint-pots out. Every penny counted and it was a crime to waste even a rope yarn. We carried no spare canvas and if a sail blew out I was sent ashore to have it mended. It was absolutely hand-to-mouth and as trade declined it got worse.

'By now, pretty all the commercial shipping had gone apart from a few herring boats and an occasional paddle-steamer. *Emma Louise* usually had the place to herself. It was like a ghost dock.'

In the summer of 1953 she went, too, and Bristol Channel working sail could be found only on postcards in the seafront shops.

Stan joined the *Mary Stewart*, a de-rigged steel 72-foot former schooner which traded briefly in the Bristol Channel in the mid-1950s. 'Bobby Parkhouse was skipper and I did three coal trips before she was laid up, and later sold to Spain. Even as a motor-boat there was nothing for her in the coasting trade.'

Stan never went coasting again. He worked for the local council and was seven years coxswain of Minehead lifeboat before becoming harbourmaster on the death of his father in 1972. By the time Stan retired in 1981 Minehead had become a purely recreational port with half-a-dozen charter angling boats and moorings for small yachts and motor-launches. The herrings, which had traditionally been

Minehead harbour today.

a major source of winter income for Minehead fishermen, inexplicably disappeared in the 1980s and have never returned.

Stan was happy to talk about the old days. Over tea in his waterfront cottage he showed us a few photographs and a small watercolour – all he had to remind him of his days on the last of the down-homers. And the *Emma Louise*? 'Captain Herbert had her for about a year and never did anything with her – there was no trade for sailing ships any more. It was said he didn't have the money to repair her and eventually the shipyard wanted her out of the way and towed her on to the mud up the Torridge with the other hulks, and that's where she stayed.

'A schoolmaster took off her figurehead and it's now in Appledore museum, along with a nice little model and a photograph of my dad. There's not much left of the old ship now. You can see her from the new bridge over the river at Bideford and she's a sorry sight. It's a pity things have to end like that. But that's what they call progress, I suppose.'

8
Through the bean-sticks to Porlock

We thought you was coming yesterday. Where ee been?

I pointed the boat at the narrow gap between two slender withies marking a dip in the shingle bank and I saw Wilberforce close his eyes. A northeasterly swell and a rising tide did the rest. Seconds later we were over the bank in a flurry of white water and into what looked like a small waterlogged village green. We had arrived unscathed, against all the advice of the *Bristol Channel and Severn Pilot*, in the harbour at Porlock Weir.

Tucked into the southwest corner of Somerset's Porlock Bay, there has been a harbour of sorts at Porlock Weir since the fifteenth century. From the shelter of the tiny drying dock, you can hear the sea breaking on the beach on the other side of the bank and there are two ancient pubs, the Ship and the Anchor. But it's sensible not to get too cosy – the sea, it seems, is not too keen on having a harbour at Porlock Weir and over the centuries has done its best to get rid of it, either by blocking

Two ketches in Porlock Weir dock in 1898, waiting to load bricks and tiles.
Herbert Henry Hole / John Gilman collection

the narrow entrance with shingle or by sweeping over the bank to create a saltwater lake which several times has threatened to engulf the village.

The good news is that it's never succeeded. For centuries Somerset's westernmost and most unlikely Bristol Channel port had a busy coastal trade, its own fleet of smacks and ketches, a boat-builder appropriately named Noah, a thriving mackerel and herring fishery and some of the tastiest oysters on our coasts. Today, Porlock Weir is a tasteful tourist destination with a dozen shoal-draught yachts anchored in the tiny pool at the entrance to the small drying dock which accommodates another thirty or so assorted fishing craft and dayboats.

The Bristol Channel pilot cutter *Breeze* lies in an apparently terminal state on the quay and the best-selling novelist Margaret Drabble has a weekend home a pebble's toss away. But if you've come looking for oysters, you'll be disappointed. Porlock Weir

Two ketches aground, beside the channel, at the turn of the twentieth century.
Graham Haw collection

Harbourmaster and oyster-catcher Preston Ley.
Ben Norman collection

was once famous for its oysters, which were dredged in the bay from tidal pools built by medieval monks. They were then 'perched' in the shallows and turned every three days. Most were sent by boat to Bristol and later by train to London – but all that remains now is Oyster Perch Cottage, and a couple of oyster-dredges hanging on a pub wall.

Porlock's oyster beds were virtually abandoned in the 1890s, and an attempt to work them in 1914 with the refitted local oyster-dredger *Laureate* ended on the outbreak of war. Another effort was made after the 1939–45 war when the then harbourmaster, Preston Ley, took a dredge off the pub wall and sailed his father's fishing boat into the bay to try his luck. Preston remembered years later, 'We had no winch on board and we had a warm time of it hauling and casting. At the end of the day we had collected about three-dozen oysters. It simply wasn't worth it.'

That Porlock was ever a viable port is a tribute to the skill of mariners prepared to sail 100-ton engineless smacks and ketches over a featureless bank and down something that for all the world looks like a country lane marked out with bean-sticks. At night, the unlit entrance was lined up with the lights of the Anchor

Hotel. Today, despite engines and electronic gubbins, you are still advised not to approach Porlock Weir at night or in even moderate north or northeast winds. The anchorage is badly exposed from these quarters and the holding is generally poor. Entry between the two tallest bean-sticks at the eastern end of the channel should not be attempted until at least one and a half hours before high water.

Porlock's last oyster-boat *Laureate* in the foreground, 1907.
Ben Norman & John Gilman collections

Typically, we came over the bank on a northeasterly, against all the rules, living to tell the tale, and finding a fascinating miniature harbour dating from 1422. Throughout its history there's been a continual struggle to keep the narrow tidal entrance clear of shingle. A sluice and lock gates were built in the nineteenth century and new lock gates were installed in the inner harbour in 1913. Lock gates are operated by chain winding gear but are usually left open and the inner harbour allowed to dry. There's a firm bottom for taking the ground and a quay to lie alongside. Occasionally the gates are closed and opened to clear the channel of shingle, but

Porlock Regatta Day before the First World War.
Dovery Manor Museum

the retained water in the pool is seldom more than about a metre.

But despite navigational problems, which meant that cargo was often offloaded over a tide from the beach, Porlock Weir prospered. In the 1900s over 100 small ketches worked the 70 miles of Somerset coast, the majority visiting the Weir with coal and taking away limestone and timber. Only local boats came in unescorted. The rest were piloted by fishermen who acted as part-time pilots and stevedores, who knew the ever-shifting shingle and could warp and kedge a 100-tonner into the tiny dock.

Regular traders included Captain John Lewis's local smack *Dolphin*, which brought coal from Welsh ports, and *Mistletoe*, a 23-ton ketch built by David Banks of Plymouth in 1890 for Captain Tom Ley, who had her specially strengthened for taking the ground on the Porlock shingle. She was later sold to Exeter and, after being fitted with a 26 hp engine, worked the small south-coast ports. Another regular arrival was the Welsh-built topmast sloop *M&E*, skippered by Walter Webber of Minehead with the help of his brother, Jesse, which brought coal weekly from the Eley River. Other cargoes included household appliances, limestone, and even a piano for a local hotel.

As recently as the 1920s, when most commercial smacks and ketches had become motor-sailers, Walter Webber insisted that *M&E* still worked by sail alone. Eventually she became uneconomic and was sold to Wales as a hulk. Today her remains lie in a creek below Haverfordwest.

The *Emma Louise*, by then the last trading ketch in the Bristol Channel, regularly brought coal to the Weir until the early 1950s, as did the *Democrat*, a Braunton-owned 70-foot auxiliary ketch built in 1909. In 1950 the *Democrat* carried her last cargo of coal to Porlock Weir. She was sold away, and lost off the French coast in 1954 on passage from Appledore to Jersey.

Tranquil Porlock Weir today.

As trading declined during the last years of the nineteenth century, the inner dock became a graveyard of derelict craft, many the property of a local farmer, John Redd, who fancied himself as a ship-broker. He bought numerous craft which did not turn out to be the bargains he had hoped and which were eventually reduced to firewood. One of Farmer John's less fortunate buys was the 40-ton ketch *Caerleon*, after local skippers said it was like trying to sail a haystack. She was eventually neaped in the inner harbour and finally burned.

Another ship which languished in the inner harbour for many years was the smack *Ranger*, 24 tons, built in 1797 and registered at Cowes. She was bought by

Farmer John for his coal business, but abandoned as being too expensive to repair. She was bought for a bargain price in 1894, by Captain Henry Pulsford of Porlock, one of the last of the epic breed of coastal skippers, who repaired her and used her in the coal trade for the next decade. *Ranger* was finally broken up in 1907. Captain Pulsford went to sea in 1851 at 16, was a skipper at 23 and a shipowner two years later. He died in 1931 at the age of 96.

As our brief foray in *Yankee Jack* soon showed, Porlock Bay is no place to be when there's north or east in the wind, making the whole stretch of shingle from Hurlstone Point to the Gore into a lee shore. Hundreds of vessels over the years have blown ashore here. For instance, in December 1906, the 40-year-old ketch *Susanna* (skipper Tom Rawle), on passage to Porlock Weir with coal from Lydney, missed the early evening tide and had anchored in Porlock Bay to await next high water when a northwesterly forced Rawle to run for the shelter of Minehead Harbour.

Missing stays outside Minehead, *Susanna* was blown onto a lee shore, miraculously escaped damage, floated off on the next tide and made the Weir 24 hours late. The harbourmaster's only comment: 'We thought you was coming yesterday. Where ee been?'

© Steve Guscott

Epic rescue

Porlock Weir was the scene of one of the most dramatic of all lifeboat launchings. On a bitter January night in 1899, the Lynmouth rowing lifeboat was called out to the sailing vessel *Forrest Hall*, in difficulties in a northwesterly gale. The lifeboat stood no chance of being launched at Lynmouth but it was thought it might be possible to get her away in the lee of Porlock Bay, over ten miles away.

It took forty men and women and twenty horses ten hours to manhandle the lifeboat across Exmoor and down the perilous 1-in-4 Porlock Hill. Hedges were dug up, ditches filled in and a cottage demolished to get the seven-foot-wide boat through the narrow lanes.

At six in the morning, the lifeboat was finally launched at Porlock Weir and stood by the *Forrest Hall* until a tug arrived. The lifeboat then escorted her across the Bristol Channel to Barry. The crew were without food or sleep for 24 hours. Four horses died as a result of their labours. They had performed a feat which, over a century later, has become a lifeboat legend. A re-enactment of the overland haul took place on 12 January 1999, the hundredth anniversary (see photograph above). A hundred Lynton and Lynmouth villagers took part, including descendants of the original lifeboat crew.

Leaving Porlock on the flood, we paused briefly off a small beach two cables east of Hurlstone Point where in February 1913 the French schooner *La Mouette*, 170 tons, built in 1869, went aground in ballast on passage from Saint-Nazaire to Cardiff for coal and was promptly neaped for three days. Two men swam ashore, climbed the cliff and walked to Porlock to telegraph for a tug from Cardiff.

William 'Fiddler' Pollard – perhaps Porlock's most illustrious son.
Dovery Manor Museum

Meanwhile, the French skipper Josef Maheo put out three anchors astern. He had heard that the tug had been delayed by fog and suspected that the ominous calm heralded a northeasterly gale.

He was right. The ship was still neaped on the third night when the storm struck, dragging her up the rocks and breaking her back before the tug could get warps aboard. A day later, when the exhausted crew were finally taken off, the locals moved in. Everything that could be removed was taken and her barometer and bell found their way into a local pub. Within months, all that remained of *La Mouette* was her stem and keel, jammed between boulders on the beach.

For the connoisseurs of the curious, Porlock Weir has a special charm. Robert Southey wrote some of his worst poetry in the bar of the Ship Inn, Coleridge messed up the ending of *Kubla Khan* after being interrupted by 'a person from Porlock', and you'll find a replica of the tatty yellow Reliant van used in the television comedy *Only Fools and Horses* parked round the back of the harbour. I don't know why.

In the village, next to rows of houses called Turkey and Gibraltar and round the corner from Beelzebub Terrace, is Oyster Perch Cottage, once the home of perhaps Porlock Weir's most illustrious son, fisherman William 'Fiddler' Pollard. He acquired the nickname after buying a violin on a trip to Ireland and teaching himself to play it well enough to perform in the local pubs. His face became known to millions in the 1920s as the old salt on packets of Wills Capstan Navy Cut tobacco. Ironically, Fiddler, who posed convincingly with his pipe on Porlock beach, was a lifelong non-smoker.

9
Disneyland in Lynmouth

*The world's most horrible port
to bring a loaded sailing ship*

No one in his right mind would ever have made a port in a cleft in a thousand-foot cliff face, with rocks on one side and heavy overfalls on the other, and certainly no one in his right mind would sail into it, particularly not in a blustery northwesterly. Wilberforce and I did, mainly, it has to be said, because Wilberforce was anxious for some chips.

The *Bristol Channel and Severn Pilot* had done its best to warn us off with 'the tricky approach is certainly not recommended to strangers', but there's something about the mere sight of Lynmouth, Devon's most easterly Severn Sea port, which seems to lure the sailor, as the Sirens tempted Odysseus. OK, the analogy's maybe a bit over the top, but Lynmouth really is an extraordinary place.

Approaching from the east, the tiny port is hidden by the gaunt 700-foot headland of Foreland Point, its lighthouse guarding the two-mile-long Foreland

Two vessels unload their cargoes by General Rawden's shower tower in the early 1890s.
Lyndale Photo Graphic Ltd

Ledge. The combination of headland, ledge and a strong ebb produced violent overfalls which kept us busy until we reached the comparative shelter of the shoaling Sand Ridge and were able to tidy up *Yankee Jack* and lay a course for the town three miles away in the middle of Lynmouth Bay.

To port, the Hollerday and Countisbury hills dropped a sheer 800 feet into the sea, claimed to be the highest cliffs in England, while to starboard, beyond the town, the Valley of the Rocks, a miniature mountain range, lay in Wagnerian grandeur. A few marker posts took us across an uneven shelf of drying rocks and boulders into the mouth of the River Lyn, in which the harbour lies. The entrance is narrow with a nasty surge and the thought of approaching it in a heavily laden engineless ketch makes you appreciate once again just what sailors these down-homers were.

An early view showing Lynmouth's dramatic backdrop.
Lyndale Photo Graphic Ltd

It's also easy to be distracted by the almost Disneyland delights which are all around. A tower, more suited to the Rhine, sits on the end of the harbour wall, built in 1850 by a retired general, George Rawden, to provide himself with seawater showers by pumping up water at high tide. Above our heads, as we tied up to a fishing boat in the small drying basin and wrung the water from our socks, the cars of Lynmouth's water-powered cliff railway rose and fell silently up the near-vertical track, connecting Lynmouth to Lynton, its sister-village, 900 feet above. It was built in 1890 and paid for by tabloid press tycoon George Newnes. It's a unique contraption and the town is very proud of it. Had Wilberforce not suffered from vertigo we would have been delighted to take a ride.

Access to the harbour is up to two hours either side of high water. There are drying moorings for around thirty small craft and fishing boats. We were the only visitor that day but there has certainly been no shortage of visitors in the past: Lynton first became a holiday destination when the Napoleonic wars prevented the rich and famous travelling to the Continent. Percy and Mary Shelley were to be seen on the harbour wall at high tide launching fleets of glass bottles containing his revolutionary poem *The Devil's Walk*. There's no record of any of them surviving the world's second-highest tide.

R D Blackmore planned his novel *Lorna Doone* in the Rising Sun pub, and

Robert Southey wrote a poem on the beach and called Lynmouth the 'most idyllic place I have seen outside of Italy'. Unfortunately it's not always like that. The truth is that Lynmouth has been constantly at war with the water since a harbour was established in the twelfth century. Nor does the peril come only from the sea: the River Lyn, swollen by Exmoor rain, has caused havoc nearly

The ketch *Nautilus* is seen in this late nineteenth century photograph showing the newly constructed cliff railway.
Ben Norman collection

a dozen times, the worst in August 1952 when 90 million gallons of floodwater roared through the village and the harbour after nine inches of rain fell in 24 hours. Thirty people died and over ten million pounds' worth of damage was caused.

Despite the hazards of trading from Lynmouth, a dozen locally owned ketches were still working the harbour up to the 1914–18 war, bringing in limestone, culm and coal and taking out pit-props and oak bark from local woods. Up to five vessels could be accommodated in the harbour, and cargoes transported to Lynton by the cliff railway. Sailing coasters worked Lynmouth until the late 1940s, including the

A harbour promenade in Edwardian Lynmouth.
Lyndale Photo Graphic Ltd

Lynmouth's foreshore below Countisbury cliffs.

Lily and the *Emma Louise*, when insurance problems and competition from the railways finally put paid to the trade.

One of the last of the down-homers to work regularly from Lynmouth was George Richards, master of the ketch *Mary*, owned by local businessman E J Pedder. Richards had skippered the *Mary* since he was eighteen and for 20 years carried cargoes of beer and flour from Bristol. Shortly before his death at 89 he remembered life in the coastal trade: 'It usually took two days from Bristol to Lynmouth, but once we did the 80 miles between daybreak on a summer's day and four in the afternoon. On the other hand, when the wind was in the west, we could be in sight of Foreland Point for a fortnight, and once we were at sea for a month between Bristol and Lynmouth!'

George eventually came ashore to go herring-fishing with his brother. His successor on the *Mary* was sacked after a month for refusing to sail on a Sunday. 'I packed in before my luck ran out,' George Richards said. 'A lot of ships were lost because of the temptation to overload them and increase the profit on each sailing. In the Bristol Channel the weather can change so fast.'

A typical tragedy befell the 60-ton ketch *Topsy*, loaded with coal from Newport, which foundered off Lynmouth in an autumn gale in 1910. According to the *North Devon Journal*,

> She was seen rolling heavily off the harbour under bare poles when she suddenly sank without any hope of assistance. The crew of four all died and their families have been thrown into distress and are in great poverty. A subscription has been started to aid the widows and orphans and much sympathy is felt.

A few months later another of E J Pedder's fleet, the ketch *Three Sisters*, went aground in heavy swell in the entrance to Lynmouth harbour, loaded with coal from Lydney. Once again the *North Devon Journal* reported:

The harbour today.

> The vessel was in danger of breaking up and Mr Pedder with the coastguards rowed out to the stranded vessel. Recognising the hopelessness of any effort to refloat the ketch until the cargo had been discharged, Mr Pedder set men to work to make a cart road over the ridge and borrowed carts from local farmers. Within a few hours a large portion of the cargo had been brought ashore and the owner had the satisfaction of refloating the vessel on the next tide, evoking much applause from a crowd of residents and visitors.

Three Sisters was undamaged and sailed for Wales on the next tide. She was lost in the English Channel in 1921.

Northeasterlies were the winds Lynmouth down-homers feared, usually in December to February, when gales could set in for days and drive huge seas into the river mouth. Typical of these was the gale of January 1891, when the pilot cutter *Cambria* was lost off Lynmouth. A local newspaper reported:

> George Dibden and John Union, crew of the *Cambria*, had put their pilot aboard a steamer when the wind, which had been blowing hard from the northeast, increased to hurricane force. All the cutter's sails carried away and she became unmanageable. They drifted in the Channel all night in a blinding snowstorm. The following morning, finding they were drifting on to rocks near Lynmouth, they abandoned the boat and took to their punt in the hope of safely running ashore. One of the oars broke, the punt was swamped and the men thrown into the breakers. Dibden managed to save himself but Union would almost certainly have been drowned had not Captain Philip Burgess, of the ketch *Nautilus* of Lynmouth, plunged into the foaming surf.

It was the second time Philip Burgess had saved a life – the previous year he had leapt into the sea to save a crewman swept overboard during a gale off the Foreland.

The following year, Lynmouth saw yet another epic rescue, witnessed by a retired clergyman, the Reverend W H Thornton, who wrote an account of the saga:

> I was sitting in my room one stormy morning when I was told there was a wreck in the bay. My heart grew sick within me as I saw a small vessel come round the rocks from the westward. She was the *Superb*, a 50-ton ketch registered in Gloucester on passage from

The tower today.

Barnstaple to Bristol. Early in the morning she encountered a heavy sea which carried away her masts and left her drifting at the mercy of a westerly gale. When I saw her she was about two miles off, her masts broken off short and four human beings lashed to their stumps.

The great tangle of spars and rigging hanging over the side was causing her to lean over to leeward. A strong sea was running with the current and the helpless craft was heading straight for the North Foreland. No one could doubt that the ship and crew were doomed – Lynmouth at that time had no lifeboat and the sea was too rough to launch a dinghy.

The coastguard, Lieutenant John Hodges, was in bed with a fever but he insisted on getting up and dressing smartly. He called for eight volunteers and stepped into the heaviest broad-bottomed boat they could find. The men showed no sign of excitement. If they were to risk their lives they meant to do it with as little civility as possible in the manner of true-born Englishmen! There was no kissing of wives, hugging of children or shaking hands with friends.

I shall never forget how the boat looked when the first wave hit her as she left the shelter of the pier. She stood up like a horse and I thought she was gone and all nine with her. But she righted herself and the men pulled strong. Presently they reached the wreck which was now less than half a mile off the Foreland rocks, and managed to rescue two men, a woman, a boy and a shaggy dog. All were barely alive, but survived when taken back to the safety of Lynmouth.

Another salvage crew went out to the *Superb* and anchored her – the sea was beginning to subside. Later she was sailed to Porlock under jury rig and beached. She was to have another ten years of life as a Bristol Channel collier. Lieutenant Hodges took off his wet clothes and went back to bed to finish his fever comfortably. Dear old fellow. He was living a year or two ago and, for my part, I could wish him immortal.

George Richards, whose father was in the rescue boat, always maintained the drama typified the spirit of the place he always called 'the world's most horrible port to bring a loaded sailing ship. In Lynmouth we always put others first in those days,' he said. 'I always think that rescue would have made a lovely poem – if anyone could have poemed it.'

10
Ilfracombe – in search of herrings

Corky had a donkey named Tintack

Ghosting along amid the cat's-paws of a gentle southwesterly breeze, *Yankee Jack* skirted the green conical buoy of Copperas Rock. Turning southwest to round Widmouth Head and Rillage Point, there was Ilfracombe, barely two miles ahead, its chapel, on a high rock, silhouetted in the last of a rosy summer sunset.

The magic of the moment wasn't lost on Wilberforce. 'Let's get in and have cod and chips,' he said. 'That smell is driving me mad.' We later learned that there are 31 establishments in the Devon harbour town of Ilfracombe producing fish and chips in various forms, and all of them seemed busy that night as the scent of frying drifted on the breeze across the darkening water.

'You can have cod if you like,' I said, hardening up the mainsail for the last leg into harbour. 'It's a nice Ilfracombe herring for me.' It seemed a logical choice:

The inner harbour, 1880s. The ketch (left) is *Jane*, in front of the schooner *Albion*.
Ilfracombe Museum

Ilfracombe's pretty harbour a century ago.
David B Clement collection

Ilfracombe was once the herring capital of the Bristol Channel. The only problem, as it turned out, was that I was about 75 years too late.

Despite modern maritime research, the movement of herrings – still warmly spoken of in Devon as 'silver darlings' – remains largely a mystery. One theory is that they swim down from the Arctic, encircle the British Isles, spawn and return to whence they came. But over the years, someone seems to have forgotten to pass on details of this route to the herring. Today, while Scottish fleets still report record catches, the silver darlings give the Bristol Channel an increasingly wide berth.

As late as 1925, 'herring trains' left Ilfracombe with boxes of up to 200,000 prime fish aboard and several dozen Ilfracombe boats made a good living in summer and autumn drift-netting for herring down the coast as far west as Hartland Point. Over a pint in the harbourside Ship and Pilot, one of Ilfracombe's 28 pubs, charter boatman Jim Harding remembered his father Alf telling stories of bringing in boatloads of herring during a particularly spectacular glut in the early 1920s and having to give most of them away.

'They counted herring in casts – three herring to a cast and 104 casts to a meaze. All the boats were coming home full to the gunwales and everyone in Ilfracombe was sick to death of herring. Soon my dad was selling them for less than ten shillings a meaze to hawkers, known as dowsters, who took them round the villages, but eventually they didn't want any more, and one night my dad had to throw 100 meaze of herring onto the quay at Ilfracombe and give them away. Some went for salting or smoking and the gulls took the rest.

Jan 'Corky' Bushen (2nd left) with fellow dowsters and his donkey Tintack, 1920.
Ilfracombe Museum

'Herrings were part of life when I was a lad. We had them boiled in milk or baked in vinegar in the oven. My dad swapped them for fruit and veg and even for petrol for his boat. Sometimes the town crier would ring his bell when a herring boat came in and people would rush down to the quay to buy the big ones. The dowsters would have the rest. Men like Ernie Ralph, Bill Irwin, Corky Bushen and Jan Conibear were very well known in the district with their donkey carts. Corky had a donkey named Tintack. They're all long gone and so are the herring.

'Even ten years ago it was worth taking a drift-net out between October and Christmas, but now it's a waste of time. You won't find a commercial herring-drifter in the Bristol Channel. They give all sorts of reasons – over-fishing, pollution, and the water warming up – but the fact is that the herring have gone and you won't find a local fish in this town for your supper.'

The inner harbour c.1880s. On the right is the ketch *Kate,* which sank off Lundy Island in 1896.
Ilfracombe Museum

And sadly, so it proved. In the busy harbour area, with restaurants and pubs catering for every taste from classic English, Mexican tapas, Caribbean, French, Italian, Indian and Chinese, not an Ilfracombe herring could be found. The posh new restaurant on the Quay, owned by the controversial artist Damien Hirst, could offer a side dish of herrings pickled in sherry vinegar (not formaldehyde), but no one seemed sure of its provenance.

Happily, the bustling resort, its 11,000 population doubled in high season, offered many consolations, including a friendly yacht club, an award-winning theatre, and an obliging harbourmaster who settled us in a cosy corner of the inner harbour.

Indeed, Ilfracombe's harbour is its jewel – the deep rockbound inlet, naturally secure from virtually anything but a northeast gale, is perhaps the safest and most accessible haven on the Severn Sea's south shore and the only one in which a trading ketch or schooner could anchor at half-ebb. The six-acre inner harbour is protected from the east by a fifteenth-century stone breakwater. It dries to a firm sandy bottom, and can be entered two or three hours either side of high water depending on draught.

The outer harbour can be entered at any state of the tide and there is a minimum depth of 1.8 metres off Promenade Pier. Anchor fore and aft, if staying overnight, and prepare for a bumpy ride if there's any north in the wind. Remember, too, that this is still the Bristol Channel: tidal streams can reach three and a half knots off the entrance at springs and there may be overfalls, especially on the ebb.

But usually both harbours are a snug refuge – Lantern Hill has given the harbour protection ever since Ilfracombe became a port of embarkation for Irish-bound troops in the thirteenth century, breaking the force of the winter gales which sometimes sweep over the fourteenth-century chapel of St Nicholas, patron saint of sailors, on the hilltop. The chapel has had a varied career as a laundry, café, a church of various denominations and home for a family of thirteen. Today a tourist centre, it has a fixed red navigation light, an improvement on the oil-lamps and candles of the past.

No wonder Ilfracombe was for centuries a popular and busy port. In 1810, 122 vessels totalling nearly 7,000 tons were registered there, and although the port lost its registration in 1840 – in future all vessels were registered in Barnstaple – it continued to thrive for another half-century.

Ilfracombe has long had a reputation for producing fine sailors. Nelson said of Captain Richard Bowen, who served with him during the attack on Santa Cruz, 'A more enterprising, able and gallant officer does not grace his Majesty's navy.' And many Ilfracombe sailors migrated to south Wales to join Swansea copper-ore barques and square-riggers in the coal trade. By the 1850s nearly 1,000 ketches and schooners were trading with Ilfracombe, as well as dozens of fishing smacks and sloops shipping coal and limestone. More than twenty Bristol Channel pilot cutters from Bristol, Newport, Cardiff and Barry regularly used Ilfracombe for victualling and repairs.

Two paddle steamers arrive with tourists, c.1890.
North Devon Maritime Trust

The last years of the nineteenth century were boom times for maritime Ilfracombe. There was a flourishing timber trade with Scandinavia. Limestone shipped in from Wales was discharged onto the beach. Cattle from Ireland, supervised by officials known as 'tide-waiters', were hoisted overboard from the outer harbour to swim ashore. But things didn't always go quite according to plan. In 1893, the *North Devon Journal* reported:

> When 20 wild bulls ran ashore up the beach this week, local people locked their doors. But regretfully one elderly lady died on the spot after hearing bellowing at her door.

The last vessel entitled to use Ilfracombe as her port of registry was the smack *Little Western*, which foundered in the Thames estuary in 1878. She was owned by 29 people in the town. By the 1890s the coal trade from Barry, Cardiff and Swansea had reached its peak with at least one ship a day discharging on Ilfracombe's south wharf. The fleet of a dozen local colliers included the ketches *Florence*, *Snowflake* and *Cicelia*. Built in Jersey in 1867, *Cicelia* was one of the last sailing vessels in the Newfoundland salt-fish trade, making at least ten Atlantic voyages a year. She switched to coastal trading after the First World War and was bought by Fred Bennett of Ilfracombe and his son Arthur in 1922. *Cicelia* was still in Ilfracombe ownership when in 1935 she dragged her anchors in a storm off St Ives and was wrecked on Penolver Rocks.

Another locally owned favourite was the ketch *Kate*, which sank off Lundy in heavy seas in 1896 after having discharged her cargo of building materials for the construction of Lundy island church. The last sailing ketch to trade from Ilfracombe was the *Mary Stewart*, built of iron in Montrose in 1876 and working out of Ilfracombe for 30 years. In 1944 she went ashore at Amroth, south Wales, in a storm but was recovered and repaired. *Mary Stewart* traded out of Minehead until 1958. She was laid up for some years and finally converted into a yacht in 1963.

Ilfracombe harbour today.

But while Ilfracombe has always been regarded as a safe haven, the same can hardly be said for the surrounding coast. To the west is Baggy Point, where great slabs of sandstone rise 200 feet out of the sea, and the sombrely-named Morte Bay, graveyard of over 200 vessels in the last two centuries. In 1844 alone, fifteen vessels came to grief in sight of Lantern Hill during a northwesterly storm. One was the 148-ton brig *Frances* of Whitehaven, blown into the Bristol Channel on passage from Honduras to London, which ran ashore on the rocks at Marlhoe Bay, to the west of the town. *The Illustrated London News* reported:

> The brig is laden with a cargo of mahogany and dyewood and is so much embedded among the rocks that in all probability ere long she will all go to pieces. At about midnight on Wednesday last, about 200 wreckers of a most desperate character made their appearance on the beach to plunder the wreck.
>
> However their motives being communicated to Lt. John Coleman, the chief officer at Ilfracombe coastguard station, he met them with his small party of men and drove them back, but not before they had a severe conflict in which the wreckers got the worst of it. The vessel is reported to be fully insured. All hands were saved.

As maritime trade declined, Ilfracombe found other ways of profiting from the sea. A late Victorian resort, aspiring to become the Brighton of the southwest, sprang up amid the fishermen's cottages. There was even a song, *Dear Old Ilfracombe by the Sea*, published in 1900 in the hope of encouraging visitors. It seems to have worked: Ilfracombe's famous residents have included Beatrix Potter, Peter Sellers, Henry Williamson, Joan Collins and Olympic gold medallist Jonathan Edwards.

But the herring have gone elsewhere, and to Wilberforce it was no great loss. 'I've gone off the idea of fish and chips,' he announced. 'Do you fancy a Chinese take-away?'

II
Sharpshooters at Bideford

What do you know about boats in a thing like that?

To anyone with childhood memories of reading Kingsley's historical romance *Westward Ho!* there's magic in the name of Bideford, where Amyas Leigh and Salvation Yeo trod the cobbles 'under its soft Italian sky'. For Wilberforce, however, it will always be the place where someone shot him with an airgun.

We had planned to sail from Ilfracombe to Barnstaple Bay, through the buoyed channel across Bideford Bar and into the wide estuary of the Taw and Torridge rivers and from there to the historic ports of Appledore and Bideford a few miles upstream. Then the plan was to drop the mast, pass under the 24-arch Long Bridge at Bideford after a spot of lunch, sail or row six miles up the narrow and largely deserted river Torridge to Great Torrington, another forgotten port, and return on the ebb in time for tea. Inevitably, it didn't work out quite like that.

The shallow and shifting Bideford Bar, at the mouth of the Torridge, where *Westward Ho!* sands meet those of Saunton, has kept the Appledore lifeboat busy

Busy nautical scene at Appledore Quay, 1923.
© *Francis Frith collection*

for the past 180 years rescuing over 500 souls from the violence of its winds and waves in heavy offshore weather. We didn't care to be added to that number, and consequently when a force six northwesterly was forecast, we chickened out, put *Yankee Jack* on its trailer in Ilfracombe and launched it on the calm water of the Appledore Quay slipway little more than an hour later.

Appledore is only a village but it remained a major sailing-ship port until after the Second World War. Today, while its wide windswept quays accommodate the occasional coaster, the seafaring heart seems largely to have gone out of the place, and the cottages in the tiny cobbled alleys are now neat retirement homes. There have been quays at the point where the

The *Emma Louise* (centre) at Appledore Regatta, c.1920. *Stan Rawle collection*

Taw and Torridge meet since the fourteenth century, and Appledore became a free port at the time of the Armada and remains so. In the nineteenth century you could take ship from Appledore to Canada and its six yards were claimed to be the best in Britain for building and repairing sailing coasters. The Appledore furling gear, of blessed memory, precursor of modern boom roller reefing, was invented here around 1900.

Walk away from the river up the hill to the top of the village and you will find that not everyone has forgotten Appledore's nautical past. North Devon Maritime Museum, housed in a fine double-fronted Georgian building with a figurehead on the portico, has a vast collection of models, memorabilia, pictures, photographs and documentation going back to the ninth century, and a very helpful voluntary staff who are delighted to share their treasures. Without the photographs and information gathered during a delightful afternoon delving into the Appledore archives, this book would have been much the poorer.

To the south of the port once stood a tall tower known as Chanter's Folly, named after a Bideford merchant who built the tower in 1800 to catch the first sight of the arrival of his ships. The story goes that when Chanter kept the first watch after the tower was completed he saw his son's ship wrecked on Bideford Bar and the entire crew drowned. He never set foot in the tower again. It became dangerous and was finally demolished in 1952.

There were herons and curlews watching from the estuary sandbanks as we rolled *Yankee Jack* down the Appledore slipway on the first of the flood, joining a fat man in a red coat who was shouting at a woman, presumably his wife, who was limply holding the painter of a twelve-foot plywood cabin-cruiser. The boat, painted an unpleasant grapefruit yellow, had apparently slipped from its launching trolley, been speared by a rusty bedstead and suffered what appeared to be terminal injuries.

When Wilberforce offered to help, the man told him to mind his own business. 'What do you know about boats in a thing like that?' he shouted at the flatner, now floating happily in four inches of water. 'The lifeboat will be out to you in a minute, I shouldn't wonder. Bloody death trap.' As we rowed in silence from the

slipway and turned south towards Bideford, some three miles distant, Wilberforce was obviously brooding on the incident. 'I shouldn't have let him get away with that,' he said. 'I should have said something really clever.' It wasn't until we rowed under the tall concrete bridge that carried the north Devon link road over the Torridge that Wilberforce regained much of his good humour.

Appledore Quay from the south, *c.*1890.
North Devon Maritime Trust

Bideford's seafaring days are also largely over, and when we stopped for lunch *Yankee Jack* had the ornate Town Quay to itself. Yet, at one time, more tobacco was imported through Bideford than anywhere else in the UK and nearly thirty customs officers were needed to handle revenue business. After the Second World War, the increased size of ships brought about a decline in Bideford's status as a port but over 50,000 tons of coal, timber, cement and gravel were still being discharged there in 1951 – and even today there's talk of a deep-water terminal in the estuary to handle container traffic.

Today Bideford seems to have turned away from the river, seeking its prosperity from inland, and it's hard to appreciate just what an important port it once was.

In the seventeenth century there was prosperous trade with America, Spain, France and Italy and more ships sailed from Bideford than any other port apart from London and Topsham on the Exe. The Elizabethan sea hero Sir Richard Grenville, who fought and sank fifteen Spanish ships with his solitary frigate *Revenge*, and died gloriously in the process, brought a Native American to Bideford in 1588 and christened him Raleigh after his cousin Sir Walter. Sadly, although he was treated with what was described as 'great kindness and civility', the visitor died within a year.

A ketch moored at Bideford Quay, 1907.
© Francis Frith collection

We lunched too long in Bideford, mainly because Wilberforce insisted on the crab salad that was on the menu, which meant that the café proprietor had to go out and buy or borrow a crab. As a result we had less than two hours of flood tide and reaching Great Torrington was out of the question. We would go as far as we could up the Torridge until the tide turned.

Bideford's Long Bridge, built in 1460 and spanning 677 feet of the river, has been called the most beautiful in the kingdom – and it is certainly one of the most hazardous for navigation. The tide sluices through the narrow arches, but until the 1920s large rowing lighters, as well as gravel and limestone barges which could lower their masts, regularly made the uncertain journey up-river through the bridge.

The bridge at Bideford today.

That afternoon, as Wilberforce rowed cautiously through the centre arch, we encountered a more bizarre hazard. As we emerged into the sunlight, *Yankee Jack* was showered with airgun pellets. Two found their way into Wilberforce's fortunately thick woolly jumper and I later found one in my hat. We shouted and waved our fists and the artillery fire, which appeared to come from bushes on the starboard side, stopped as abruptly as it had started. We never discovered why we had been attacked or by whom. As far as I knew, Wilberforce hadn't upset anyone since we left Appledore.

We reached Halfpenny Bridge at Weare Gifford some three miles up river from Bideford. There were still stacks of limestone on the foreshore, discharged by barges for some long-extinct lime-kiln. Alongside the river runs the Tarka Trail, in memory of Henry Williamson, author of *Tarka the Otter*, who had lived nearby.

At Halfpenny Bridge we went ashore for ice-cream before coasting back to Bideford on the ebb, where we found Steve Clarke standing on the quay. He's the man behind the epic five-year restoration of the town's most treasured nautical heirloom, the 200-ton three-masted tops'l schooner *Kathleen & May*, the last UK vessel to trade under sail and now fully rigged and resplendent in black and gold on Clarence Wharf on the opposite river bank. 'She looks great, doesn't she?' Steve said. 'I've lost count of the times when I thought we'd never do it. When we found her, she was dead in the water.'

The *Kathleen & May* at Appledore – still trading under sail in the 1960s.
Peter Loughlin / Kathleen & May *Trust*

The story of the *Kathleen & May*

The *Kathleen & May* was built in north Wales in 1900 and for thirty years worked out of Bideford, owned and skippered by the legendary Tommy Jewell, until she was finally laid up against Appledore Quay in 1960, facing an uncertain and increasingly gloomy future. Later she was acquired by the government-funded Maritime Trust, which spent nearly £2 million over the next decade turning her into a floating museum before the money ran out and a succession of private owners drove her onto the rocks of bankruptcy.

In 1996 the *Kathleen & May* was towed into Gloucester docks and largely forgotten, until Steve Clarke, then 48 and proprietor of a plant-hire company, walked by the sheeted hulk. A flapping tarpaulin at the stern revealed the name: *Kathleen & May*, Bideford – Steve Clarke's home town.

Steve Clarke, mastermind of the restoration project.
© *John Nash*

'I didn't know what she was and had absolutely no interest in boats or the sea, but I saw she was from Bideford and had this feeling she should go back there as a centrepiece of the regeneration of the town. I decided then and there to make an offer and to get funding to restore her and take her back home. If I had thought about it, I wouldn't have done it. From that moment the *Kathleen & May* took over my life.'

Next, Steve persuaded Appledore boat-builder Alan Hinks, creator of replicas of the *Golden Hinde* and the *Nonsuch*, to survey the boat. 'I told him that so long as he promised not to take her to sea but restore her as a static exhibit, I'd come on board as consultant,' Alan told us. 'But it wasn't long before Steve moved the goalposts and decided to restore her to seagoing condition, which has more than doubled the cost.'

On the strength of promised grants of £350,000, the *Kathleen & May* Preservation Trust took possession of the schooner in February 1999, sheathed the hull in one-inch ply, and towed her down the Bristol Channel. But the triumphant return to Bideford lost some of its sparkle on finding that all the funding had fallen through. 'So here we were with a boat and no money,' Steve Clarke remembered.

The *Kathleen & May* during her refit.
Clare Kendal / Kathleen & May *Trust*

'I had no alternative but to put £100,000 from my business into the venture to keep things going while we looked for more finance.' Some money came from the Irish port of Youghal, where the schooner had been a regular visitor for twenty years, but massive grants were still needed. But at least the *Kathleen & May* was back home – 37 years after Tommy Jewell sailed away with a cargo of coal. A few months later he had sold her for £4,000.

Built by Ferguson and Baird on the Dee in north Wales in 1900, she was bought by the Jewell family of Appledore for £700 and stayed in their ownership for the rest of her working life, mainly in the coal and china clay trade between West Country ports and Ireland. After Tommy Jewell could no longer make a living with her, the schooner changed hands almost yearly until 1970, when the Maritime Trust came on the scene, bought her for £8,500, and moved her to Plymouth for a refit scheduled to cost £25,000 and take six months.

Even after the Trust had spent its £2 million the *Kathleen & May* was still not in seaworthy condition, and she needed a massive rebuild which would include half the double oak frames, the entire 800 cubic feet of three-inch topside planking and the elegant semi-elliptical stern replaced in 35 tons of prime oak. And that was only a start. Still on Steve's shopping list was 3,000 feet of decking, a 500 hp diesel, 4,000 square feet of sails and complete replacement of masts, spars and standing and running rigging. His enthusiasm was infectious. Local people came forward

Becalmed but graceful –
the fully restored *Kathleen
& May*.
Steve Clarke / Kathleen & May *Trust*

to help financially and to give a hand. Clarence Wharf, onto which the schooner was craned, was rented for a nominal £1.

Several of the half-dozen shipwrights gave up their own businesses to work on the project. One skilled chippie, a habitual speeder, given 200 hours of community service after his last conviction, was allowed to serve it on the *Kathleen & May*. The schooner's maiden voyage in restored condition was to Youghal in August 2001. The town proclaimed it a public holiday.

It was nearly three years after this triumph when we saw the *Kathleen & May* in Bideford, but her future was still by no means certain, in spite of a refit costing more than £1 million and a busy schedule of corporate entertainment, filming, port visits and media promotions. With operating costs at around £1,000 a day, including interest on outstanding loans, and no substantial public funding yet forthcoming, the schooner needed to work to survive.

Captain Tommy Jewell died in 1985 but his daughter Hester Ryan, who had often sailed with her father as a schoolgirl and who still lived in Appledore, was certain that the story of the old ship's return would eventually have a happy ending. 'It's wonderful to see her back again,' she said. 'I know my dad would have been so pleased.'

We had stayed too long in Bideford. The ebb was in its last hour and the mud up to our knees as we hauled *Yankee Jack* onto the bottom of the slipway ... to find the car clamped and a demand for an extra parking fee for the trailer. Wilberforce thanked me for an eventful and interesting day.

I2
Vertically challenged at Clovelly

Iron walls of rock amid a howling waste of spray

At the time, we had no intention of going ashore at Clovelly, and that would have suited Wilberforce just fine. He apparently had childhood memories of being bitten by one of the donkeys which in those days took tourists up the village's near-perpendicular main street, and had no wish to repeat the experience. He also didn't fancy walking up that hill.

Yankee Jack was anchored in the southwest corner of Barnstaple Bay on a shiny summer's morning waiting for the tide to take us down-channel, but there was Clovelly, a mere couple of cables away, hanging down a cliff like a string of pearls on a dowager's green blouse. There was a tiny sandstone quay, and a pub and fishing boats drawn up the beach. It was the first chapter of *Treasure Island* come to life and surely Jim Hawkins, Squire Trelawney, Blind Pew and the Black Spot could not be far away? It was too good to miss. 'We can anchor off the beach and have a quick look,' I told Wilberforce. 'Stop sulking and I'll buy you a pint. And keep away from the donkeys.'

Clovelly luggers drying their sails *c.*1880.
North Devon Maritime Trust

Clovelly is unreal. It's a private fishing village of about 100 cottages which some lunatic built on a vertiginous slope about 600 years ago, and no one has been allowed to change it since. About 500 people live there, spending their lives at 40 degrees and hiding from the half-a-million or so tourists who visit the place every year. Every house is immaculate and appears to be empty. Clovelly is north Devon's *Marie Celeste.* No wheeled vehicles are allowed on the tiny cobbled street. Groceries and other essentials are slid up and down the cobbles on sledges shaped like enormous tea-trays. The donkeys help out when they can, but mostly they stay at the top of the village having their photographs taken.

By wading ashore we got into Clovelly for nothing, but if you come by road you will have to attend a visitor centre and hand over four pounds to the Clovelly Estate Company, run by the family which has owned the village since the Norman conquest. This cheered Wilberforce up a bit but he still remained very doubtful about the wisdom of visiting Clovelly.

Of course, the place was real once. It was a fishing village whose inhabitants knew poverty and hardship. After all, this is north Devon's Iron Coast, where prevailing westerlies can turn a millpond into ten-foot waves in the time it takes to smoke a cigarette. Clovelly was once a busy fishing port famed for its herring and mackerel. Charles Kingsley wrote *Westward Ho!* while living in the village, and a waterfall on the beach gave him the idea for *The Water Babies*.

Once, the tiny harbour with its quay and Red Lion pub was the only safe haven between Appledore and Boscastle but scarcely anyone but fishermen, farmers and the crews of limestone ketches knew of the place – until Charles Kingsley, whose father was rector of Clovelly, moved there in 1855 and immortalised it in *Westward Ho!* Half the characters in the novel lie in Clovelly churchyard. The Iron Coast hasn't changed much since Kingsley described it as 'darkened with the grey columns of the waterspouts stalking across the waves before a northern gale towards the iron walls of rock amid a howling waste of spray.'

Picarooners and longboomers beached in the quaint harbour, c.1890.
© Francis Frith collection

Kingsley took Clovelly to his heart. For six years he spent every moment that he could in the village and then after an absence of thirteen years returned and wrote to his wife, 'I cannot believe my eyes: the same place, the pavement, the dear old smells, the dear old handsome loving faces again.' Kingsley's father also loved the village, writing to a friend, 'The street is so narrow that if you lean out of your bedroom window you can grasp the hand of your neighbour on the other side of the street.' The Reverend Kingsley was a popular figure who had apparently impressed the locals as 'a man who feared no danger and could steer a boat, hoist and lower a sail, shoot a herring net and haul a seine as one of themselves'.

Clovelly may be partially sheltered from the prevailing westerlies but even so onshore winds can raise a swell, so always approach the harbour, idyllic though it may look, with caution. There is a useful anchorage a little east-southeast of the harbour entrance which can be a good place to wait for sufficient rise of tide. An approach is best made from the northeast near high water: over the years a steep pebble ridge has built across from the shore side of the harbour, restricting safe access to boats of about 4.5 feet draught. The deepest water lies close to the pier-head. In calm settled weather yachts can dry out on the firm sandy mud alongside the inner wall of the pier. The harbourmaster, who runs one of the pleasure boats, will help with any problems.

An unknown smack leaves the quay in light airs, c.1885.
G S Reilly / David B Clement collection

The unchanging face of Clovelly owes much of its existence to the Cary family, who inherited it in 1370 and have never allowed any houses to be sold, or any alteration or development. It is a village in aspic, and maybe none the worse for that. For centuries before tourists appeared, Clovelly was a self-sufficient fishing port, its sandstone quay curving out in an eastwards-bending semicircle to protect a fishing fleet which in good times numbered more than a hundred.

The harbour empties at low tide and vessels are stranded, or as the local term goes, 'sewed' – no problem for the 'stone boats', limestone-carrying ketches like *Mary*, *Thomasina* and *Express*, specially built to take the ground, and which until the 1930s brought Welsh limestone into Clovelly from Caldy Island and Aberthaw. Kiln fires were started with wood and overlaid with layers of limestone and culm (coal-dust), brought from Newport. This was largely a winter occupation – boys roasted potatoes on the fires and fishermen were glad to warm their backs when the wind was in the east.

But fishing was Clovelly's main livelihood, carried out by a unique fleet of drifters and trawlers, known as picarooners and longboomers. The name picarooner appears to be derived from picaroon (Spanish *picarón*), a sea-robber, and the boats, mainly built around the corner at Appledore, were seaworthy 15- to 16-footers reaching their final evolution around 1870. A picarooner had a deep keel and wide waterways surrounding a small well, and was rigged with a dipping lug forward and a standing lug on the small mizzen with bumkin and outrigger. They were shallower than the older local boats and so able to enter harbour earlier on the tide.

Clovelly longboomers, of which none survive, were heavy carvel-built decked smacks. Early versions had a curving stem and broad cutaway forefoot with a tapering narrow gutted stern and pronounced tumblehome producing a heart-shaped transom. Similar features are found on Galway hookers. Later cutters adopted a straight stem and square forefoot with a fuller deckline and broader transom. They were around 30 feet in length and, unusually for British trawlers, worked their beam trawls over the starboard side.

For centuries, herrings were the lifeblood of Clovelly, and during the season catches were unloaded on the quay and counted in a curious manner – somewhat

Herring boats landing their catch in the 1930s.
Paul Ashton Ellis / Sheila Ellis collection

different from Ilfracombe. Three fish were picked up at a time and thrown into a large round basket to constitute a cast. Forty casts made up a 'long hundred' and ten more casts, plus one more for luck, made a tally. There were four tallies to a meaze, pronounced mayze, believed to be of Norse origin. Try working all this out at the checkout in Tesco.

It wasn't unknown for a Clovelly boat to bring nine thousand herrings ashore after a single trip. They were the staple food of the Barnstaple Bay area until the early twentieth century, when they could often be bought for a penny each. The hook for the scales still hangs on Clovelly quay. In 1900, more than fifty Clovelly picarooners and longboomers fished daily, usually for herring, and wives and daughters would be on the beach to help 'shake the nets'.

Herrings were poured into baskets known as mawns and taken on sledges up the village street to waiting carts which took the fish to Bideford to catch the Billingsgate fish trains. Cod was caught in winter and the main summer catches, apart from herring, were turbot, sole, plaice, gurnard and mackerel. In 1850, when fishing reached a peak, the harbourmaster recorded a total of 72 boats in Clovelly: 'Six large boats, 50 small boats and 16 boats employed in the taking of large fish. God has been pleased to send us his blessing of a great fishery among us.'

But the price of herrings was often tragically high. In 1821, 60 Clovelly boats were caught in an unexpected autumn storm in Barnstaple Bay, drowning 31 village fishermen. Over 20 boats never returned. When another storm drowned

The harbour today at low tide.

Boats on outhauls from waterside cottages.

21 Clovelly men and wrecked 14 boats five years later, Charles Kingsley's father comforted the sorrowing relatives and held services on the beach for survivors.

Nor were the worst gales confined to winter: on a summer's day in 1736 a sudden storm whipped up thirty-foot waves which engulfed the picarooner of Charlie Lyall as he fished a few yards from the beach. As his wife Kate watched from her cottage window, Charlie was drowned before her eyes. Demented with grief, she was known as Crazy Kate for the rest of her life. Crazy Kate's Cottage remains a few yards from the beach.

From Elizabethan days Clovelly had lived on herring fishing, but by 1880 the season had shortened to only two months a year and the village increasingly relied on tourism, with notices announcing 'hot water for tea' appearing in many cottage windows. By 1895, Clovelly boasted three hotels and many lodging houses, and tourists landed in their hundreds from steamers from Bristol, Barry, Tenby and Ilfracombe.

Fishing had all but stopped by the 1970s when there was yet another dramatic decline in herring. The last man to remember the golden days of boats laden to the gunwales with silver darlings was Oscar Abbott, who died in 1976 aged 88. While still a schoolboy, Oscar would leave school after lessons, join his father's boat, fish with him all night and be at school at nine the following morning. He remembered that he would fall asleep during lessons, and even as he was playing with his pals in the school yard. His wife claimed that he fell asleep during their wedding ceremony after walking up the hill to the church.

Such stories only confirmed Wilberforce's belief that the heights of Clovelly could wreak havoc on heart, lungs and shoe-leather, and he stayed stubbornly at sea level in the bar of the Red Lion until it was time to leave.

13
Faint hearts at Hartland

Behind us lay Lundy, sitting in the water
like a half-submerged crocodile

To the tune of *The Red Flag*, Wilberforce sang in an unpleasant tenor, 'From Pendeen Head to Hartland Light, A drowning coast by day or night.' As Hartland Light was approaching on the port bow and the glass had been dropping all morning, I felt they were sentiments we could well do without, particularly as it was at least the tenth rendering since we had left Clovelly little more than an hour earlier.

We were bound for Hartland Quay, or at least what's left of it, which isn't much – and that was a sobering thought, too. Hartland Point, a grim promontory, complete with lighthouse and coastguard station, marks the southwest frontier of the Bristol Channel. A vicious shoaling race stretching two miles offshore runs past the point at over four knots at springs. No wonder a nearby gaunt outcrop is known as Tense Rocks.

Hartland Quay in 1878 – today hardly a stone remains.
Hartland Quay Museum

This is the Iron Coast – massive cliffs rising straight from the sea and battered by Atlantic storms generating waves recorded as up to 80 feet high. Anyone wanting to build a port in such a frightening and precarious place must have been out of his mind. But a couple of miles round the corner, dead south of Hartland Point, that's exactly what someone did. By the late eighteenth century, Hartland Quay was a busy port with a fleet of trading sloops, a thriving fishing industry and even its own privately printed banknotes.

If it was madness to build a port on this Atlantic lee-shore with its crashing waves and merciless reefs, the courage and tenacity of the men who brought their engineless ships into Hartland Quay was even more extraordinary. Not that they all lived to benefit from their bravery. Over a hundred vessels sank in the Hartland area in the nineteenth century and over a dozen have been lost since the last war despite modern navigational aids.

The original idea was to anchor *Yankee Jack* briefly under the khaki-coloured cliffs at slack water in Quay Pool behind the remains of the breakwater, have a quick drink at the pub, walk round the tiny museum, allow Wilberforce to buy some liquorice allsorts at the shop, and scurry off to Bude before anything awful happened. But by lunch-time, with the wind rising from the northwest and no clear passage apparent through the rocks, we chickened out. Behind us lay Lundy, sitting in the water like a half-submerged crocodile, and in front were the iron-bound ribs of the Warren headland. It was

The schooner *Mary Barrow*, with a cargo of coal from Swansea, beached at Hartland in 1908.
Hartland Quay Museum

no place for heroics in a 20-foot open boat. 'We'll make for Bude while there's still water in the harbour,' I told Wilberforce. 'And if you sing that song again I'll throw you over the side.'

There had been a harbour of sorts at Hartland since the Middle Ages but not until the sixteenth century was any sort of quay built in an attempt to give protection from the prevailing westerlies – an astonishingly ambitious project involving a 40-foot-wide base of huge stones, floated into place with scores of empty barrels and bound together with iron staples set in lead. Many of these stones still lie where the harbour once was.

The quay, some 40 feet high, threw a protective arm around the shipping that was soon regularly calling at Hartland bringing in lead, coal, building materials and lime for the area's meagre soil. Fishing flourished, too: nets were strung across the harbour mouth and up to a thousand mullet could be caught on one tide.

In 1790 a visitor to the quay found 'an excellent inn, over a dozen decent cot-tages, lime kilns, maltings and a commodious little pier where fishermen and coasters find good shelter'. The first of the fleet of sturdy Hartland traders was the sloop *Blessing* (32 tons) owned by Thomas Hockin, who rented the harbour in 1789. The Hockin family soon had a considerable fleet of smacks and sloops, mostly around 50 feet. They included the *Susanna*, built in Appledore in 1860 and lengthened by 10 feet to 62 feet to increase cargoes of limestone and coal.

Hartland in 1814, in an aquatint by the artist William Daniel.
Hartland Quay Museum

When business was slack the Hockins sent *Susanna* coasting the length of the Bristol Channel in search of work, but her home harbour was by far her most perilous port of call. Moored in Quay Pool during a storm, she reared and rolled so violently that she was expected to smash herself to pieces before morning. In fact *Susanna* not only survived, but outlived the harbour itself. Said to have brought the first cargo of guano ever landed in England into Hartland Quay, *Susanna* was eventually re-rigged as a ketch and worked until she was broken up in 1924.

Hockin's son Frank carried on the tradition by buying the new Clovelly-built sloop *Dasher* and the smacks *Sprightly*, *Roebuck*, *John* and *Speedwell*. The *Stucley*, a long-term mainstay of the Hartland fleet, ended her days in Ireland as a scrap-metal barge as late as 1929. But there were continual casualties: in five years, the Hockins lost four ships – the *John*, the *Rose*, the *Mary* and the *Edward and Ann*. The *Edward*

Sinister rocks to the west of Hartland Quay.

Cruel Coppinger – pirate king

Hartland's most legendary figure is 'Cruel Coppinger', a pirate and smuggler said to be the sole survivor a ship wrecked nearby in 1792.

Thanks to his biographer, the Reverend R S Hawker, the eccentric vicar of nearby Morwenstowe, Daniel Herbert Coppinger was transformed from a minor villain into a gothic monster.

The bare facts are that Coppinger, a Danish sailor, married a local girl and was later gaoled for debt. But in Hawker's version, after being saved from the sea, Coppinger and his gang of cut-throats lured ships onto Hartland rocks, looting the vessels and murdering the crews.

According to Hawker, revenue officers eventually hunted down the pirate, who escaped aboard a local ship and sailed from Hartland into the teeth of a storm. Ship and pirate were never seen again.

© Pat Dennis

and Ann sank in a gale within sight of horrified watchers on the quay, drowning the master and the ship's boy.

As the toll of Hartland ships mounted, Fanny Hockin, a member of the family, came to so dread shipwrecks that she kept a lamp in her window every night as an aid to sailors, and appreciative ships dipped their ensigns as they passed her house in daylight. One observer wrote, 'Even in calm conditions, great walls of water advance with unhurried deliberation to the shore, falling and receding with irresistible rhythm.'

Indeed, there never seemed a right time to enter Hartland Quay: too little wind and the loss of steerage-way was a constant hazard; too much, particularly from the west, and there was terrible risk of a ship becoming embayed among the rocks before reaching the shelter of the breakwater. Even then, a master's problems were not necessarily over. A newspaper reported that in 1851 the vessel *Speedwell* 'was lying strongly moored in Quay Pool when the tide created a ground-swell of such power as to knock out some of the stanchions, injure her pump, companionway etc., and tear her stern out.'

At the entrance, coasters would be met by hobblers – usually local fishermen – in their rowing boats, who would make all secure, and hold ships off the walls using 'junks' – thick cables which took the snatch out of moorings in a heavy swell. Because of this swell, which blighted the harbour on even the calmest days, loading and discharge usually took place when vessels took the ground at low water. Cargoes were winched out of holds and loaded into carts drawn up alongside. In the early 1800s harbour workers were paid a shilling a day and women fourpence less.

Local historians say the most unusual vessel to call at Hartland Quay was probably local MP Sir George Stucley's yacht *Deerhound*, a schooner-rigger steamer made notorious by picking up the captain and crew of the Confederate warship *Alabama*, sunk off Cherbourg in 1864. Four years later she was part of the ceremonial procession which opened the Suez Canal, and she was later arrested for running guns to Spain. *Deerhound* eventually sank in a gale off East Africa in 1879.

But over the centuries, Hartland Quay's fight with its greatest enemy, the sea, was destined to be a losing battle. No structure then known could withstand the full force of Atlantic gales, which exerted pressure of four tons a square foot on the harbour walls, and workmen were constantly repairing the damage. In 1840 Thomas Pullman and five men worked on the walls for 140 days and put in a bill

Hartland Quay as it is today.

for twelve pounds three shillings and sixpence. Their labours were largely in vain. In 1841 the pier-head collapsed and was rebuilt with stone brought in by the *Susanna*, the *Sprightly* and the *Prince of Wales*.

Only months later the sea again broached the walls, causing £12,000 worth of damage, but the work was never properly completed and when, in 1887, a violent storm virtually demolished the main pier, the then owner, George Stucley Buck, refused to spend any more money on repairs. In 1893, the ketch *Rosamond Jane* discharged Hartland Quay's last cargo, and three years later the major structure had disappeared.

A hotel was built and Hartland Quay became a popular summer holiday destination – and remains so to this day. In 1976 a modest slipway down to Quay Pool was built out of debris of the port by local volunteers, and this is used in calm weather by anglers and trailer-borne small fishing boats. Today no one would know much about the history of Hartland Quay were it not for the efforts of one of our finest marine illustrators, Mark Myers, who moved from California some thirty years ago to live on the windswept north Devon coast.

Past president of the Royal Society of Marine Artists, Mark first came to north Devon in 1968 to join the *Nonsuch* Project, in which a replica of the 1668 Hudson's Bay Company vessel was built in nearby Appledore. 'I fell in love with the area and particularly Hartland. I found it hard to believe that there had been a busy port in such a dangerous spot. The more I learned about it the more fascinated I became.' The result was the definitive book, *Hartland Quay: the Story of a Vanished Port*, co-written with Michael Nix and now in its ninth impression. The two also founded the small but fascinating museum above the sweetshop next to the hotel.

Mark still sails the north Devon coast in a 17-foot dayboat. Wise fellow, he keeps it at Bude.

14
Bude – where boats had wheels

Navigating must have been like trying to thread a needle while bouncing on a trampoline

W ilberforce had been looking forward to arriving in Bude. He had heard that boats there were fitted with wheels, which struck Wilberforce as an eminently sensible idea.

So when he called up to ask whether we could come in, he was a bit surprised when the harbourmaster asked: 'Are you sure?'

To be fair, the harbourmaster did elaborate later. 'It's not that I want to put visitors off,' he said. 'We love visitors. It's just that Bude can be a difficult place to get into – and an even more difficult place to get out of. You can be stuck here for weeks.' This is because in my humble opinion there should never have been a harbour at Bude in the first place, and whoever decided to build one must have been seriously short of things to do, or was trying to get out of redecorating the bathroom.

Bude Haven – ironically, that's its official name – is not a harbour but a beach, one of the biggest and whitest in the West Country. A surfers' paradise. The

Shipping moored in Bude canal in 1875, with four smacks waiting for the tide by Barrel Rock
Bill Young collection / Bude Museum

harbour begins about a quarter-mile inland behind the massive lock gates of the Bude Canal – the only lock in the country that opens directly onto an ocean. Connecting the lock with the open sea is a drying channel running across the beach and navigable about two hours either side of high tide. You can lock into the canal when the water reaches five-and-a-half metres. Navigating an engineless heavily laden ketch or schooner into the 33-foot entrance must have been like trying to thread a needle while bouncing on a trampoline.

The port in its heyday, 1897. Among the moored ships are the *Stucley* and the *Wild Pigeon*.
Bill Young collection / Bude Museum

There is usually a long Atlantic swell rolling in from seaward, and even moderate onshore winds dramatically increase the breaking seas. Strangers are advised to enter Bude only in quiet weather or with offshore winds. You approach Bude in bad weather or at night at your peril. Over sixty ships have been wrecked on this piece of iron-bound coast in the past century, and over twenty of them off Bude.

The entrance looks deceptively simple. To starboard as you approach the bay is Barrel Rock, marked by a barrel fixed to a ship's propeller shaft. Leave this to starboard and follow two pairs of leading marks to the lock entrance. A piece of cake – at least it is under engine in a glassy calm – but according to Bude fisherman Cliff Bowden such conditions are pretty rare, even in summer. 'The slightest Atlantic depression can cause a big ground-swell. That means surf, and surf means trouble. That's when you have to wait out behind the Barrel and hope for a bit of smooth water. You can be out there waiting for fifteen or twenty minutes. The trick is to ride in just behind the wave – the opposite to a surfer. It's a bit strange because you can't see where you're going because of the wave.

Making a dash for Bude with Barrel Rock to starboard.
North Devon Maritime Trust

'Then there's a point coming in when the waves seem to suddenly slow right down before picking up again. That's when you have to throttle back. You don't want to get in front of a wave because then your propeller will be in the surf and turning in fresh air.'

Which once more raises the question: why a port at Bude? There was nothing to bring in or take out. There was no fishing fleet, no industry to speak of, no serious agriculture. All Bude had going for it was that it was situated in the only break in twenty miles of formidable cliffs. Then, in 1825, everything changed dramatically: Bude had a canal, and with it the prosperity which until then had only been a dream. Now ships could safely unload while afloat instead of being beached on the sands.

Tub-boats, with their
wheels under water,
and the ketch
Stucley of Padstow.
Bill Young collection /
Bude Museum

Ironically what brought Bude most of its prosperity was something the town had previously dismissed as worthless – sand. It had acres of the stuff, rich in lime and ideal for fertilising inland soil. To take it where it was needed, two canals were dug, one to the River Tamar near Launceston and the other into the heart of Devon. It took six years to dig the 35-mile waterways. There were only three locks, including the giant sea-lock. Otherwise, in place of locks there were gentle slopes fitted with iron rails which ran into the water at each end.

Up these the 20-foot oblong tub-boats – of which Wilberforce had heard – ran on 14-inch wheels. They each carried four tons and worked in trains of four or six, carrying up to 50,000 tons of sand a year. They were hauled up the slopes by chains moved either by waterwheels or by the gravitational force of water buckets rising and falling in deep wells. Heath Robinson was obviously alive and well on the Bude canal.

Sadly but inevitably, the coming of the railways killed off the Bude canals in less than sixty years, but the canal basin and its sea-lock remained a bustling port with ship-owners, agents, shipyards, brokers, merchants and banks busily engaged in seaborne trade. The most successful Bude Haven shipyard was established by Robert Stapleton in 1830 and was operated by the family until it closed in 1917. Ships built at Bude included the ketches *Lady Acland* and *Jessamine* and the schooners *Elizabeth Scown* and *Annie Davey*, but Stapleton's soon became known as ship lengtheners and rebuilders.

Spectators watch the stricken
Austrian barque *Capricorno*
aground off Bude on 28
December 1900. Only two
of the 14 crew survived. The
gulley between the rocks is
now a swimming pool.
Bill Young collection

Some of their finest work was done on the sloop *Ceres*, built at Salcombe in 1811, converted to ketch rig and lengthened by 15 feet in 1865. In 1813, *Ceres* had carried military stores for Wellington in the Peninsular War. In 1856 she was bought by Bude's Captain Henry Petherick and stayed in the family for four generations until she sank off Baggy Point in November 1936. The crew were rescued by Appledore lifeboat. Over the years Stapleton's reckoned they had replaced every piece of timber in the *Ceres*.

Robert Stapleton has left a fascinating reminder of the shipbuilder's art in an account of lengthening the ketch *Lady Acland* by 13 feet in 1903 with no powered equipment of any kind:

> We hauled her out ... took out her masts and much of the planking, then cut her in half.
> New ways were built under her forrard, well-greased and with slides on them. The forrard

half of the vessel was pulled away by our men using crab-winches, my uncle watching from a bit of rising ground ahead to see that the end moved straight. I stood amidships and held a thirteen-foot batten in the gap. When I signalled that the gap was wide enough, the winching stopped. Everything had to be in perfect alignment.

We put in the new keel in two parts. The forrard half was of English elm ... the after half was of American elm. When this was done, a new keelson was put in and we planked her up again. At the finish it was not easy to see where the cut was made.

Vessels in the channel at high tide.
Bill Young collection

In her new guise, and renamed *Agnes*, the ketch would sail for another 54 years. In 1957 she was wrecked in a West Indian hurricane on passage to Australia.

At its peak, the port of Bude was handling over 300 vessels a year and exporting sand, gravel, timber, grain and bark. Over a hundred people worked on the docks and in ancillary trades. But while all may have been busy and cosy in the basin, the Atlantic lay in wait on the other side of the lock gates – graphically illustrated early one morning in February 1904 when Captain John Hallet moored the ketch *Wild Pigeon* in the lock, hoping to leave on the morning tide. Leaving his crew asleep on board, Captain Hallet stood with the harbourmaster at the gate looking out onto the bay. A huge ground-swell made it unlikely they would sail that day.

A local newspaper reported what happened next:

As they watched, an enormous wave, estimated at least 30 feet high, came up the estuary from seaward. Sensing disaster, Capt Hallet shouted to his crew, the mate Richard Saxon and the captain's two sons, James and Archie, to come on deck.

They jumped ashore just as the wave struck, caving in the massive lock gates. The *Wild Pigeon*'s ropes parted and she went out of the locks like a shot from a gun into the harbour where she was swept across rocks and on to Summerleaze beach. She later broke in half and was a total loss. Another ketch in the lock, *Jessie*, was severely damaged but was salvaged and later repaired.

The ketch *Wild Pigeon*, wrecked in 1904 by a wave that stove in Bude's lock gates.
Spencer Thorn / Bill Young collection

The Iron Coast of Cornwall took few prisoners, and the folk of Bude became accustomed to risking their own lives in the hope of saving others from the unforgiving sea. In October 1862, the square-rigger *Bencoolen*, on passage from Liverpool to Bombay with a crew of 32, lost her main and mizzen masts in a westerly gale and was blown onto the rocks off Bude breakwater in mountainous seas. Twenty-five of the crew tried to reach the shore on a raft made of spars and booms but it capsized and all but two were lost. Only six men were saved from the

Barrel Rock and the channel across Bude beach today.

Looking out through the restored lock gates.

The lock and the town.

wreck and the debris of the *Bencoolen* was strewn on beaches for miles around.

The dangerous coast and the limitations on tonnage imposed by the sea-lock contributed to Bude's steady decline as a port, and by the late 1920s it was handling less than one ship a month. The docks finally closed to shipping in 1930. A bridge was built at the far end of the basin, cutting off the canal from the docks and sealing its fate as a commercial waterway. Today less than two of the original 35 miles contain water.

After years of neglect, the harbour was restored in 1991 and the lock gates rebuilt from greenheart oak at a cost of £500,000. The basin is now a busy pleasure-boat venue with pubs, restaurants and an interesting little museum. Berths are quiet and sheltered and the quays are only a short walk from the holiday centre of the town. It's a nice place to stay. I had a coffee with Paul Johnstone, who had brought his converted Looe hooker up from St Ives the previous week and had locked in without difficulty on a calm morning tide. He said he intended to stay another week.

Wilberforce had disappeared. I found him in the museum eating an ice-cream and enthusing over a restored wheeled tub-boat with the curator. Apart from not having pointed ends, it was the same size as a flattie. Later I caught him staring reflectively at *Yankee Jack* with one of those looks that I have come to know and thoroughly mistrust. Finally, under pressure, he did admit that he was working out where we could put the axles.

15
Called to the bar at Padstow

A local man shot a mermaid who was carrying a bag of sand

Wilberforce is usually automatically attracted to bars, but this one was an exception. Throughout the 25-mile passage westward from Bude on a warm summer's morning he had been muttering that if I had any regard for him as a friend or any sense of responsibility as a skipper, I wouldn't even think about going into Padstow.

Normally you couldn't have kept Wilberforce away from somewhere like Padstow, a place he had never visited. It's a pretty little holiday town with over a dozen pubs, enormous full-fat Cornish ice-creams, cafés on every corner, Rick Stein's world-famous seafood restaurants and even a shipwreck museum for when it rains.

Padstow is also probably the safest port of refuge on the north Cornwall coast, lying two miles up the River Camel, one of the most attractive and unspoilt estuaries in the West Country. The problem is that stretching across the river at

A relaxed Edwardian scene at Padstow harbour. Moored is the *Guiding Star* with a Barry pilot cutter in the background.
RIC / David B Clement collection

the point where the Camel joins Padstow Bay is the Doom Bar. And that's what got Wilberforce into such a stew. He had read about it in a book of Cornish shipwrecks, and there's no denying that the Doom Bar has had a pretty bad press over the years.

More than 600 ships have come to grief on the bar – a vast drying area of sand extending from Stepper Point in the west to Trebetherick Point in the east. There was once even a society dedicated to helping shipwreck victims who managed to get ashore from this godforsaken place. In fact, except in northwesterlies and providing you get the tides right and stick carefully to the buoyed channel, a modern boat with a decent engine usually has little to fear from the Doom Bar. Even the name is misleading: it's actually a derivation of dun or dunne, meaning sand.

But this was certainly not the case when large and none-too-weatherly sailing coasters were regularly negotiating the Camel estuary with no recourse to a powerful diesel. The main problem was that on entering the narrow channel through the sand at Stepper Point a sailing ship could get becalmed in the lee of the Point or thrown sideways by eddies onto the sand.

The harbour in the late 1890s.
Reg Watkiss Archive

To help prevent this, Padstow's Association for the Preservation of Life and Property from Shipwreck had the novel idea of installing three huge capstans on Stepper Point for winching ships through the narrow channel. An 1895 pilotage guide states:

> The capstans are 27 feet above sea level. On arrival of a vessel in the offing during the prevalence of adverse winds a hawser will be conveyed by a pilot boat to the vessel to aid its passage over the bar.

Of course, capstans have long been used to haul fishing boats up beaches, but so far as I know they've never been employed in this way anywhere else, and sadly they're no longer on Stepper Point. A pity – they'd be a timely reminder of how real sailors did things in the old days. But now we have engines and radios and depth-sounders and so there's absolutely no excuse for making a drama out of navigating the Doom Bar.

'Don't try to enter Padstow too early on the tide,' advised the harbourmaster, Trevor Platt. 'About three hours before local high water is the ideal time to start the approach. That means you'll only have a short wait before entering the inner harbour.'

From Stepper Point, the navigational channel runs southeast towards Trebetherick Point before turning south and following the buoys. A cable from the harbour the passage runs close inshore. 'Don't be tempted to give this point too much clearance,' Trevor warned. 'There's plenty of water close inshore. Stand too far off when there's a flood running and you can be pushed out of the channel onto the sand.'

Armed with this information, *Yankee Jack* motored gently through the tranquil Doom Bar on a windless afternoon. In fact we were eating Swiss roll and drinking tea in highly civilised fashion as we passed Gulland Rock, where St Geolland, an Irish saint, was said to have spent his old age. The story is that he set up a bell on a post to warn mariners of impending storms. One winter he fell ill and when a violent storm threatened he was unable to leave his bed and ring the bell but he heard it tolling and saw the ringer was a seagull he had befriended. St Geolland is now the patron saint of Cornish seabirds. I thought it a nice little tale but Wilberforce just said 'Do you want that last bit of cake?'

We arrived at Padstow's retained-water inner harbour just as the tidal gate was opening and moored next to a Belgian trawler. Wilberforce was strangely silent as we stepped ashore into a throng of holiday-makers and the overwhelming scent of suntan oil. I think he felt the Doom Bar had let him down. But he did allow me to buy him a very large ice-cream.

Other visitors have enjoyed Padstow's hospitality if not its ice-cream, including Sir John Hawkins, on his return from the West Indies, Sir Martin Frobisher, after his

Fishing boats in the harbour in June 1906 with the schooner *Guiding Star* in the background.
Herbert Hughes / © Royal Institution of Cornwall (PADhs003)

search for the Northwest Passage to China, and Sir Walter Raleigh. Sadly none of them was there when we arrived. There has been a port at Padstow since the sixth century. But then it was called Alderstowe, Petrockstowe or Lodenek, and handled cargoes of fish and wine.

Even then there was a sand bar across the river, caused, so the legend goes, by a local man named Jan Treadeagar, who shot a mermaid who was carrying a bag of sand. Before she died she cursed Padstow and predicted that eventually the river would be blocked by sand. In fact it very nearly happened. In 1829, shipping authorities were so alarmed by the build-up of the Doom Bar that it was planned to blast a cutting across Stepper Point 'so that ships could hold the wind blowing through it.' The ambitious scheme was started but never finished. Eventually the excavation was turned into a quarry, which remained operational until the 1960s.

Today the site has a navigation beacon which marks the entrance to the Camel estuary. Originally a fisherman from nearby Hawkers Cove was paid to hang an oil-lamp from the beacon every evening. Another beacon was erected on a site near to where Trevose Head lighthouse now stands. The 40-foot tower, designed to hold a fire beacon, is still on the charts.

By the sixteenth century, when the first stone pier was built, Padstow was the main north Cornwall smuggling port, despite the attentions of Customs and Excise, who vainly tried to control smuggling with a small army of officials. These included a customs inspector, an inspector of the preventive water-guard, a tide-waiter (who boarded ships before they moored), a landing-waiter and an officer of excise. Even so, by the mid sixteenth century, the value of contraband landed at Padstow was reckoned in modern terms at over a million pounds a year.

The schooner *Lord Devon* of Salcombe unloads at the quay.
North Devon Maritime Trust / Edward Blight collection

Despite navigational difficulties, Padstow prospered. By 1850 it was the busiest port in north Cornwall. Twenty ship-owners registered over 100 vessels in Padstow and that year more than 500 ships used the port, which handled nearly 30,000 tons of cargo. Timber was shipped from Scandinavia and Canada, and a fleet of smacks, schooners, brigs and barquentines brought in slate, agricultural products and coal. Larger ships, including square-riggers, moored in the Pool, a deep-water anchorage just beyond the harbour.

In the late nineteenth century, Padstow had five busy shipyards, the most successful being that of John Tredwen, who built the town's first lifeboat, the *Mariner's Friend*. It saved six lives in its first year. Tredwen's most famous ship, the topsail schooner *Mary Jane*, jammed on the launching slipway for four days and slid off of her own volition the following Sunday. From then on she was known in Padstow as the *Sabbath Breaker*. Another Tredwen creation, the schooner *Emily*, was known as the yard's fastest ship – until she left Padstow one clear night in 1872 to sail to Plymouth and never arrived. No trace of her was ever found.

One yard launched thirty ships between 1860 and 1870, and as many as ten sailing vessels were arriving or leaving on one tide. There were dozens of thriving mercantile businesses – sail-lofts, chandlers and boat stores, now cafés, shops and apartments.

But as Padstow's shipping trade flourished, so did the toll of victims on the Doom Bar. In just one year – 1882 – twenty ships were wrecked and over forty lives lost. They included five of the crew of the lifeboat *Edward Albert*, going to the rescue of an American schooner which had capsized on the bar in a gale. In 1900 Padstow's steam lifeboat, *James Stephens*, capsized, drowning eight crew and three fishermen they had rescued from the Doom Bar.

The following year, as the rowing lifeboat *Arab* went to the wreck of the ketch *Island Maid* on the bar, a French brigantine, *Angèle*, running in under bare poles before a gale, made a violent change of course to avoid the ketch and lifeboat and herself ended up on the bar. A local newspaper reported:

> The lifeboat failed to reach the *Angèle* in tempestuous seas and returned to Padstow. When asked to launch for another attempt, the crew refused and a scratch crew was sought in Port Isaac.

They eventually reached the *Angèle* and saved the captain but four other crew were lost. No action was taken against the Padstow crew. It was decided they had taken as much as was humanly possible.

By the turn of the century, the Great Western Railway had stolen much of the trade previously carried by West Country coastal shipping, but ironically the railways turned out to be the salvation of Padstow's fishing trade. Fish carried from the port by rail increased from 24 tons in 1900 to 3,000 tons in 1908. Fish were carried from the trawlers straight onto Billingsgate-bound trains which left Padstow every afternoon. Even old passenger coaches were adapted to carry fish, mainly herring and pilchards, up to London.

Harry Nancarrow, whose family have fished out of Padstow for centuries, told us that his grandfather bought three houses in the town from his fishing profits before the First World War. 'Then other fishing fleets started to muscle in – a lot of boats came from the east coast for the winter fishing. They called our fishing grounds the Klondike. My grandpa said that the east-coasters cleared off when German submarines started sinking the fishing fleets – thirteen Padstow boats were sunk in one day – and they never came back.'

A thriving fishing port at the turn of the 20th century.
RIC / David B Clement collection

With both the docks and the fishing industry in decline after 1918, Padstow fell on hard times. Even tourists kept away, which was hardly surprising: a guide-book of the time described the place as 'one of those antiquated unsavoury fishing towns best viewed from a distance', and added, 'Few will deliberately visit it for its own sake.'

Things are very different nowadays. The shellfish trade is again booming, thanks mainly to the influence of Rick Stein – some are now calling the place Padstein – and there's a national lobster hatchery on the quay. The retained-water harbour is full of leisure boaters and the dredged outer harbour can now take freighters of 2,000 tons. It's a busy and friendly place to visit.

When *Yankee Jack* left the estuary on the top of the tide, it was as bright and smooth as silver foil. There wasn't a breath of wind and the Doom Bar was once again as docile as an old sleeping dog. But despite the sunshine and a bag of doughnuts, still hot, Wilberforce was in a grump. Once again the Doom Bar had been a deep disappointment. 'Calls itself a bar,' he muttered. 'It should take a few lessons from Bideford.'

The same corner of the harbour today.

16
No breakfast in Wadebridge

I'll draw you a chart. Pass me that beer-mat

It was not very often that *Yankee Jack* in full sail was overtaken by two middle-aged ladies on bicycles, and Wilberforce was not best pleased. 'Can't we start the engine?' he asked when we were also left astern of a family of Dutch cyclists and a sturdy toddler on a tricycle. 'I can't take much more of this.'

I did point out that it was at Wilberforce's insistence that we were making the four-and-a-half-mile detour up the River Camel from Padstow to the market town of Wadebridge when every sane bone in my body had cried out that we should have taken the early morning tide from Padstow and pressed on to Newquay, where there was a proper harbour, albeit a drying one, and we at least knew where we were going.

We were on passage to Wadebridge, mainly to stop Wilberforce rabbiting on that in the dim and distant past he had enjoyed the finest all-day breakfast known to man in a café near the ancient bridge and that he would die happily if only he could eat another.

The Camel, rising far away on remote Bodmin Moor, is one of the most attractive and unspoiled rivers in the West Country, and Wadebridge was once one of Cornwall's busiest and most prosperous estuary ports. The granite which built London's Blackfriars bridge was shipped by sail from there in 1834. So was the

The busy town quay a century ago.
Peter Tutthill collection

stone for the new Eddystone lighthouse which was completed in 1882. By 1900, Wadebridge was a major clay and iron-ore port, with four shipyards and thriving mercantile businesses. It was not unusual to see a dozen schooners and ketches crowded against the busy quays.

Wadebridge was flourishing in ways unheard of since it was the centre of the Cornish wool trade in the sixteenth century, but sadly its maritime prosperity didn't last. The river was relentlessly silting up, and by the late 1950s Wadebridge was to all intents and purposes high and dry, and ship-owners refused to send their vessels there. This was mainly because the ever-shifting shingle and sand bars between Padstow and Wadebridge made it impossible to buoy a safe channel, and ships going aground on a falling tide could find themselves neaped for a fortnight.

Today no commercial shipping ventures up to Wadebridge, the docks and wharves have gone, and alders, willows and Indian balsam flourish in the silted-up berths. Warehouse-style riverside

Late Victorian regatta on the river.
Peter Tutthill collection

apartments start at £200,000 and are snapped up while they're still pretty pictures in an estate-agent's brochure, but apart from dinghies and a few shallow-draught yachts and motor-cruisers, there's little movement on the Camel above Padstow or the village of Rock on the opposite bank, burial-place of Sir John Betjeman. They make the Cornish Crabber range of gaffers there, too.

It had seemed sensible to know where we were going, which was why, while Wilberforce complainingly loaded the boat, I was to be found in the Shipwright pub in Padstow looking for local knowledge. Apparently there was no detailed chart of the Camel estuary. 'You'll be all right so long as you go up on the flood and keep to the right, or is it to the left?' said an Ancient Mariner at the bar. 'I'll draw you a chart. Pass me that beer-mat.'

Returning with a map which could have been drawn by a demented octopus, I fortuitously bumped into harbourmaster Trevor Platt. 'From here to Wadebridge is very much by guess and by God,' was how he put it. 'There are no channel markers but if you want to try it you should find the deepest water in the middle.'

It was nearly three hours after low water before we could float across the drying sands north of Padstow and make for Cant Hill, a mile to the east. Round the corner is Cant Creek, graveyard of half-a-dozen trading ketches. Only their keels remain.

After the sandbanks off Camel Quarry there was unimpeded water for nearly two miles leading up to the narrow channel approaching Wadebridge. We were jilling along comfortably in a light westerly breeze along the southern edge of the estuary and it was here that Wilberforce got so upset.

There may not be much water-borne traffic on the Camel but there's still plenty of activity on the nearby land. The Camel Trail follows the river bank for 18 miles along the now-defunct Southern Railway line, the seventh line in the UK to use steam locomotives. Today it caters for thousands of cyclists every year, and most of them seemed to be out that afternoon, enjoying the novelty of bicycling faster than a boat. Eventually I did succumb to Wilberforce's request to start the outboard and soon the seventeen-arch fifteenth-century bridge, said to be built on bales of wool, came into view and we ran the boat ashore by the sailing club on the outskirts of the town.

Pleasure-boats moored at the quayside, *c.*1900.
Peter Tutthill collection

Today, three arches of the ancient bridge are hidden by a row of shops and another ten obstructed by islands of silt and sand. It was hard to believe there were still people in Wadebridge who remembered when half the town's workforce crewed its ships or worked in its port. Indeed, every vestige of Wadebridge's maritime past seemed to have magically disappeared.

Once there was a regular ferry service from Padstow to Wadebridge. It ran until the nineteenth century, when it was made redundant by the railway. It carried freight as well as passengers and cut the road journey by three miles. Now the trip can only be made by a shallow-draught boat on a high tide.

Over a drink with local historian Paul Fennell, we learned that Wadebridge had in fact been a major maritime centre since the Middle Ages. Before the bridge was built in 1450, ships rode up on the tide to the ancient village of Egloshayle, which is now the north side of Wadebridge.

For many centuries lime-bearing sand had been carried up the Camel estuary for the use of farmers further inland, and by the eighteenth century a fleet of barges was regularly transporting sand to dumps on the river bank above Wadebridge. 'Barges like that must have drawn at least four feet or even more,' Paul said, 'and they seemed to operate on all states of the tide. There must have been a hell of a lot more water in the river in those days. Something pretty startling must have happened. Now you can go aground in a Mirror dinghy.' Wilberforce said he blamed the government and pointed out it was my round.

One dramatic solution, which sadly came to nothing, was a grandiose nineteenth-century scheme for cutting a ship canal to link the Camel in the north with the River Fowey in the south, a distance of about 13 miles. This would have enabled vessels travelling down the Bristol Channel to cross to the English Channel without rounding Land's End, so saving at least 80 miles. The scheme was

proposed by local MP Sir William Molesworth and actually received parliamentary consent in 1796 but was dropped for financial reasons despite efforts to revive it by none other than Isambard Kingdom Brunel.

But even without the canal, Wadebridge prospered. In 1865, over 500,000 tons of goods were handled, including iron ore, china clay, coal, nitrates, timber and general hardware, and lack of

The railway sand quay.
Peter Tutthill collection

water between the fortnightly spring tides – a traditional problem for Wadebridge – was solved in a novel way. On small tides vessels left the port without the last portion of their cargo, but shipmates were reluctant to lose freight by short-shipping a cargo. Hence there grew up the curious custom, as far as I know unique to Wadebridge, of sending the last few tons down to Padstow by barge at the cost of the ship. A few hours later the freight would be transferred to the ship, which would then sail with a full cargo.

Studies have shown that estuary ports like Wadebridge would never have prospered in the nineteenth century if it hadn't been for the passing of the Merchant Shipping Act in 1854. Under the previous 1772 Tonnage Act, only length and beam measurement were used when calculating cargo capacity, on which port dues were levied. So ship-owners deepened the holds of their vessels without increasing length and beam. This meant that ships were unstable when light and drew too much water to enter shallow rivers like the Camel when loaded. But the Merchant Shipping Act did away with the incentive to build ships with deep holds, and with new shallow-draught sailing vessels Wadebridge and other tidal ports finally came into their own.

In the coming years, Wadebridge almost doubled its shipping tonnage with a fleet of coastal trading ketches and schooners including such West Country classics as *Three Brothers, Emma Jane, Maud, Lizzie, Charlotte, Flying Foam, Emma Louise, Water Lily* and *Gipsy Queen.*

Berths were booked weeks or even months ahead, which prompted ship-owner Robert Neal of Padstow to write to a Wadebridge shipbroker in 1873: 'I have a new vessel hear about 170 tons and we was thinking to launch her next spring. Can you load her with clay for Runcorn the spring after next?' He was referring to the tide, not the season. The ship was the *Peace*, one of the finest schooners ever built at Padstow.

The Camel, from the old bridge.

Sadly, trade dropped away steadily over the years, particularly after Padstow, down-river, dredged its outer harbour to accommodate freighters of up to 2,000 tons. No one needed to edge their way up to Wadebridge any more. In 1943 the

Peter Herbert's ketch
Agnes in difficulties
on the river in 1955.
Robert Simper collection

Appledore ketch *Bessie* brought a load of coal to Wadebridge, the last cargo the port would handle for twelve years until Peter Herbert of Bude delivered a cargo of animal feed in his 70-foot auxiliary ketch *Agnes*.

The Padstow pilot Tommy Morrissey took the ship up to Wadebridge Mill but, when mooring up, Peter Herbert underestimated the force of the ebb-tide under the bridge and the head-ropes parted, swinging the ketch across the channel. An old man watching from the bridge remarked with quiet satisfaction, 'I was waiting

Ten of the bridge's arches
are now silted up.

for that to happen. You should have had a rope running up to the top window of the mill.' Two years later *Agnes*, now fitted out as a yacht, was wrecked on a Barbados reef and was a total loss.

After the *Agnes* there was a slight revival in harbour trade but sadly it didn't last. A few months later the German motor-vessel *Flut* brought in a consignment of timber, the port's last cargo. As there was no outward cargo, *Flut* made a 90-mile journey in ballast to Par, on the south coast, to load china clay. As the crow flies, Wadebridge to Par is just fourteen miles.

We found Wadebridge an interesting and friendly town – at least until Wilberforce discovered that the café providing legendary breakfasts was now a Taiwan takeaway. It was closed. On the largely silent trip back down-river on the ebb, the Camel Trail was almost deserted and no cyclists overtook us, which was just as well. Further humiliation on top of the all-day breakfast disaster could well have been more than even Wilberforce could bear.

17
Newquay – pilchards and pilot gigs

You could say this is the harbour no one knows

Two hundred years ago, the town of Newquay relied on pilchards for its living. Now it depends on people – up to 80,000 a week in the summer arrive in the north-coast town which has become Cornwall's largest and busiest holiday resort. By sea, Newquay is some fifteen miles southwest of Padstow but, as Wilberforce and I soon found, in terms of culture-shock the distance is immeasurable.

A glance at the chart will show that Newquay is set in a shallow west-facing bay a mile-and-a-half wide, flanked by Trevelgue Head to the north and Towan Head to the south. Padstow is still basically a fishing village but Newquay is a place of huge beaches backed by cliffs and topped by the most remarkable jumble of B&Bs, vast hotels, amusement arcades and sundry bits and bobs of anarchic architecture to be found almost anywhere outside Las Vegas. There are over a hundred establishments selling chips (Wilberforce claimed to have counted them) and shops that sell shouting electronic toys.

Schooners, brigs and gigs in late Victorian Newquay.
J Rosewarne / David B Clement collection

Circling the bay on a calm hot August afternoon in order to line up the narrow entrance of the harbour on the southern side, *Yankee Jack* was rocked by speedboats driven at suicidal speed by holiday-makers who greeted us in Midlands accents. They seemed to be having a good time. And all around, on the wide white beaches, their compatriots lay in rows in various states of roasting, frying and braising. The air, as Wilberforce pointed out, was so heavy with the fumes of sun-oil that one struck match would probably have blown Newquay halfway to America.

The *Hind* and the *Mary Wighton* aground in the harbour – a horse and cart help with the unloading.
© RIC (NWQhs094)

Holiday-makers started to arrive in Newquay at about the same time that the shoals of pilchards decided to leave, and in summer now outnumber the resident population by four to one. Many come to surf on the Atlantic rollers – Australian lifeguards brought surfing to Britain in Newquay in 1965 and international championships have several times been held at the town's Fistral Beach, on the south side of Towan Head.

This lump of rock is topped by the vast baleful structure of the Atlantic Hotel, and nearby is an eighteenth-century whitewashed building called Huer's House. Until the late nineteenth century a man known as the Huer would keep watch for the red-stained water indicating shoals of pilchards entering the bay and alert the fishermen below by shouting 'heva, heva'. The inhabitants of Newquay assured us this was the origin of the expression hue and cry. As Wilberforce observed, it was almost worth coming to Newquay just to learn that.

Newquay harbour lies to the north of Towan Head and was once the centre of a village called Towan Blystra, which in 1439 was allowed by the Bishop of Exeter to build a protective groyne known as New Quay. Towan Head keeps the worst of the Atlantic out of the harbour, which is tucked between east-facing rocky coves, but the west-coast Admiralty pilot which belonged to Wilberforce's father, and which his son carries at all times in a Tesco bag, did warn that no attempt should be made to enter the harbour in a ground-swell or during an onshore gale.

We had no such problems on that calm summer afternoon and soon *Yankee Jack* was firmly moored on the north quay of a drying harbour which was surprisingly busy, surprisingly picturesque – and surprisingly empty of holiday-makers. 'You could say this is the harbour no one knows,' said the harbourmaster Captain Malcolm Gater. 'I get people who have been coming on holiday to Newquay for years saying things like 'We never knew there was a harbour here.' In fact, after decades of commercial decline, Newquay is once more a thriving port with a fleet of over twenty full-time fishing boats working crab and lobster pots, and long-lining and netting in the off-season.

We learned that the iron-bound coast has its own horrors, like the Old Dane, a reef just north of the harbour where waves can turn to surf as they close on the wide and shallow beach, producing a swell that can turn the harbour mouth into a maelstrom. 'Get it wrong,' said Captain Gater, 'and the backwash can spin a power-ful boat like a twig.' The current generation of pot-haulers have other problems too – big deep-sea boats, mainly foreigners, who wreak havoc by ploughing through strings of carefully laid pots. 'It's Russian roulette,' Ron Eglinton told Wilberforce. Ron is retired after a lifetime at sea but has two sons operating family boats.

'You can put out a string of sixty pots and if a beamer or a scalloper has been through in the night you can lose the lot. All those pots gone, at £50 apiece, never mind the time you spend looking for them. We've had a hundred disappear in a single night and you can imagine what that does to a small boat's income.'

Topsail schooners by the jetty, c.1915.
Jordan © RIC (NWQhs013)

They rarely see a pilchard in Newquay nowadays. They inexplicably disappeared from north Cornwall waters in the mid nineteenth century, leaving several hundred men and women who had been employed in the Newquay pilchard fishery out of work. Some forty vessels were used for pilchard-seining and curing cellars were built into the rock-faces surrounding the harbour. So heavy were catches that a harbour railway was built to connect the town with the quays, running through a tunnel in the hillside.

The average Newquay pilchard seiners were 25- to 30-foot half-deckers with a standing-lug mainsail and gaff or sprit mizzen. There was a fish-hold amidships, plus a tiny cuddy with a coal stove, barely four feet of headroom and two narrow bunks. Despite the spartan facilities, it was not unusual for seiners to stay out for a week or longer when the pilchards were shoaling along the Iron Coast.

It's not too melodramatic to say that pilchards were almost life and death to a place like Newquay. The average wage was around 12 shillings a week in the 1860s and fish was the staple diet. Every cottage usually laid in about 1,000 pilchards for winter use, curing them in large earthenware pots known as 'bussas'. When fish were split open and dried in the sun they were known as 'scroulers.' The usual price was ten pilchards for a penny or as low as sixpence for 120 when there was a glut, as on a day in November 1834, now part of Newquay folklore, when an estimated 20 million fish were caught in 24 hours. A local newspaper reported:

> Day and night, the silvery catch was carried into the fish cellars in hand barrows and dumped on the floors to be seized by children who piled them into ever-growing heaps according to

size. The smallest fish were sold at 10 pence a cartload for manure. At dusk, candles threw flickering shadows on the stone walls of the cellars and work went on all through the night. The best pilchards were salted and packed in barrels for export to Mediterranean countries, particularly Italy, where they are much esteemed.

Then suddenly the pilchards swam away, leaving Newquay and other north-coast fishing ports desperate for alternative income. In Newquay's case a saviour appeared in the form of Mr J T Austin, who had made a fortune from Par harbour, fifteen miles away across the peninsula on the south coast, and was anxious to repeat the experience. Soon after Austin acquired Newquay harbour, two Acts of Parliament allowed him to dramatically develop the port. His plans included

The railway took pilchards from Newquay's bustling harbour to Billingsgate.
Charles Woolf © RIC (NWQhs093)

building a railway link to Par with an extension to an important group of iron and copper mines and china clay pits. By 1860, Newquay ships were exporting iron, copper and clay to France, Germany, Scandinavia and Holland as well as to major UK ports including London, Liverpool and Southampton.

Shipbuilding thrived in Newquay: the mining and clay industries needed shallow-draught vessels capable of working small tidal harbours and for forty years four Newquay yards kept the harbour busy and prosperous. In 1880 nearly 200 vessels were owned and managed in the port. They included the classic ketches *Belle of the Plym*, *Fairy Maid* and *William Henry* and the brigantine *Agnes Louisa*. A high proportion of Newquay's population took up shares and formed companies, including the Newquay Maritime Association, a marine insurance firm.

A similar view today.

It was all too good to last. The opening of the main railway line through Cornwall hastened the demise of small seaports and Newquay's seaborne trade steadily declined. By the end of the 1914–18 war the town owned only two sailing coasters, and in November 1922 the schooner *Hobah* brought in Newquay's last commercial cargo – a consignment of agricultural fertiliser. Now nearly every trace of the commercial port has gone, apart from the remains of the trestle bridge which once carried the railway to the stone jetty that sits like an island in the middle of the harbour. And of course the tunnel which took fish trains into the town.

Now it's blanked off with huge wooden doors. Fisherman Phil Trebilcock opened them up to show us the immense dark cavern and Wilberforce expressed surprise that the tunnel hadn't been made into some sort of tourist attraction.

'Don't say that,' Phil Trebilcock said. 'It's the perfect place to keep the gigs.'

You don't have to be in Newquay long to realise that along with pilchards, pilot gigs have a hallowed reputation in the town. Newquay was the last mainland Cornish port to have working gigs and today Newquay Rowing Club's headquarters on the quay houses eight classic vessels, including the one which is the benchmark for gig-building around the world – the *Treffry* (pronounced Tref-rye), built in 1843 and still in racing trim.

Newquay Rowing Club, founded in 1921, is the most senior and influential of the fifty clubs now racing traditional gigs and, as secretary, Phil Trebilcock is rightly proud of its history and traditions. 'We have over five hundred members and more than a hundred row regularly,' he said. 'We've even made a CD of sea-shanties. We're real gig enthusiasts down here.'

To outsiders, using 30-foot lightly built shallow six-oar rowing boats, planked in elm barely a quarter-inch thick, on the exposed rocky coasts of the Southwest Peninsula has always smacked of maritime madness, but today gig rowing and racing has never been more popular. Over 2,000 rowers competed in the 2005 world championships in the Isles of Scilly. Paradoxically, it's largely the length and lightness which provides the stability that enables pilot gigs to live in virtually any sea. By the early nineteenth century at least 200 gigs were stationed around the Southwest, roaming fifty miles out into the Western Approaches in all weathers to deliver pilots to ships, plus ferrying passengers, animals and merchandise and even relieving lighthouses.

Racing gigs at Newquay.
Ralph Bird collection

It was in the summer of 1843 that John Peters and his son William, boat-builders at the tiny Polvarth yard on the Fal at St Mawes, accepted a starkly simple commission from a Newquay pilot: 'Build me the fastest gig ever!' The Peters yard not only rose to the challenge but in the process made maritime history by producing the *Treffry*, a boat which, it's generally accepted, has never been bettered as an example of the gig-builder's art. The finished job was so beautiful that John Peters refused to paint her in his usual white livery and instead she was polished with linseed oil.

Today, *Treffry* and other nineteenth-century gigs from the Peters yard, *Dove* and *Newquay*, are still in competitive trim, and race annually for a silver trophy so valuable it's kept in the bank. Over the years, *Treffry* has been the most consistent winner. No wonder that under Cornish Pilot Gig Association rules, all new gigs are today built exactly to her lines and dimensions. In 2003, she celebrated her 160th birthday and her 80th year with the Newquay Rowing Club.

So gigs are alive and well in Newquay, but what of pilchards? We saw only two during our stay, and they were on the town's civic crest.

18
St Ives – art for art's sake

The drowning coast lay patiently in wait
only just around the corner

To be honest, I wasn't terribly looking forward to sailing into St Ives. My only previous visit, when crewing a yacht on passage from France to Bristol, had been at night in a heavy swell when we'd come within a whisker of ending up on a nasty excrescence known as Heva Rock after mistaking some traffic signals in the town for port and starboard buoys. I'd wondered at the time just what was the significance of the orange one.

This time it was a warm sunny morning and the pretty town was bathed in sunlight but I still felt a mild twinge of what Edwardian yachtsman Claud Worth had astutely identified as 'morbid apprehension'. It was a Sunday and Wilberforce, always ready to spoil a chap's day, had reminded me that in the not-too-distant past the population of St Ives took a very dim view of anyone doing anything remotely nautical on the day of rest.

Apparently it all started about 150 years ago when St Ives – some 25 miles down the coast from Newquay – was Cornwall's leading pilchard landing port. Its record

Crowds gather on the shore to welcome a deep-sea visitor. Trading vessels continued to service St Ives into the twentieth century.
St Ives Museum

catch was 8,000 barrels – a total of 24 million fish – and fishing was the lifeblood of the town. Except on Sundays.

By 1850, the St Ives fishery employed over 500 people and 200 fishing vessels were registered there but the port was empty and silent on Sunday. The town was a Methodist stronghold – John Wesley visited St Ives 27 times – and non-conformist gospels banned Sunday work. So when in 1860 an Essex lugger brimming with pilchards moored up on the outer pier and began to unload, a furious band of Cornishmen soon arrived and threw the fish back into the sea.

Shortly afterwards half-a-dozen east-coast smacks arrived on another Sunday and attempted to auction their catch on the quay. Again there was a protest which ended in a fight. When the smacksmen tried to take their fish to the nearby port of Hayle, which had no religious restrictions, St Ives fishermen set fire to their carts. The following year a fleet of fifty mainly east-coast vessels approached St Ives on a Sunday with heavy catches but, seeing an angry crowd on the quay, sailed into Hayle instead. The custom of 'keeping the Sabbath' died hard and most St Ives boats wouldn't go to sea on a Sunday until fish became an essential part of the local diet at the outbreak of the First World War.

Boys rowing exquisite clinker skiffs c.1900. Note the washing line in the background.
St Ives Museum / Comley collection

In the summer the St Ives lugger fleet went seining. There was a saying, 'Corn up in shock, fish in to rock', and it was only at harvest-time that the seine nets were worked.

They were a quarter of a mile in length and would be shot around a pilchard shoal, usually at dusk. At the start of the season, St Ives boats would need to search beyond the Scillies for shoals, but fish came nearer the north Cornwall shore as the season advanced.

Cork buoys were attached to head-lines, allowing the nets to sink deep enough to let vessels pass over them without damage, but as an added precaution primitive flares made of oil-soaked rags in tin cans would warn off shipping when a lugger was lying to her nets. The catch of a St Ives drifter was divided into eight shares – four for maintenance of the boat and nets and four to the men, including the master, who got the same as the rest of the crew. The only one to lose out was the ship's boy, who was only allowed fish which fell into the sea when the nets were being hauled and which he tried to retrieve with a net on the end of a pole. In the 1880s a fair week's share came to about eighteen shillings a man.

But almost as important to his family as a man's wages were the fish they could buy – at about a shilling a hundred when catches were good. As in Newquay, our previous port of call, families would store large quantities of pilchards for the winter, salting them in barrels. Other fish were pressed and the oil extracted to use in cottage lamps. In October, at the end of the pilchard season, St Ives luggers would fish for hake or sail around Land's End looking for herring.

Unlike their south-coast counterparts, many St Ives pilchard drivers were double-ended with a sharper entry, a finer run and a more upright stem. As the St Ives harbour dried out, they had to be able to take the hard sandy bottom without damage and without falling over, hence heavy rubbing strakes and bilge keels. Some were three-masters of up to 50 feet but remained open boats or half-deckers, with the crew sleeping in their oilskins or wrapped in sails under the forepeak.

Mounts Bay luggers were said to perform better in light airs but St Ives boats,

A classic period photograph showing luggers aground at low water, c.1900.
St Ives Museum / Comley collection

built by such local yards as Francis Adams, William Paynter, Arthur Rosewall and Henry Trevorrow, were reckoned to hold their sails better in a blow. They often needed to: St Ives Bay can still be a perilous place in a northeast or northwesterly gale and even a fresh onshore wind can generate a nasty swell which makes it difficult to take the ground safely. And remember that from Land's End to Hartland Point has gone down in history as the drowning coast, witnessing more shipwrecks than any other British shoreline of similar length.

In an attempt to make St Ives a more acceptable port of refuge, John Smeaton, of Eddystone lighthouse fame, was commissioned to design an outer pier in 1770. This improved protection from the northwest and gave the port a period of prosperity that reached its peak around 1860. Pilchards were exported to Italy, and fruit, hides and wood were imported from Spain, Greece and South America. There was also a regular passenger service to Ireland.

Privateering and smuggling added to the excitements of the busy little port. St Ives businessmen licensed and fitted out privateers to hunt down enemy vessels during the Napoleonic wars and smuggling activities were carefully chronicled by Captain John Tregarthen, the town's customs officer in the 1840s, in his official diary:

January 3: The Negroes from the French brig *Perle* taken on shore by Habeas Corpus and ordered to be clothed and sent to London.

February 8: The Preventive Boat at St Agnes took a small cutter with 120 kegs of spirits.

March 6: Capt. Moses Martin of the Preventive Service with the assistance of the pilot gigs and their crews took a smuggler with 339 tubs of spirits and a crew of six.

April 25: The French brig *General Foix* brought in by the *Caesar*. Four men washed overboard by heavy seas. All sails carried away. Vessel the most valuable prize ever brought in. Sugar, coffee, rum etc.

The people of St Ives had long become accustomed to risking their own lives in the hope of saving others from the sea, and after three men had been drowned

Topsail schooners and young shell-collectors, *c.*1890.
St Ives Museum

in 1840 vainly trying to rescue the crew of a sailing ketch in a violent storm, the townsfolk built and maintained their own lifeboat. Over the next hundred years its successors saved 477 lives and 31 bravery medals went to St Ives crews. Ten of them were awarded in the winter of 1873 when the town's rowing lifeboat, *Covent Garden*, was called to a schooner and two ketches in distress in heavy seas off Clodgy Point.

She made no headway and was eventually driven back to a nearby beach, her crew exhausted. A second crew volunteered to take out the boat and managed to rescue six seamen before they also succumbed to exposure and exhaustion. The *Covent Garden* was launched again by a third crew who managed to rescue another man, a fourth crew brought back one, and a fifth team of volunteers returned with five, making a total of thirteen. A sixth crew was standing ready to try again but by then the wind had increased to storm force and the sea was too rough to launch.

The Iron Coast of Cornwall has continued to take few prisoners. In 1938 the St Ives lifeboat capsized during a rescue operation, losing five crew, and a year later came an even worse disaster. In the early hours of 23 January 1939 the St Ives lifeboat, the *John and Sarah Elizabeth Stych*, was launched in a ninety-mile-an-hour storm to carry out a rescue off Cape Cornwall, eleven miles away. It took eighty helpers to launch the boat into the darkness of a wild winter's night.

The 2,000-ton steamer *Wilston*, bound for France with coal, was sinking and sending up red flares. When still only a mile from shore the lifeboat was hit by a massive wave and capsized. When she righted herself four of the eight-man crew were missing. The petrol engine

View from the fish cellar across the harbour.

had stalled, and while the mechanic John Griffin tried frantically to start it the boat capsized again and Griffin was drowned.

As wind and sea swept the boat across St Ives Bay towards Godrevy Head, the lifeboat rolled over once more and this time only one man, William Freeman, a 36-year-old fisherman, survived. Ironically he was a volunteer who had never previously been on a lifeboat rescue. When the *John and Sarah Elizabeth Stych* hit the rocks of Godrevy Head a few minutes later, William Freeman managed to scramble ashore and made his way to a nearby farmhouse.

The next day the wreck of the *Wilston* lay on the Longships reef, her crew

Some of today's fishing fleet at low tide.

drowned, her back broken, and flags flew at half-mast in St Ives. When the lifeboat was found her engine was still in working order. She was burned where she lay to discourage ghoulish souvenir-hunters. Seven members of the crew were posthumously awarded the RNLI's bronze medal for bravery and only William Freeman survived to have his medal pinned on his jacket. He later recorded an account of the tragedy for BBC radio but it was said that few people in the town could bear to hear it. Nearly every family in St Ives lost a relative in the disaster. The coxswain's wife lost her husband and son, eight children were fatherless and a widow was expecting a child.

But in today's bustling holiday town, such tragedies are now distant history. The shoals of pilchards finally swam away in 1924, inexplicably never to return, coastal trade tailed off to the occasional coal-boat, and St Ives, much to its surprise, found economic salvation in its scenery.

A marine painter, George Fagan Bradshaw, started the St Ives Society of Artists in 1927 and within ten years over a hundred painters, potters, sculptors, artists and illustrators had studios in cottages in the town – including Laura Knight, the Newlyn School doyen Stanhope Forbes, Ben Nicholson, Barbara Hepworth and Bernard Leach. Stanley Spencer painted seascapes during his honeymoon. Virginia Woolf put Godrevy lighthouse in a novel.

Today there are more fishermen and fishing boats in paintings in St Ives's forty galleries and craft centres than go to sea. The flower-decked holiday-let cottages and streets of double-parked Volvos are a backdrop for gourmet restaurants, and up-market coffee-houses and boutiques. Tate St Ives, opened in 1993, has just welcomed its two-millionth visitor.

The view from the town across St Ives Bay is still as breathtaking as ever and not surprisingly the place is chock-a-block with tourists from spring to autumn.

Parking is a nightmare in St Ives but there is plenty to see once you are there. Barbara Hepworth's house and garden are much as they were when the sculptress died in 1975 and round the corner from Smeaton's pier is the town museum, run by enthusiastic volunteers who will tell you anything you want to know about the history of St Ives. There is a wonderful collection of mining, fishing and maritime artefacts and the curator kindly kept the place open an hour beyond closing time while we rooted among a treasure-trove of photographs which have brought this chapter to life.

That evening we moored fore and aft off the harbour wall and grounded gently on hard white sand. At high tide the water was so clear that it magnified tiny pebbles and shells like a microscope. In this prosperous and peaceful place it was hard to remember that beyond the lighthouse the drowning coast lay patiently in wait only just around the corner.

Hayle but not hearty

Once one of the most important industrial ports of the Victorian era, Hayle, deep in the southern corner of St Ives Bay, finally closed to commercial shipping in 1977 and ever since has been the subject of elaborate regeneration plans, none of which has unfortunately yet come to fruition.

No serious dredging of the entrance channel has been carried out for over thirty years, and while the port is still used by a large shellfish fleet, strangers are advised to consult the St Ives harbourmaster about the current state of the Hayle Channel, which is notorious for its rip-currents and undertows. In calm conditions, adventurous types with shallow-draught craft can edge their way through the sandbanks about an hour before high water. The massive but largely derelict quays dry to soft mud and sand.

Regatta week at Hayle in 1909.
Sarah Foot and Michael Bossiney

Today, looking at the sad wasteland surrounding the docks, it's hard to imagine how vibrant and impressive an industrial centre Hayle once was. Over 500 people once worked on the harbour quays. A young blacksmith, John Harvey, set up a

The steamship *Hayle*, launched in 1893, in her home port, c.1900.
Reg Watkiss Archive

foundry which by 1850 was employing over 1,000 workers making steam engines, mining pumps, winding gear and, later, iron ships. The Cornish Copper Company moved from Camborne to set up a massive copper-smelting plant, resulting in a bitter dispute with Harvey over access to the sea. Eventually Harvey built his own dock and tidal reservoir, still existing as a unique piece of industrial archaeology.

A visitor to Hayle in 1860 reported a 'busy scene of bustle and industrial prosperity comparable to much larger northern and midlands towns', but in fact even by then Hayle was already in decline and Harvey's foundry finally closed in 1903. The last major industrial employer, Hayle power station, shut in 1977.

A massive regeneration scheme, backed by the Prince of Wales, includes a revitalised harbour, industrial heritage centres and a new generation of shops, restaurants and leisure facilities. In the meantime, the town which 150 years ago was at the summit of its industrial glory waits nervously for something to happen.

Panoramic harbour view in 1906.
*J C Burrows ARPS /
Reg Watkiss Archive*

We found that many people are delighted that Hayle has remained largely undiscovered and are anxious that it keeps its idiosyncratic charm. There is a three-mile stretch of golden sand in one of the very few sheltered estuaries on Cornwall's north coast. Behind the beach are the Towans – a windswept stretch of dunes on which fishermen's huts have been converted into an eccentric collection of holiday homes.

One evening we were taken by friends to one of Hayle's culinary gems – a Thai restaurant treasured by those in the know for the quality and cheapness of its food and the frankness of its proprietor, a man of apparent nautical background.

Hayle's shellfish fleet now uses the dockside warehouses.

After a superb meal we were perturbed to find that neither cheques nor credit cards would be accepted for payment on the grounds that they were operated by 'robbing bastards who won't get a penny from me'. But apparently payment was no problem: 'Go out of the front door, steer a course 287 degrees magnetic and you'll find all the money you want.' The course, followed with the aid of Wilberforce's pocket compass, took us straight to a building-society cashpoint.

19
Sleepless in Newlyn

Pretty pictures of girls on the beach
tucking their skirts into their knickers

Newlyn has always seemed to me to be the marine equivalent of the last chance saloon. Tucked away in the far western corner of Mount's Bay, there's nowhere else to go before Land's End, some twelve miles away, unless you count Mousehole, a couple of miles further on, which I don't. They're inclined to seal up their harbour entrance with boards in bad weather and that's the only time you'd really want to go in. So Newlyn harbour, behind two long piers and accessible at any state of the tide, is the ideal choice for an overnight stay en route for the Scillies or Brittany, or if you've forgotten something vital for the voyage. I once went into Newlyn to buy a pint of milk for our tea when delivering a motor-boat to Ireland.

While the rocks, shoals and assorted dangers surrounding nearby Penzance harbour are allotted nearly a page in the *English Channel Pilot*, Newlyn is a doddle. You simply steam through the 150-foot-wide entrance between the north and south piers and you're in 40 acres of completely protected water with long stone jetties to moor against and a quaint little town to explore. At least that's the theory,

Bystanders admire the
Newlyn fishing fleet,
c.1880.
Reg Watkiss Archive

spoiled only by the fact that Newlyn is now England's largest fishing port, with a fleet of over 170 beam trawlers, long-liners and crabbers working around the clock – and fishermen don't take very kindly to pleasure-boaters getting in the way.

There's no room in Newlyn for visitors' moorings and you raft up where you can, preferably against a fishing boat that doesn't look as though it's likely to cast you adrift in the middle of the night. Keep away from the North Pier, which tends to the needs of the deep-sea trawlers of W Stevenson & Son, now the largest fleet under one ownership in Britain, with gear and nets piled high on the quay and everyone in a hurry. In the middle of the harbour, parallel to North Pier, is Mary Williams Pier, where boats are smaller and have a more relaxed attitude. If they are sailing at three in the morning, they will usually tell you beforehand, but not always, and it's rare for yachties to get a decent night's sleep in Newlyn.

The Newlyn lugger fleet in the 1880s.
Reg Watkiss Archive

I never quite understood why, if you have to go fishing in the middle of the night, you need to wake everyone else up in the process. One evening some years ago I arrived in Newlyn in *Shamrock*, our 80-year-old retired Colchester oyster smack, in company with a plastic yacht. We both rafted up alongside a rusty sidewinder trawler whose crew reluctantly took our lines with the ritual warning, 'You can't stay here – we're sailing later.' At 4 am we were woken by lights and commotion, but no one told us to move so we stayed where we were and went back to sleep. In the morning we found that the trawler had gone. *Shamrock* had been silently moved and carefully moored and fendered alongside a nearby crabber. The yacht had been untied and allowed to drift onto a nearby mud-bank where it stayed aground, but luckily unharmed, until the next tide.

Seeing the mate of the sidewinder in a pub the following day, we asked about the discrepancy in the treatment of the trawler's unwelcome guests. 'We saw the numbers [fishing registration] on your boat and reckoned you were one of us,' the mate said. 'We couldn't care less about yachts.' I suppose we shouldn't have been surprised: the somewhat perverse solidarity of Newlyn fishermen is legendary, and in the past has got them in a lot of bother in one way and another.

If we thought Sunday fishing had caused problems in St Ives, it was nothing compared with the commotion caused when a fleet of Lowestoft drifters arrived in Newlyn on the Sabbath in May 1896 and began to unload a catch of mackerel, resulting in what became known as the Newlyn Riots. According to a report in the *West Briton* newspaper:

> Three hundred Cornish fishermen arrived on the North Pier and despite the efforts of the police and the coastguard, forced their way on to the Lowestoft vessels and threw a large quantity of fish into the sea.
>
> The visiting boats were advised to put to sea but when they did so they were followed by at least six Newlyn craft. Eight Lowestoft boats were boarded in the bay and severe damage inflicted to equipment including sails. In addition, further fish were thrown overboard.

When the local boats returned, chains were stretched across the entrance of the harbour to prevent Lowestoft boats from entering. Due to the inflammatory nature of the situation the Newlyn Magistrates decided that no action should be taken against the rioters until feelings had subsided and the authorities had all matters under control.

There was little chance of that. Next day, hearing that the Lowestoft drifters intended to dock in nearby Penzance, over 200 men marched from Newlyn but were beaten back on the outskirts of the town after hand-to-hand fighting with police and coastguards. The situation was only resolved when a gunboat full of troops arrived in Newlyn. No criminal charges were ever brought against the rioters. While an official inquiry held later in the year ruled that it was not illegal to land fish on any day of the week, visiting fleets tended to steer clear of Newlyn from then on, preferring to land fish in Penzance or Plymouth.

There has been a harbour at Newlyn since the fourteenth century, but its growth as a major fishing port came only in the eighteenth century when its fleet of luggers and seiners became the biggest and most prosperous in Cornwall. In January and February they fished for mackerel off south Devon, following the shoals westwards to Mounts Bay for a couple of months. They moved to Irish waters for the herring season, returning in July to catch pilchards until September.

Luggers returning to port, c.1900.
Reg Watkiss Archive

Nor were they just coastal craft. In 1854 Captain Richard Nicholls and six crew left Newlyn in the 15-ton lugger *Mystery* – bound for Australia! She was built in Newlyn and owned by Nicholls, Job Kelynack, Richard Badcock, William Badcock, Lewis Lewis, Charles Boase and Philip Matthews. Fishing was bad, the tin-mining industry was in virtual collapse, and the men met in Newlyn's Star Inn to discuss the possibility of emigrating to Australia. When Job Kelynack suggested selling *Mystery* to pay their passage, his brother-in-law, Richard Nicholls, on leave as skipper of a 700-ton brig, said 'No, we'll sail her there. I'll be the navigator.'

Mystery was decked in fore and aft and her bottom sheathed with zinc. She left Newlyn in November 1854 and arrived in Melbourne, Australia, 115 days later after a seven-day stop in Cape Town. The *Cornish Telegraph* reported:

Captain Nicholls put into Cape Town for stores and water and the sight of this tiny craft no bigger than a ship's boat caused the greatest astonishment among the locals. As the regular mail-boat had not turned up the skipper agreed to take letters to Melbourne where in due course he arrived safely without serious incident other than having to ride at a sea-anchor for several days in the worst of westerly gales.

On arrival, *Mystery* was sold for £150 and became a pilot cutter. She was eventually wrecked in Keppel Bay, Queensland in 1869 but all her crew were saved. Philip

Matthews and Lewis Lewis remained in Australia, but the other five eventually returned to England. Job Kelynack, Charles Boase and the Badcock brothers returned to fishing in Newlyn and their descendants still live in the town. Richard Nicholls, after surviving the longest voyage ever made at that time by so small a craft, was knocked down and killed in Charing Cross Road, London by a horse-drawn cab. A plaque on the wall of the Newlyn Royal Mission to Seaman commemorates what is thought to be the first recorded epic voyage of a fishing boat converted into a yacht.

On a wet Monday, Newlyn has the grey severity of some Scottish fishing ports. Many of the picturesque dockside cottages were knocked down, despite public outcry, in the 1930s, but even before that there wasn't a lot to write home about, as Dr Johnson's great friend, the elderly Mrs Piozzi, found in 1810. She reported: 'No milliners' shops, no rooms, no theatre, no music meetings, no pleasure – and no expense.' As she had arrived from Bath expressly to save money, that suited her fine.

Nowadays, Newlyn lands fish worth around £20 million a year, more than any other port in the UK, and yet prosperity is not immediately apparent. There are a few galleries, pubs, cafés, fish and chip shops and chandlery stores but little in the way of trendy high-street shopping, and a recent study into the future of the port linked to a possible £57 million development programme detected a 'clannishness' which it was thought could be hindering Newlyn's progress as a major tourist venue.

Like Watchet, where our voyage began, Newlyn has always been a working port, not a seaside resort. Its gritty history rather than its scenery brought fleeting fame, if not fortune, when an extension of the Great Western Railway to west Cornwall was completed in 1877. That was when artists began to arrive in the town, drawn by the purity of the light, the low cost of living and the picturesque hardship of the fishing community.

Newlyn, as it was in the 1900s …
St Ives Museum

By the mid-1880s the Newlyn School of painting had been established and nearly thirty artists were working in the town, painting everyday outdoor life in the *plein air* tradition originally started by the Barbizon School in France, where followers of Gaugin had chronic-led the poverty and misfortunes of Breton fishermen and their families on the cruel coasts of Brittany. One of the first to arrive in the town was Walter Langley, from a working-class background in Birmingham, soon hard at work depicting the hardships and dangers of life at sea. He was followed by Stanhope Forbes, whose picture *A Fish Sale on a Cornish Beach* was the talk of the 1885 Royal Academy summer exhibition, and Frank Bramley, whose *A Hopeless Dawn*, depicting women waiting vainly for a fishing boat's return, became a quintessential Newlyn masterpiece. Bramley, along with Walter Langley, Henry Tuke, Norman Garstin and Ralph Todd, concentrated on the tragic side of life in the seafaring community.

They were on to a winner. By 1888 several artists were successful enough to have studios built on a meadow overlooking the harbour. Anchor Studio, built for Stanhope Forbes and his artist wife Elizabeth Armstrong, has become a listed building and there are plans to restore it to its original Victorian state. Less successful painters lived with local fishing families and used their pictures as currency for board and lodging.

... and as it is now, still a fishing port.

By the early twentieth century, the Newlyn School, once hailed as 'uncompromising realism' and 'absolute fidelity to nature', was going out of fashion and the First World War further lessened the public's appetite for harrowing pictures of poverty and danger at sea. Ever adaptable, the Newlyn artists looked to other markets. Laura Knight, who had lived with her husband Harold in Newlyn for twelve years, became celebrated as a painter of portraits and horses. Dod Proctor (born Doris Shaw), a pupil of Stanhope Forbes, exchanged painting fishermen for nude female figures. The *Daily Mail* bought one of her pictures for the Tate Gallery. Henry Tuke gave up bleak seascapes to paint naked boys on sunlit beaches, which caused his contemporaries some concern. The patriotic Stanhope Forbes painted soldiers going to war.

The painter and sculptor Alexander Hollweg, who lives in the house once occupied by another former Newlyn artist, Garnet Wolsley, said that Garnet saw which way the wind was blowing and by 1910 'was painting pretty pictures of girls on the beach tucking their skirts into their knickers'.

Alex's grandfather, the celebrated Vorticist artist Edward Wadsworth, painted marine abstracts which are now in the Tate Gallery and successfully tried his hand at designing camouflage for dreadnoughts. He also spent a short time painting in Newlyn during an epic hike from London along the Southwest Peninsula in the summer of 1920. 'My grandmother disliked Newlyn intensely,' Alex said. 'She thought it was a very dull place.'

Although nowhere near the number to be found in St Ives, there are still many artists in Newlyn today. You can see Norman Garstin's classic painting *The Rain It Raineth Every Day* in the renowned Penlee House gallery in Penzance and there is a permanent Post-Impressionist Newlyn School exhibition in Newlyn's Orion gallery. Wilberforce particularly asked to see *A Fish Sale on a Cornish Beach*, of which he had had a copy in a children's encyclopaedia. A modest request and one, as so often in Wilberforce's life, which was doomed to disappointment. The picture, he was told, was in a gallery in Plymouth.

Mousehole — sea salts and sail

Mousehole, pronounced 'Mouzel', has nothing to do with mice. One theory is that the name derives from the Cornish *Moeshayle*, meaning 'at the mouth of the river of young women'. Precisely what that means is sadly lost in history, but Wilberforce means to do more research another time.

Mousehole men, hauling a boat ashore, *c.*1890.
© *Judges /*
David B Clement collection

Back in the thirteenth century Mousehole was the main port in Mounts Bay, and it remained so until Penzance and Newlyn, less exposed to southerly gales, began to gain ascendancy as commercial fishing harbours. But even as late as 1850 over 400 fishermen were working on Mousehole luggers, which fished as far afield as the North Sea herring grounds.

These were good days for the tiny village. In addition to the fishermen, Mousehole gave work to 370 packers, 45 fish curers, and four cooperages, which made the barrels in which salted pilchards were packed for export. It was said that everyone in Mousehole earned his or her living from fish.

Fishing from Mousehole was always hazardous, and great baulks of timber close the harbour against winter gales. It was at the height of a November storm in 1907 that the Thames sailing barge *Baltic*, bound for Newlyn with cement, went aground outside Mousehole. Her crew and the captain's wife and daughter were rescued by six fishermen who manhandled the crabber *White Lady* over the timber baulks. The *Baltic* was salvaged and returned to Essex, but a young Irish sailor on board settled in Mousehole and married the harbourmaster's daughter.

Mousehole today. The harbour entrance is closed against winter storms.

A legendary figure in the village was Dolly Pentreath, said to be the last person to speak Cornish as her native tongue. She sold fish, smoked a pipe and was claimed to have a voice you could hear as far away as Newlyn. It was said that when a press-gang landed to take up Mousehole fishermen for the navy Dolly took up a hatchet and drove them back to their boats. She died in 1777 at the age of 102 and is buried in the neighbouring parish of Paul.

At one time Mousehole even had its own maritime court, sitting outside and as close as possible to the sea to hear cases involving seamen, shipping merchants and fishermen. It was a principle of early maritime law that such people had the right, on arrival in port, to appeal to a maritime court to right a wrong or injustice. Detailed records were not kept but it's known that the Mousehole court dealt with disputes over the price of fish, damaged cargo, careless pilotage, injury at sea, collisions and breaches of contract.

After the Second World War, facilities at Newlyn had improved so much that most of the Mousehole fishing boats moved there, but the village hasn't forgotten its past. Every two years there's a Sea Salts and Sail maritime festival which invites back remaining Mounts Bay luggers and stages displays of local crafts, photographs and memorabillia. 'Mousehole has a vast amount of history that is rapidly being lost,' one of the organisers, Leon Pezzack, told us. 'We were once one of the main fishing ports in the Southwest, and the festival is a wonderful way of making people aware of our heritage.'

The village has had a long and often traumatic relationship with the sea and its lifeboat, stationed at nearby Penlee since 1913, carried out many heroic rescues including saving the crew of the legendary battleship *Warspite*, driven ashore in a gale while on tow to the scrapyard in 1947. But the most traumatic night in Mousehole's recent history was in December 1981 when the lifeboat *Solomon Browne* was launched into 40-foot waves to aid the brand new bulk carrier *Union Star*. On her maiden voyage in ballast from Denmark to Ireland, the *Union Star* was blown ashore in a hurricane near Land's End after her engines failed.

On board were Captain Henry Morton, his wife, two teenage stepdaughters and a crew of four. In appalling conditions, the lifeboat managed to get alongside the *Union Star* and take off four survivors. While attempting to rescue the rest, the *Solomon Browne* smashed against the ship and disintegrated. Everyone on board the *Union Star* and Cox'n Trevelyan Richards and his seven crew were drowned. The lifeboat station was moved to Newlyn after the disaster and all the *Solomon Browne*'s crew received posthumous medals. A quarter-century later the obvious scars may have healed but the village has not forgotten. The lifeboat house has been preserved as a memorial, and every year on 19 December the Mousehole Christmas lights are switched off in memory of the men who gave their lives.

Rosebud approaching Big Ben.
Morrab Library

Rosebud's epic voyage

On a grey morning in October 1936, to the sound of hundreds of people singing 'Fight the good fight', the motor trawler *Rosebud*, skippered by Cecil Richards, left Newlyn harbour on a 450-mile voyage to London to deliver a petition signed by over 1,000 townspeople to the House of Commons complaining about the local council's draconian decision to pull down nearly 200 cottages, fishing lofts and workshops on the waterfront.

Penzance council had decided the properties were beyond repair and planned to demolish the lot and move the occupants to a new estate on the outskirts of town. A committee of fishermen, artists, shopkeepers and local residents failed to persuade the council to change its mind and repair the historic buildings and it was decided to send the *Rosebud* up the Thames with a petition.

The voyage made the national newspapers but whether it actually made any difference is still undecided in Newlyn. Demolition started, but only one block of houses was destroyed before the outbreak of war put a stop to all building activity. After the war, the houses of Old Newlyn were regarded as part of the town's historic heritage and were restored and repaired. Sadly, *Rosebud* was less fortunate. She was decommissioned and rotted to bits in a creek near St Ives.

20
Speechless in Porthleven

Are you looking for a house?

Porthleven, a pretty little granite town, and England's most southerly port, sits on the eastern edge of Mounts Bay and puts a brave face on things. It retains an old-world charm and in the summer its harbour is busy with pleasure craft and a small fleet of lobster and crab boats. We rafted up against an old Penzance long-liner – there was no room alongside the quay in the inner basin – and Wilberforce hurried ashore. He had set his heart on an ice-lolly.

But this is not really how Porthleven wanted things to be. For nearly a century the place yearned to be a major commercial port but simply never quite managed it. The tin-mining centre of Helston, only three miles inshore, preferred to ship its cargoes from Penzance or Newlyn and the massive Victorian quays, built with such high hopes, were used largely by the local pilchard fleets.

The reason wasn't hard to find: Porthleven spends most of its time on a lee shore. It is rare to find a Cornish harbour which faces southwest, directly into the prevailing wind, but Porthleven does, and over the years it has paid a heavy price for being in the wrong place at the wrong time. We found that even a light wind and a moderate sea can make entry into Porthleven cove more worrying than it should be.

It was in 1811 that an Act of Parliament was obtained for the construction of an artificial harbour to provide a safe haven for wind-bound vessels forced to shelter from the Atlantic gales which roared unchecked into Mounts Bay. The task proved longer and more expensive than the newly formed Porthleven Harbour Company had imagined

Luggers and mackerel-drivers shelter in Porthleven's pretty harbour, c.1900.
St Ives Museum

and the work, which included employing Napoleonic War prisoners to remove 380,000 tons of mud and gravel, largely by hand, took over fourteen years.

Finally completed in 1825, the harbour was opened with a feast of roast beef and plum pudding for the whole village, but the celebrations were short-lived. A few months later the harbour was completely destroyed by a storm, prompting a local dignitary, Davies Gilbert, President of the Royal Society, to complain that 'Credulous persons had been induced to contribute large sums of money for the purpose of rebuilding the harbour under the vague pretence of saving human life – a senseless undertaking which has utterly failed in its object and made the harbour even less suitable for boats than it was before.'

Nevertheless, by 1850, Porthleven had a 100-strong fishing fleet employing nearly 300 fishermen and packers. In 1855 the harbour company was bought by Harvey and Co of Hayle, who installed lock gates allowing ships to remain afloat at all states of the tide. It was hoped this would bring a resurgence of coasting trade, and for a while Porthleven did fulfil its dream of becoming a busy boat-building and ship-owning port, until the mining slump of 1880 scuppered its hopes for good, although occasional small cargoes continued to arrive until after the First World War.

Local fishermen provide authenticity for this Victorian postcard.
Pictorial Stationery Co. – Peacock Series / David B Clement collection

The fishing fleet of Mounts Bay luggers and mackerel-drivers returned to enjoy free range of the impressive granite quays, and ironically it was fishing that brought a new and unexpected prosperity to the Porthleven waterfront. In the 1880s fishing accounted for over 80 per cent of Mount's Bay's income. Penzance alone had 300 lug-rigged mackerel-drivers, and when skippers needed a new boat it was invariably to Porthleven that they came – where the yard of Kitto and Son was producing some of the finest West Country fishing boats ever built.

Richard Kitto had served his apprenticeship at Symonds' yard in Penzance. In 1847 he received a testimonial from the King of Norway 'in recognition of his gallant services' during the rescue of the crew of the Norwegian schooner *Elizabeth*, wrecked off nearby Mullion, and three years later he opened his own business in Porthleven. Soon Kitto's yard was the biggest and busiest in the area, employing over 100 shipwrights and building a variety of craft including 50-ton coastal schooners. The firm also made nets on Cornwall's first net-making loom, brought from Bridport in Dorset.

By the turn of the century, Kitto's had customers as far away from Cornwall as Ramsgate, Brighton, Folkestone and parts of France. They built some of the first steam trawlers for Lowestoft and Yarmouth, but luggers, fast becoming an anachronism, remained Richard Kitto's first love. A Kitto lugger wasn't lofted out, but built by eye from a half-model to the ideas and specifications of the customer.

Pilchard-drivers and crabbers in Porthleven harbour, c.1900.
W M Harrison / Reg Watkiss Archive

For a fisherman in Folkestone Kitto's built a 40-foot carvel-built decked dipping lugger of Norwegian red deal on sawn oak frames. She was named *Happy Return*, and was to remain in Folkestone, in a variety of manifestations, for the next 93 years.

Descended from the three-masted Cornish smuggling luggers of the late eighteenth century, the classic Kitto drifter evolved from open boats and half-decked pilchard-drivers in which the crew slept as best they could in heavy oilskin capes. By the mid-1850s, decked luggers were being built to over 50 feet, working fleets of drift-nets up to a mile and a half long. By the 1880s Porthleven boats had evolved gradually from round-bowed to a more yacht-like profile, prompting judges at the 1883 International Fisheries exhibition in London to declare that, in their opinion, the Mounts Bay lugger fleet was the world's finest.

Certainly the fleets of Newlyn, Penzance and Porthleven were superb sea-boats, manned by fishermen who thought nothing of fishing seventy or eighty miles offshore, and which rode the seas beautifully. Distance never seemed to daunt Mounts Bay skippers. The lugger *Nelly Jane*, built by Kitto in 1897, sailed from Scarborough to Mounts Bay in 56 hours in 1905 with only two nights at sea in a strong northeasterly blow. On another occasion, *Nelly Jane* sailed 600 miles in 70 hours. Fishermen reckoned a lugger's best point of sailing was on the wind, when speeds of ten knots were commonplace. The favourite amount of wind was known as a two-mizzen breeze, when a big mizzen sail was set on the foremast and a smaller one aft.

The *Happy Return*'s rededication at Penzance in 2003.
The Mounts Bay Lugger Association

Porthleven boats fished all year round and carried three fleets of nets. The mackerel season was from January until June or July and luggers often sailed over 100 miles to meet the shoals as they came north. The foremast was lowered when the nets were out and the boats and nets 'drove' with the tide – hence the name mackerel-driver. Summer herring-fishing started around July until August or early September off Ireland and the Shetlands, or in the North Sea until October, out of Whitby and Scarborough. After that, they followed the pilchard shoals out of their home ports, often hand-lining for hake in October and November. When the pilchard season was over, herring and mackerel nets were put on board for fishing out of Plymouth or mackerel-driving off the Scillies. If the holds were empty, skippers often brought home potatoes or coal.

In those sunlit days, no one ever imagined that fish stocks would run out, but by 1910 numbers had fallen dramatically and twenty years later no sailing luggers were working in Mounts Bay. Even Kitto's yard closed in 1959 when the founder's grandson, James Richard Kitto, finally retired. The nearby Loe Bar, a great barrier of sand and flint, is now a Site of Special Scientific Interest.

Meanwhile, in the English Channel, *Happy Return* was crabbing, long-lining and trawling under the succession of owners. In 1971, she had her last commercial skipper – Peter Barrett – who fished her continuously until 1987 when she drove ashore in a storm and was an insurance write-off. Peter bought her back, and after extensive repairs she became the UK's oldest working fishing boat until

decommissioned by MAFF in 1998 and destined for the breaker's yard. Fortuitously, the Mounts Bay Lugger Association happened to be looking for an authentic mackerel-driver to restore and heard about *Happy Return*. Peter Barrett eventually persuaded the authorities to allow her to return to Cornwall for restoration and in May 1998 he motored the lugger 300 miles to Penzance. She had a wheel-house, no rig, and looked like a little old trawler, but her basic lines were still there, and the Association knew that with time, effort – and a lot of money – she could be restored to how Kitto's built her.

The *Happy Return* bowls along in a two-mizzen breeze.
The Mounts Bay Lugger Association

And so it was that five years later, in March 2003, after a £90,000 rebuild *Happy Return* was launched in Penzance Harbour, watched by an emotional Peter Barrett and by relatives of the original owners. 'It was like a dream come true,' Dr Mike Hope, a trustee of the Association, told us. 'There had been so many problems and setbacks. But there she was, for all the world like a new boat, back where she came from.'

Today, the *Happy Return*, crewed by Association volunteers, is used regularly as an educational and sail-training ship and is a major attraction at French and UK sea festivals. After nearly a century away from Mounts Bay, *Happy Return* is finally back – to stay.

Sadly, Porthleven's massive slip hadn't seen a locally built boat launched since the late 1970s – although Wilberforce discovered that two Porthleven-built trawlers were still working out of Brixham. Today the town, with narrow streets climbing steep hillsides, is a pleasant mix of fishing port and holiday resort with restaurants, pubs, galleries and gift shops trading alongside fishmongers and chandlers.

Stroll along the quay and you will pass a three-storey building which was once pilchard-curing cellars. Next door is the Wreck and Rescue Centre, formerly a clay store housing up to 7,000 tons of china clay from the Tregonning Hill quarries, which was exported to Europe and even America. Either side of the harbour are two cannon from the frigate HMS *Anson*, which took part in the battle of Brest against the French in 1794. The *Anson* was wrecked on Loe Bar in 1807 with the loss of 120 of her crew.

Over a beer in the Atlantic Inn with local historian Alan Spencer and lobster fisherman Roy Bolitho, we learned that a hamlet of fishermen's dwellings was established in the cove in the fourteenth century. Boats were kept behind a shingle bar in marshland fed by a stream. Alan said that the stream still flows through the valley and divides the village into two parishes, Sithney to the east and Breage to the west.

Roy said there were seven generations of Bolithos in local churchyards but many of his forebears had died at sea. 'Even today, with big powerful boats, a lot of fishermen won't come into Porthleven,' he said. 'You've only got to see the place in a southwesterly gale to know why. I've seen waves go right over the Institute clock-tower and that's seventy foot high. No wonder we shut up the harbour with baulks of timber in the winter and the fishermen have to move to Newlyn.'

Porthleven today – a pleasant mix of fishing port and holiday resort.

Alan Spencer complained that Roy was giving Porthleven a bad name. 'Tourists love it, and look at the harbour – it's full of yachts,' he said. 'We have concerts and gig-racing. There's always something going on.' Roy Bolitho finished his pint and held out the glass to Wilberforce. 'You can show me *your* appreciation of the place by getting me another,' he said. For once, Wilberforce was speechless.

That evening, as long warm shadows spread along the quays, Wilberforce and I went in search of any remains of Kitto's yard. We found nothing. Asked 'Do you know where Kitto's is?' an elderly man carrying three mackerel in a Kwiksave bag pointed down a narrow street and said, 'Are you looking for a house?' It was a minor mystery which was quickly solved. Kitto's, we discovered, was a large Cornish estate agents.

The holy headland of Penzance

For nearly a century, Penzance laid claim to be Cornwall's major port. By the 1850s, half of Cornwall's tin was shipped from its wharves to Turkey, Italy, Russia, France and Holland, and there were 27 registered ship-owners in the town. But 25 years later Penzance's major export was people.

During the first six months of 1875 nearly 11,000 emigrants left Penzance for Australia and the *Mecca*, a locally-owned 400-ton barque, made regular sailings to New York, 'with very superior accommodation for both cabin and steerage passengers and every precaution to promote the health and comfort of passengers by regularly fumigating the ship during the voyage'. Both the *Mecca* and her sister-ship the *Oregon* offered to provide passengers with letters of introduction to contacts who 'can put them in the way of procuring employment'.

A much shorter voyage – the 28 miles to the Isles of Scilly – was less well organised: in 1827 the Scilly packet was dismasted in a gale and only the fact that many of the passengers were experienced seamen enabled the ship to make Penzance safely. Four years later the same vessel caught fire and, according to the *West Briton* newspaper, 'terror and confusion on board was very great and 17 passengers found there were no lifeboats in which to make their escape'. The passengers' fate is unknown.

Penzance harbour in 1869. The paddle-steamer (centre) is the *Earl of Arran*, wrecked in 1872 on the Penzance–Scillies service.
Robert Preston / Reg Watkiss Archive

Today Penzance – ancient Cornish for 'Holy Headland' – with a permanent population of 20,000, relies on tourism rather than its harbour for its prosperity. Part of the dock has been filled in to make a car-park, but maritime history is everywhere. The first news of Nelson's victory and death at Trafalgar in October 1805 was announced on the balcony of the Assembly Rooms, now the Union Hotel. A Penzance lugger had got the information from HMS *Pickle*, racing up-channel with government dispatches for London.

A glorious three-acre subtropical garden is an unlikely find in the middle of a busy town but there's one in the middle of Penzance. It surrounds Morrab House, a nineteenth-century mansion which is now an independent library and archive

A late Victorian dockside scene showing two barques in the floating harbour.
Reg Watkiss Archive

– once again staffed by volunteers who could not have been more helpful in providing photographs and information. When Wilberforce recently remarked that Mr Morrab must have done all right for himself, I said that surely everyone knew that the word was Cornish for 'land near to the sea'? It seemed unnecessary to mention that I had been put right by a friendly lady librarian when I had made the same mistake.

In the season Penzance is a busy yacht haven with limited moorings, and often it's necessary to raft up alongside trawlers and other working vessels, prompting proposals for a new 200-berth marina

and an improved ferry terminal, which are currently seeking EU funding in an effort to re-establish Penzance as what it has historically always been: the first major port of call for the Atlantic voyager.

21

Making a packet at Falmouth

The streets sparkled with gold epaulets, gold lace hats and brilliant uniforms

Sailing vessels and steamers at Falmouth's coaling arm.
David B Clement collection

The first time I dropped anchor in the Fal estuary, on a dark and stormy night some thirty years ago, I had just lost my ten-year-old son at sea and was in no mood to appreciate the delights of the world's third-largest natural harbour. To be less melodramatic, Tim wasn't lost, just temporarily mislaid, but I wasn't to know that at the time.

We were three days into a family holiday, cruising towards the Scillies in our 44-foot Colchester oyster smack *Shamrock* in company with *Wind Dance*, an elderly Hillyard sloop owned by my good friend John Owen, a farmer who invariably sailed alone. Mid-afternoon found us motoring across a flat windless sea under a cloudless sky some five miles south of Salcombe on a course which hopefully would bring the Lizard abeam about midnight and take us into Hugh Town, St Mary's, in time for an early breakfast.

By early evening, as we chugged westward at five knots, Tim, having read all his *Beano* comics and eaten all his Smarties, announced that he was bored and wanted to get off. Could he join *Wind Dance* for a while? John, motoring nearby, agreed, came alongside, and Tim was hauled aboard. The plan was that he would return in an hour for supper – but Davy Jones obviously thought otherwise, a summer gale arrived literally out of the blue, and that was the last we saw of Tim and John for three days.

By 10 pm it was black and wet and a howling southwesterly was kicking up a massive sea. It seemed sensible to curtail the entertainment for the day and run for the shelter of Falmouth, some ten miles away. There was no VHF radio in those distant days but I assumed John would see what we were doing and have a similar sense of self-preservation. I had forgotten that like Captain McWhirr, in

Merchant shipping and yachts anchor side-by-side in this dramatic scene of Falmouth's heyday of sail.
William Sharman / David B Clement collection

Conrad's short story *Typhoon*, John tended to be heroically single-minded in the face of danger.

As it transpired, it never occurred to him to divert from his course, and *Wind Dance* plunged on into the gale, pitching so deeply into the waves that Tim, not a timid child, was certain they would die. 'This is really good fun,' John shouted above the scream of the wind.

It took us three hours in a breaking beam sea to reach Falmouth, the safest of all West Country harbours. The sky was lightening as we anchored off the town. There was hardly a ripple on the water, but outside the gale still roared in the bay. We were storm-bound all the next day and it was a slight consolation that the coastguard had no reports of any yacht sunk or in difficulties. We finally arrived on the Isles of Scilly two days later to find *Wind Dance* moored unharmed in Hugh Town and Tim, pale but cheerful, fishing from the dinghy. John said it had been an interesting but not particularly eventful trip.

I related this little parable to Wilberforce to show what a valuable refuge for sailing craft the Fal estuary has always been. Its mile-wide entrance, between St Anthony's Head and Pendennis Point, can be entered day and night in all weathers and at all states of the tide. Only Plymouth Sound can rival it as a West Country safe haven, providing you steer clear of the dreadnoughts.

The Fal estuary is a drowned river dating from the last Ice Age and winding some eleven miles through steep wooded valleys to the city of Truro. The first four miles, known as Carrick Roads, are at no point less than a mile wide, a huge expanse of sheltered water with creeks and inlets, accessible at all times and in all weathers – perfect for small-boat sailing, even in a Channel gale. To port is Falmouth, tucked behind the Pendennis headland, a busy seaport handling ships of up to 150,000 tons, and neighbouring Flushing and Penryn. A mile upstream is Mylor, once the smallest Royal Navy dockyard in the country and now a busy yacht harbour and marina. A mile further on is the narrow entrance to Restronguet Creek with its ghost port of Devoran.

From here on, the river narrows dramatically. Silent and sepulchral, it remains so deep that mothballed freighters and rusting obsolescent tankers can moor under the trees at King Harry Ferry, some eight miles from the sea, waiting for some economic miracle or, more likely, the blow-torches of the breaker's yard.

Old wharves and creek-side churches appear without warning from deep foliage and herons sit motionless at the water's edge.

You can still motor up-river to Truro if you have the time and the inclination. It has been a port since the twelfth century and on spring tides a few small freighters still find their way to the Town Quay. The channel is tortuous and littered with sand bars and low-tide mud-flats.

The eastern bank of Carrick Roads contains further delights. The village of St Mawes, hidden behind St Anthony's Head on the northern side of the Percuil River, was from

The Devoran smack *Daisy* moored at St Mawes.
RIC / David B Clement collection

medieval times a busy port and fishing harbour and today is a safe and popular yacht haven. Two miles upstream, the tiny anchorage of St Just Creek is snug in anything but a strong southwesterly.

Henry VIII built two castles – at St Mawes and Pendennis – to guard the entrance to the Roads, and they were the making of Falmouth. Previously it was called Smithwick and was little more than a village, but after it changed its name in 1660 it soon eclipsed Penryn – a mile away up a muddy creek – as the estuary's main port.

It was in the passage between the two castles that the tale of my son's disappearance was neatly rounded off by his arrival at the wheel of his top-of-the-range Moody 35 yacht with central heating and en-suite bathroom. He was no less welcome for being thirty years late. In fact we had arranged to meet up that morning. A successful musician and media composer, Tim now lives in Falmouth with his young family and moors his boat at Mylor, which became the rendezvous for our stay. We went ashore for milk and in Mylor churchyard I showed Wilberforce a gravestone which read:

Here lies Joseph Crapp, shipwright
Who died on board ship June 1770
Aged 40.
His foot did slip and he did fall
'Help, help,' he cried and that was all.

Wilberforce said the inscription only confirmed his view that we must be mad to go sailing.

It was Sir Walter Raleigh, returning from discovering the coast of Guinea, who was the first to see the possibilities of Falmouth as a major deep-water port and persuaded his friend, the financier Sir John Killigrew, to build a customs-house, quays and a market. In 1688, Falmouth became a Post Office packet station, first dealing with mail to and from Spain and then to the rest of Europe, America and the West Indies. By the 1820s there were forty packet-boats based in Falmouth, mostly small neat brigantines, designed for speed, armed with cannon for defence and carrying crews of forty or fifty, including a surgeon.

He was often needed. On the high seas, packets were at the mercy of pirates and privateers and regarded as fair game by the enemy during the Napoleonic Wars. Some of them fought, and even won, bloody battles against ships manned by larger and better-armed crews. Between 1812 and 1814, for instance, Falmouth packets were involved in 32 actions against the French and won 17. Legally, they were not ships of war and were not supposed to use their guns unless first attacked. If they had no chance of escaping or winning, masters had orders to strike their colours and sink their mails.

But many packets never hesitated to fight

A Falmouth Quay Punt racing in the harbour, c.1910.
Robert Simper collection

Errand-boys of the sea

As Falmouth became a major deep-sea port in the Victorian age a new species of sailing craft evolved – the Falmouth Quay Punt, so called because they operated from the busy Custom House Quay. By 1880, a fleet of over thirty quay punts were indispensable work-horses in the harbour, running errands for ship-owners and servicing the needs of vessels calling at Falmouth for orders. Most were carvel-built yawls with fuller lines and deeper hulls than the oyster-dredgers. Mostly they worked within the port limits, but they would occasionally sail out into the English Channel to meet incoming ships with messages and mail and to take orders for food, chandlery and even clothes, which would be delivered when the vessel docked.

The earliest punts were open 18-footers but by the 1870s they had evolved into 25- to 30-foot half-deckers which could almost be mistaken for yachts with their deep draught, cutaway forefoot, heavy iron keels, manila running gear and wire shrouds. Yawl rig was preferred so that masts could be kept short in order not to foul the braces and yards when coming alongside a square-rigger, and because it was easily worked under jib and mizzen when short-handed or in bad weather.

The day of the Falmouth Quay Punt finally ended after the First World War when the number of sailing ships trading with Falmouth dropped dramatically. A few punts survived by fitting motors, but that cut profits to the point where there was hardly a living to be made and by 1930 all the sailing punts had all been replaced by motor-boats. Today a few quay punts still exist, but as yacht conversions. These include the 28-foot *Louis Will* and the 26-foot *Greenshank*.

back, as in the case of a ship attacked by a French frigate off Jamaica. When the master and mate were killed, the boatswain, Richard Pasco, took command, lashing the two ships together and 'pouring musket-fire into the enemy until they cried for mercy.' Thirty Frenchmen were killed. The packet captured a lucrative prize with the loss of two killed and four wounded.

Packets also carried passengers. In the early nineteenth century the fare from Falmouth to New York was £54, and £107 to Brazil. They were also trading vessels, under an unofficial arrangement which allowed officers and crew to carry merchandise to the port of destination.

In 1815, James Silk Buckingham, master of a Falmouth packet, remembered that he took 'a little trading stock of velveteens, muslins and other articles sure to find a ready sale'. Officers and crews from well-established Falmouth families were allowed considerable amounts of goods on credit. One captain took £5,000 of general goods, including watches and jewellery, his officers £2–3,000 worth of goods and the men up to £1,000 each on sale or return. Arriving in port, the goods were by arrangement 'smuggled ashore' – customs officers, the government and even the Church sharing the profits of this trade.

Returning to Falmouth, dutiable goods were landed secretly with the connivance of the customs, who took a share of the profits. According to Buckingham, packet crews traded in 'Havannah segars, port wine and other articles paying a high duty in England'. It was a lucrative business: by the early nineteenth century the packets' private cargoes were worth £4 million a year. Technically it was contraband, but it was a crime that was rarely punished, probably because Falmouth's chief magistrate, Captain Isaac Cort, was also the town's most successful smuggler. But the days of the sailing packets were numbered. The last scheduled voyage by the *Seagull* was in December 1850, and from then on the service was run by steamers operating on far stricter regulations.

The classic tea-clipper *Cutty Sark* in Falmouth, 1930.
David B Clement collection

But by now Falmouth didn't need the packet trade. It was a dynamic seaport and a major port of call for orders for outward- and homeward-bound ships. Nearly twenty countries had consuls there and in 1835, during a storm, 350 vessels rode out the weather in the harbour. The local newspaper, the *West Briton*, reported proudly, 'They left having sustained scarcely any damage, a thing unprecedented in any other port in Great Britain.'

In 1872, an average year during Falmouth's golden age of shipping, 7,500 vessels docked in the port, spending over £15,000 on pilotage, more than in any other British port except London. By now, Falmouth not only serviced ships but built them. In the thirty years up to 1880, over twenty yards were turning out from one to ten smacks, ketches and schooners a year. Fishing also flourished: nearly 200 boats were registered in Falmouth in the 1880s, employing 730 fishermen and 500 men and women in fishing-related trades.

As Falmouth prospered, so nearby Penryn, once a major English Channel port, declined. Once it had shipped out granite for the Fastnet Lighthouse, Waterloo Bridge, Billingsgate Market and Waterford Cathedral. Its shipyards turned out schooners which traded with Newfoundland and South America and shipped live cattle from Spain. But by the mid nineteenth century Penryn had lost most of its trade to its rival across the creek. Today there is no commercial shipping; there is some fishing from the Town Quay, but most of the creek is full of yacht moorings and houseboats.

Tourists relax on the waterfront at Falmouth.

Opposite Falmouth, the little village of Flushing had its own special attractions. In Napoleonic times, according to the *West Briton*, 'Flushing saw more gaiety and elegance of life than any place of its size in England. The streets sparkled with gold epaulets, gold lace hats and brilliant uniforms. There were dinners and parties every evening and three or four dances every night.'

Like other West Country ports, Falmouth was hit by the decline of the copper- and tin-mining industries, and by 1912 the number of ships using the port had fallen to under 3,000 a year when the formation of the Falmouth Docks Company brought in shipbuilding and repairing, which flourished during the First World War. Its successors are now major employers, with thriving bunkering and ship-repair facilities. Pendennis Shipyard, opened in 1989, operates the UK's largest private dry-dock – 850 feet long, and handling ships of up to 85,000 tons.

It is always hard to leave Falmouth, an elegant thriving town with its smart restaurants and cafés, old friends to see, the new Cornish National Maritime Museum to visit and the cool dark beer of the Chain Locker bar, but out on the Carrick Roads a westerly breeze was piping up and it was time for the next part of our journey.

22
Dredging up problems in the Fal

Fishery gets in the blood of all who work in it

'I can tell you that shouting "windward boat" or "starboard" won't do us a damn bit of good,' my son Tim said. 'They come straight at you regardless. We'll just have to get the hell out of here.' With that he started the engine and spun the Moody on her heel onto a reciprocal course. And not before time. Moments later a dozen Falmouth oyster boats thundered past only yards away on a broad reach, their huge rigs heeling the boats over and the crews leaning like dinghy sailors over the weather rails.

As Tim had predicted, none of the oyster boats, locked in near-mortal combat during their regular Saturday afternoon race, had altered course for the Moody, which, on the starboard tack and hard on the wind, had immemorial right of way. 'You'd think they owned the river,' Tim said, but his heart wasn't in his complaint. The racing cutters were a stirring sight. We resumed our course across the Fal estuary on that sunny summer afternoon and a few minutes later dropped anchor off St Mawes for a family picnic to which Wilberforce and I had been invited. By now the work-boats were out to sea, beyond the obelisk on Black Rock, racing hard and still grouped so closely together that their big coloured jackyard topsails looked like a bunch of exotic flowers.

An atmospheric scene on the River Fal a century ago.
W M Harrison /
Reg Watkiss Archive

Who could begrudge the little cutters of the Truro oyster fishery their day out in the sun? The last vessels in Europe to fish commercially under sail, they still dredge oysters in the chilly waters of the Fal and Carrick Roads between October and March under a Victorian bylaw which prohibits fishing under engine. It is hard, unremitting and sadly often unrewarding work when disease and bad weather lay waste the oyster beds, but today there are still a dozen cutters dredging commercially and a further thirty or so in private hands used for pleasure-sailing and racing.

In the mid nineteenth century most Fal oysters were dredged by 'foreigners' – up to 100 east-coast smacks had been counted fishing in the estuary at one time

– and by 1860 the friction between east-coast and Cornish fishermen made some sort of legislation essential. The Truro Oyster and Mussel Fishery Order of 1868 forbade oyster-fishing by mechanically propelled craft and brought all oyster stocks under local control. Soon the wandering fleets of east-coast smacks were seeking new oyster beds in France and even the Bristol Channel, and Cornish fishermen once more had the place to themselves.

Almost coincidentally the bylaws became some of the first pieces of maritime conservation legislation: the inefficiency of dredging under sail compared with under motor has conserved oyster stocks ever since and prevented the almost-inevitable over-fishing found on all other British oyster-layings. The only concession to modernity is that skippers can motor to and from the beds. If there is no wind, which is quite frequently the case in winter, they won't go, and the fishery gets a rest.

Falmouth work-boats developed slowly from a variety of vessels being used to dredge oysters, but by the mid nineteenth century a definite type had evolved: a gaff cutter of anything from 20 to 30 feet, usually half-decked and with a deep cockpit protected by

An oyster-dredger on the Fal estuary, c.1900.
Reg Watkiss Archive

a six-inch coaming. The hull was carvel-built with straight stem and stern, sharp floors, round bilge and a deep iron keel as well as internal ballast. All carried the same rig set on a pole mast – mainsail, staysail and a jib set on a bowsprit which could be half as long as the boat. For racing, a jackyard topsail and big reaching foresail were set, but topsails were never carried while working. Some later boats had roller reefing.

Racing was an integral part of oyster-dredging life, and before long some local boatyards had a reputation for building winners, particularly the Restronguet yard of the redoubtable William 'Foreman' Ferris. Leaving school at twelve after being discounted as a dunce, he became a boat-building legend, producing a succession of classic yachts, ketches and schooners and knocking up work-boats for his friends when business was slack. Foreman's great rival was Frank Hitchens at nearby Devoran. The general view was that Foreman was a better craftsman but Frank's boats were maybe faster.

Their rivalry came to a head in 1870 when the owner of the clinker-build work-boat *Zinguener*, finding she was too deep for oyster-dredging, asked for a shallow-draught carvel-built bottom to be fitted to the boat. Frank Hitchens said it couldn't be done. Foreman Ferris said he'd think about it. Next day he put *Zinguener* on the beach, chocked her up on sheer-legs and sliced the hull through at the waterline.

The job cost £22, including an iron keel, and *Zinguener* was still working a century later.

Today on the Fal they still tell stories about Forman Ferris. In his definitive book *The History of the Falmouth Working Boats*, Alun Davies recalls that Foreman's wife was also a skilled shipwright and that the two of them once went into a field with a cartload of timber, several pasties and a bottle of rum and set to work building a boat. The tale goes that Foreman built one side, his wife the other, and when they bolted them together it was a perfect fit.

Alun Davies in his oyster-dredger *Evelyn*.
Alun Davies collection

Foreman Ferris built his last boat, a punt aptly named *Granny and Grandfather*, when he was 87. Soon afterwards he died peacefully sitting in his chair talking to friends and tamping down the tobacco in his pipe. All along the Fal other small yards – Burt, Hitchens, Jacket, Green and Rutson – were also building exquisite little fishing cutters with love and care. Shortly before his death, Gerald Rutson, the last to run the family's Restronguet yard, wrote to a friend in 1961: 'It is good to recall those happy times when men enjoyed and took a pride in their work and thought more of the craft than the pay.'

Oyster-dredging is skilled and hard work. I had a couple of dredges on my Colchester smack *Shamrock* but have to admit they were mainly for show, and we never really got to grips with how to use them. On the Fal oyster banks, boats dredge with the tide because they are drifting, not sailing. Sails, usually a small jib and reefed mainsail, are backed and scandalised to drift at right-angles to the tide at about one knot. Deliberately making excessive leeway, bigger boats stream three dredges on the windward side of the boat – off the beam, the quarter and the stern. Dredges are only down for a few minutes before they are hauled in and emptied into a box-like table in the cockpit. No oyster of under two inches diameter can be kept. At the end of the drift the boat sails back to the starting-point and begins again. On a good day a boat will complete six to eight drifts in the six hours allowed for dredging on weekdays and a boat's catch could be 40–50 kilos per man. Most Fal oysters go to France or Spain, where prices are better.

It's back-breaking work: dredges are triangular metal frames weighing about thirty pounds with a three-foot-wide mouth and a twined mesh bag. They are attached to up to fifteen fathoms of rope and are usually streamed and hauled by hand. Most sailing-powered dredging is done on four banks in Carrick Roads, but beds further up-river are traditionally worked by 'haul–tow' boats, fifteen-foot punts fitted with two-barrel windlasses. The method of operating is to haul the boat up to an anchor with one barrel and then haul the dredge up to the boat with the other. Fishermen call the punts 'winks' – the nautical term for a hand-operated winch. Today there are only about half-a-dozen active 'haul–tow' punts, mainly because the up-river oyster beds are increasingly unproductive.

The fortunes of the Fal oyster fishery have varied over the years, but it's fair to say that no fisherman has made his fortune from it and most need to do other work in the off-season. There is ever-increasing competition from farmed oysters. In the late nineteenth century over fifty boats were dredging under sail, a similar number in the mid-1920s and over thirty in 1970. This fell disastrously to two full-timers in the 1980s, slightly recovering in the 1990s before Bonamia disease once more decimated the oyster beds.

In recent years the number once again rose to about a dozen, most of them GRP hulls developed by Terry Heard, a dredger-man turned boat-builder, who produced his first glass-fibre work-boat, the 28-foot *Melorus*, at his Mylor yard in 1972. I remember talking to Terry shortly before his untimely death in 1985, when I was thinking of buying a work-boat hull and converting it for cruising. He said that although he loved wooden hulls, the future of Fal oyster-dredging could well lie in plastic. A rebuild of a 100-year-old wooden cutter could exceed £20,000, and what working fisherman could afford that?

As an example, Alun Davies has finally and reluctantly parted with his beloved 1895 wooden cutter *Florence*, built by Foreman Ferris, which he'd owned for nearly thirty years, in favour of a largely maintenance-free GRP hull. 'It was a terrible wrench getting rid of her but the time and money spent on continual maintenance had made her uneconomic as a commercial working boat. It was sensible to get something modern. *Florence* has gone to a racing syndicate in St Mawes and they've promised to look after her.'

Florence racing at St Mawes.
Alun Davies collection

Sadly, times are once again hard for the Fal oystermen. For the past couple of seasons weather and catches have been poor and only seven or eight boats have been regularly dredging. At times like these, men turn to their other trades – fishing, shipwrighting, running smallholdings, anything which pays the bills until the fishery recovers. Alun Davies, the most devoted of dredgermen, reluctantly cut short his season to take a diving industry assignment in the West Indies, something he would never have contemplated when times were good.

Alun is a Cornishman by adoption. He was brought up at West Mersea in Essex, hallowed oyster country, and after school joined the Seasalter & Ham Oyster Company in Whitstable as a management trainee, eventually moving to the beds they owned on the Fal in 1965. Once he saw oysters being dredged under sail, a way of life unchanged for 150 years, his fate was sealed. He bought his first boat, the *Result*, in 1970 and oyster-fishing has largely dominated his life ever since.

Two oyster-dredgers laid up at Mylor.

He finds it hard to be optimistic about the immediate future of the Fal fishery, which oystermen claim has been neglected by the harbour authority and the local council, both of whom would like to see the area of the oyster beds used for more lucrative purposes. 'They couldn't care less about this priceless asset,' is how Alun Davies put it. 'They want to fill the estuary with expensive yacht moorings and there is even a plan for commercial mussel farms, which would inevitably take over the oyster habitat and wreck the ecology of the area.

'An added problem is that many fishermen are no longer able to afford dredging fees, which can be nearly a thousand pounds a year, and consequently the fishery is not being worked as much as it should be. Weed grows and smothers the beds, making it impossible for spat to settle, and ground is being lost by silting. Maintenance work is urgently needed on all the fisheries, particularly those up-river, but who's to pay for it?'

Fishermen were currently meeting officials from the government's fishing and environment agencies in an attempt to work out a strategy which would accommodate all the Fal's environmental and commercial issues. 'Most of the working oyster fishermen are now over sixty years old and we need a new generation to carry on,' Alun told us, 'but this will only happen if they can make some decent money. We want to see the Truro oyster fishery survive for a few hundred years so that future generations can enjoy it as we have.

'The truth is that the Fal fishery gets in the blood of all who work in it. We all know it's better not to have to work, but if it can't be avoided, then take it from me – oyster-dredging under sail, for all its hardships and problems, takes some beating.'

23
Devoran – the port killed by success

The arsenic in the water took care of the nits

W e left Mylor the next morning bound for Restronguet. It is the next creek on the left up the Fal estuary, about five miles north of Falmouth, a peaceful two-mile-long inlet in the hills leading to the small town of Devoran. It is not a place to go if you're in a hurry – and the tide usually makes sure of that. On only a few days a month is there enough water to allow a yacht of even medium draught to negotiate a channel which has silted up dramatically in recent years, leaving Devoran's ambitions to be a major commercial port literally high and dry.

Stay around the entrance of Restronguet Creek and you'll be fine. There's a 12-metre deep pool with moorings, and the celebrated Pandora Inn has its own 40-metre pontoon. Just remember that in Cornwall spring low tides coincide with closing time.

The pub was named in memory of the *Pandora*, the Royal Navy ship sent to Tahiti to capture the mutineers of Captain Bligh's *Bounty*. On the way she was wrecked on the Great Barrier Reef in 1791 and Captain Edwards, in command, was

The coaster *Greta*
and a topsail schooner
at Devoran.
© RIC (RR007)

court-martialled and dismissed the service. The tale has, however, a happy ending: he returned to Cornwall and bought the pub. Wilberforce had mussels, prawns and crab for a fiver and for £1 I had a shower in a sumptuous marble bathroom.

We played safe, left the boat on the Pandora pontoon and walked the two miles round the head of the creek to Devoran, past impressive houses tastefully concealed in trees. James Wharram, of Polynesian catamaran fame, lives in one. It would have been interesting to meet him, but we had an appointment elsewhere.

The Falmouth to St Mawes ferry *Roseland* at Devoran on a summer evening trip, 1907. © *RIC (SR0037.6)*

Today, Devoran – Cornish for 'where two rivers meet' – is a commuter suburb for Truro and Falmouth, but once there was a lordly plan to build a new town from scratch with grand buildings in classical symmetry, fronted by a major port. Devoran would become what its backers called 'a place of professional and commercial significance'.

It very nearly happened. It's hard to imagine now that this sleepy little place was once a boom town with railway lines to nearby tin and copper mines, extensive wharves and shipyards and up to a dozen barges, ketches and schooners loading or unloading timber, coal, iron, copper and tin.

As we walked by the creek, the ruins of the vanished harbour, tidied up by local conservationists, could be seen all around: the tops of granite bollards protruding from the grass, quays submerged in gravel banks and the gaunt frames of wooden steps leading down to nowhere. A series of small docks, once lined with wooden posts, were now shallow pools and the home of water-birds.

Devoran's sadly brief history began in the early nineteenth century when the Redruth and Chasewater Railway was built to bring tin and copper from the Gwennap mines to Restronguet Creek. By 1840 wharves had been built all along the creek and Devoran was a busy and thriving port. Ironically, it was prosperity that killed Devoran: waste from the upstream mines was steadily silting up the creek until the port was only accessible on the highest tides and ships began to go elsewhere.

At the same time, cheaper copper and tin were found in other parts of the world and Cornish mining became uneconomic. By the early twentieth century the port of Devoran was a relic of an extinct species. The mines have now been closed for a century, but their legacy remains in the strange orange-tinged water which still laps the creek. Legend has it that when the mines were working, children who swam in Restronguet Creek never got head-lice. The arsenic in the water took care of the nits.

We caught up with the man we had come to Devoran to see as the sun glinted on the first of the flood tide at the bottom of his garden. Ralph Bird was in the long low workshop attached to his chocolate-box cottage on the edge of the village. He was planing the gunwale of the exquisite 32-foot six-oared Cornish pilot gig he had been building single-handed for the past six months. It was the twenty-second vessel in the past two decades to come from the hands of the man now recognised as the country's finest racing-gig builder and restorer.

Not that you would get Ralph to admit such a thing in a million years. If there was a world championship for understatement, Ralph, a lean and vigorous man in his sixties, would go straight into the semi-finals. 'How do you build a gig? You just put down the keel and then set up eighteen templates we call moulds. Then you plank it up, put in the frames and the rest of the bits and pieces, and that's it, really. There's nothing complicated. It's only just a big rowing-boat, after all …'

Low tide at Devoran.

It was Ralph who in 1972 took off the lines of the legendary *Treffry* we saw in Newquay, built by Peters here on the Fal in 1843 and the benchmark for gig perfection ever since. Today, all gigs under the jurisdiction of the Cornish Pilot Gig Association, of which Ralph is president, have to be exact replicas of *Treffry*, and each is measured a minimum of three times by the Association's inspectors.

The original, still the flagship of the Newquay gig fleet, had not long emerged from Ralph's workshop after a major refit, along with even older gigs including *Newquay* (1812) and *Dove* (1820). 'Everyone wants gigs now,' Ralph Bird said. 'When I first got interested as a youngster there were no gigs in south Cornwall — we had to borrow them from Newquay, and woe betide us if we damaged them. Now there are forty clubs in Cornwall and new ones springing up everywhere. They all want boats – my next gig is going to west Wales. There are about eight

The legendary pilot gig *Treffry*, racing.
Ralph Bird collection

Ralph Bird, and one of his gigs under construction.

builders specialising in building and restoration and there's far more work than we can cope with.'

Today you can expect to wait up to two years and pay at least £18,000 for a thoroughbred racing gig. For that you get well over a thousand hours of craftsmanship, the finest seasoned oak and elm, and skill and tradition which is beyond price.

In the garden workshop of Pilot Gig Cottage, Ralph Bird was readying the as yet unnamed vessel, built for the Cornwall Rowing Association for the Blind, for her paint and varnish. Its delicacy was frightening – elm clinkered planking barely a quarter-inch thick, garboards only three-eighths – and wafer-thin thwarts supported by a central pillar.

Paradoxically it's the length and lightness of the gig and its length/beam ratio of 6.5 to 1 which provides its legendary strength and flexibility and allows it to survive in virtually any sea. 'A hull has to move with the water,' Ralph said. 'If it's too rigid it won't be fast. They got it just right with *Treffry*: the harder she's driven the more she lifts.'

Ralph admitted that the more gigs he made, the more mystifying was the alchemy which differentiates a winner and a loser. 'You try to make them all the same, but they all perform differently. I honestly can't tell you why. Maybe it's the timber you use or the way it's riveted up. I can never be sure how they will turn out until they're finished and in the water. Take the *William Peters*, the second gig I ever built in 1987. I never liked her all the time she was in the shed. Everything went wrong and I was glad to see the back of her. But she was probably the best boat I ever made.'

In his first-floor study, packed with books, pictures and half-models, with boats stirring at their moorings in the silent creek, Ralph Bird remembered how it was that pilot gigs came to dominate his life. 'I come from a long line of boat-builders on my mother's side, and when I left school I got a job in a Falmouth yard building wooden yachts. I started rowing in the Fal when I was a teenager. I became fascinated by the history of gigs. They called them longboats in Cromwell's time, but they reached their present specifications about 1790–1800, when there were at least 200 pilot gigs stationed around the Southwest.'

Eventually superseded by powered pilot cutters, many classic gigs ended up rotting on the beach, were burned or even converted into chicken-houses. 'They'd almost died out after the war and Newquay was about the only place interested in them,' Ralph Bird remembered. 'When I started helping to restore some of the old Newquay gigs you couldn't help be impressed by the craftsmanship of the old boys.'

The tiny Polvarth yard on the Fal at St Mawes, run by the Peters family since the mid eighteenth century, was still the shrine of the gig-builder's art, and it was here that Ralph Bird sought out Frank Peters, descendant of *Treffry*'s builder, then in retirement. 'I told him I wanted to know all about gigs. He was very suspicious at first, but when he realised I was genuinely interested, we sat down and talked for hours. Later we became good friends, and when I started building gigs he would come to the workshop and give me an enormous amount of information about gigs and wooden boat-building which would otherwise have died with him. A lot of older people were resentful of the younger generation but Frank wasn't like that. He did everything to encourage me almost until the day he died.'

Armed with his increased knowledge, Ralph undertook increasingly ambitious restorations at Pilot Gig Cottage. 'I had *Newquay* – she was built in 1812 and is the oldest surviving gig – *Shah* (1873) and *Treffry* in the shed, and they were virtual complete rebuilds. *Newquay* was very bad – I took pretty well all of one side out of her – and *Treffry* was another nightmare. A lot of planking had to go and she needed a lot of new frames, thwarts and knees. I try to save as much as I can but sometimes you have to admit defeat and put in new.'

By now, whether he liked it or not, Ralph Bird was a racing gig icon. 'In 1983, carpentry students at Falmouth Technical College wanted to build a gig and asked me to help out,' Ralph Bird remembers. 'I said I could spare a week or two – and ended up teaching there for seventeen years!'

With interest in West Country gig racing spreading worldwide, the future of these beautiful craft seems assured, but with true Cornish caution, Ralph Bird noted with approval that Newquay's priceless collection of historic gigs is held in trust for the town and so can never be disposed of, or sold. 'You never know what will happen in the future. Those boats are irreplaceable.'

We might have all the modern tools, materials and techniques, but it was Ralph Bird's guess that William Peters and his contemporaries probably forgot more than any modern boat-builder would ever know when it came to building gigs.

Back in Restronguet Creek, there was water around the Pandora pontoons and we left on the top of the tide with questions still unanswered. Did Devoran children still bathe in diluted arsenic? Would Tim have the kettle on when we

Another famous nineteenth-century racing gig – *Shah*, built in 1873 – before and after restoration at Brabyn's yard in Padstow in the late 1940s.
Ralph Bird collection

returned to Mylor? More to the point, who would build those frail and beautiful pilot gigs when Ralph Bird finally called it a day? ·

Truro puts its oar in

Not surprisingly, the city of Truro was all against building docks at Falmouth in the seventeenth century, fearing that it would usurp its position as the Fal's major port. But in fact Truro remained a busy maritime centre well into the twentieth century.

The tug *Empress Victoria*, with passengers aboard and a schooner in tow, on the Truro River at Malpas.
RIC / David B Clement collection

Today small coasters still make the fifteen-mile trip from the sea on spring tides, bringing coal, timber, cement and potatoes, and visitors' moorings are available for pleasure craft.

There has been a town of Truro since the twelfth century and the place became an important port two centuries later, eventually superseding Bodmin and Lostwithiel as the main centre of the tin-mining industry. By the sixteenth century, Truro was assaying nearly half the tin mined in Cornwall and exporting it through its riverside port. The town's merchants diversified into shipping and regularly traded with Rouen, La Rochelle, Bilbao, Bordeaux, Swansea and London.

During the Georgian period Truro became known as the London of Cornwall. Fine mansions were built in surrounding parks and woodland, and 1818 saw the founding of the Royal Institution of Cornwall to encourage literature and the fine arts. Although now a secondary port to Falmouth, Truro still had a fleet of over thirty seagoing vessels in 1820 and was sending tin to Russia, France, Spain and Portugal and copper ore to south Wales.

Truro became a city in 1877. Today, although it still has a silver oar among its civic regalia, Truro is no longer primarily a seafaring place but a bustling

A topsail schooner moored in Truro with the cathedral in the background, *c*.1920.
© *RIC (Teqb1023)*

county seat with a gothic-style cathedral built as recently as 1910, a museum, art gallery and fashionable shops and restaurants. Wilberforce maintains it's worth making a trip to Truro just to walk along the narrow thoroughfare called Squeeze Guts Alley.

24
Charlestown – square-riggers in the mist

A Georgian sailing-ship port preserved in aspic

Cruising boats leaving Falmouth and sailing northeast, skirting Gull Rock and the Dodman, are usually making the easy ten-mile hop to Fowey – and why not? A charming sheltered harbour and two hospitable yacht clubs make it a place always worth a visit. But this time we were sailing elsewhere, turning west beyond Black Head a mere mile from Fowey and into the great sweep of St Austell Bay, looking for the port that time forgot.

To begin with, things didn't look too promising. Spoil heaps from the clay-pits fringe the coast like huge white pyramids to remind us that St Austell Bay means business. Par is a busy clay port which gives yachtsmen short shrift, St Austell is a slightly uneasy mix of modern commerce and industrial archaeology, and the huge and crumbling 1930s entertainment complex at Carlyon Beach, where the Beatles once played, has been the subject of demolition rumours for the past twenty years. Then we saw tall masts above a band of rocks and trees in the northwest corner of the bay and England's only commercial square-rigger port was half a mile ahead in the mist.

Horse-drawn wagons attend schooners in Charlestown harbour in the late nineteenth century.
RIC / David B Clement collection

At first sight Charlestown, a harbour village a couple of miles from St Austell, is a Georgian sailing-ship port preserved in aspic with square-riggers moored at its granite quays and shipwrights, riggers and carpenters busy at their mysterious trades. But what looks like an illusory time-warp is in fact the hard-headed business venture which, against all the odds, keeps Charlestown very much alive.

The chances are that almost any galleon or man-o-war you happen to see sailing across a TV or cinema screen belongs to the Square Sail Company, which has been based in Charlestown's inner harbour for the past twelve years. 'We've had a wonderfully busy year,' Robin Davies, the managing director, told us over tea in his office. 'Just as well, with costs and insurance being what they are.' In his late fifties, he looked more like a farmer than a man who had sailed square-riggers from the tropics to the Arctic, and that's not surprising. He was brought up on the family farm on Mersea Island, Essex, by a boat-mad father who hijacked his kids as yacht crew.

Stormy seas, both meteorological and financial, have been part of Robin Davies's life since the age of 24, when he persuaded his dad to lend him £1,000 to buy a neglected Danish trading ketch and tried to earn a living under sail.

If Robin Davies needed Charlestown in 1994, the place also needed him. Fifteen years earlier it had finally given up the struggle to compete with Par and Fowey as

A schooner and a steamer in the harbour basin in the 1920s.
Robert Simper collection

a major outlet for china clay and kaolin. For the first time in nearly two hundred years it was no longer a working port and was sliding into dereliction.

But then Charlestown has always needed to keep busy. It only came into existence because St Austell wanted a safe port which could handle the tin, china clay and copper being mined nearby in quantities now too big to be shipped from nearby beaches. In 1780, Charles Rashleigh, a mining adventurer, decided to build one, and commissioned John Smeaton, builder of the Eddystone Lighthouse, to create an artificial retained-water harbour in a narrow rocky cove Rashleigh owned at West Polmear.

The port, with an inner and outer harbour, was carved by hand out of solid rock and took twenty years. Rashleigh named it Charlestown after himself and set up such adjunctive industries as rope-making, shipbuilding, lime-burning and a pilchard fishery, but it was clay which brought prosperity beyond even the canny Rashleigh's wildest dreams. By 1850, Charlestown was shipping over 15,000 wagon-loads of clay a year, and this was doubled in twenty years. There was also a large tonnage of copper ore as well as coal, timber and general merchandise and regular work for up to 200 dockers and labourers.

Charlestown was busy and prosperous but the golden days couldn't last for ever and decline, when it came with the First World War, was quick and dramatic. Most freighters had become too large for the narrow lock, although it was widened from 27 feet to 35 feet in a vain attempt to lure in bigger ships. Over the years the harbour frequently changed hands, usually with disastrous results, and it was in a sad state when in 1994, Robin Davies found it largely by chance. He was looking for a permanent home

Steamers and sailing vessels in the busy harbour in 1914. Front left is the steamer *Westdale*.
Herbert Hughes © RIC (CHShs001)

for Square Sail, which had for years been a water gypsy, pushed from port to port – West India Dock, Gloucester and Bristol – to make way for redevelopment. He never expected to find anything as idyllic as Charlestown. He loved the Georgian quays and warehouses, and the atmosphere of timeless elegance.

More to the point, it was for sale. 'I took the biggest gamble of my life and bought it from a property company which had gone bust. It was a once-in-a-lifetime opportunity.' Davies sold his homes in Bristol and Colchester and borrowed to the hilt. 'It was a hell of a gamble, but I'd do it again,' he said. 'These ships have always earned their living at sea from the day they were launched. That's what they're doing now. It's much better than being in some museum.'

Gambling was nothing new to the man who was sailing the estuaries and creeks of Essex as a boy and a few years later was dealing in boats the way a present-day Essex lad might deal in Ford Mondeos. 'My father could hardly blame me when I became as crazy about boats as he was and couldn't settle to anything else. They sent me to be an engineering apprentice but I couldn't bear the thought of being in a factory for the next forty years. Then they made me look after thousands of chickens on the farm and that was even worse.'

Eventually, Davies senior, bowing to the inevitable, lent Robin £1,000 to buy the fifty-year-old *Clausens Minden*, which he rebuilt with his older brother Tony on the beach at Brightlingsea, Essex. For a couple of years they lived on the breadline on charter fishing, and trips round the bay, eventually selling the boat at a profit and replacing it with an 80-foot Baltic ketch. Four years later, Robin Davies sold a three-masted schooner to a German sail-training association for £100,000 – 'it was like winning the lottery' – and embarked on his dream of creating Britain's first fleet of commercial square-riggers for nearly a century.

Robin Davies.
The Square Sail Company

The harbour dressed for filming.
The Square Sail Company

But first Davies needed big ships. There were some terrific bargains around, particularly from Denmark, where square-riggers were being replaced by steel coasters. First came *Kaskelot*, 153 feet, now the flagship, built in 1948 as a Greenland fisheries support vessel. Transformed by Square Sail shipwrights into a replica of a nineteenth-century three-masted barque, *Kaskelot*'s movie credits include *Terra Nova*, *The Last Place on Earth*, *Return to Treasure Island* and *The Three Musketeers*. The *Earl of Pembroke*, one of the last of Sweden's trading schooners, was built in 1945. As a three-masted eighteenth-century barque she has starred in a dozen films including *Moll Flanders*, *A Respectable Trade* and *Cutthroat Island*. Her sister-ship, *Phoenix*, a former Danish Christian mission schooner, now a two-masted brig, has changed her personality as often as an Oscar-winner actor – recent roles include Columbus's *Santa Maria*. She has also toured UK ports as a floating fifteenth-century life-at-sea museum.

'At first it was all we could do to keep afloat,' Robin Davies remembered. 'Then one day a chap just appeared on the quayside and asked if we would be interested in a film he was making. It turned out to be *The Darwin Adventure* for television. It paid well and I could see there was serious money to made in movies.'

A chance meeting with the producer of the TV sea-soap *The Onedin Line* gave Robin Davies his prayed-for big break. 'They were looking for another boat for the series and we had one. From then on we provided all the boats in the series for the next four years and I skippered most of them. *The Onedin Line* really got us on our feet.'

The *Earl of Pembroke*, once a Swedish schooner, disguised as an eighteenth-century barque.
The Square Sail Company

Once installed in Charlestown, and with some unaccustomed cash, Robin Davies lost no time in turning the eighteenth-century quayside into the most unlikely Hollywood outpost. For the five-week filming of *Frenchman's Creek*, in which the *Phoenix* and the *Earl of Pembroke* were attacked by French raiders, the film-set period houses were so convincing that several sightseers offered cash to buy them.

A storm sequence for the film *Amy Foster* showed the *Kaskelot* plunging to her gunwales when in fact the ship never left harbour. 'We rigged a cable to the top of the main mast and rolled the ship from side to side with an 18-ton crane,' Roger McGowan, the company's chief rigger, told us. 'Throw in a few thousand gallons of water and you've got yourself a storm.'

As part of Robin Davies's master plan, Square Sail also provide custom-built

The Square Sail Company's flagship *Kaskelot*, once a Greenland fisheries support vessel.
The Square Sail Company

craft for films – they completed two fifty-oared ancient Greek galleys in fifteen weeks, plus a Viking longship – and can usually transform a ship to any film-maker's requirements in a matter of days.

Wilberforce and I enjoyed our stay in Charlestown. It has largely escaped development and has remained perhaps the most unspoiled small Georgian port on the Cornish coast. There are visitors, but not too many. There is a shipwreck museum and a shop that sells delicious smoked fish. There are moorings available in both the inner and outer harbours, but once again not too many. Again against the odds, Charlestown has once more become a working port – a small amount of clay is once again being exported in around thirty ships a year, thus saving the place from being a cosy caricature of itself with no real sailoring.

And real sailoring was something which was currently occupying most of Robin Davies's waking hours. 'We are now well known in the movie business, but that doesn't generate enough income to keep this place going,' he said – hence his plan to develop Charlestown into a major maritime centre, with sail-training, shipbuilding, and eventually a dry-dock. Over a lunch-time drink, he admitted that he could probably have made a lot more money and got a lot more sleep running some small commercial shipping line. 'The truth is that once you've done square-rig sailing, you'll never be happy with anything else.'

Charlestown was one of the last ports John Short visited in *Annie Christian*. I like to think that he would have been pleased to know that the square-rigged sailing he loved and understood was alive and well in Charlestown more than a century after he sailed away.

25
Mevagissey – Fowey – Polperro – Looe

Hidden delights ... surprises at every turn

I've always thought of the twenty-five miles of coast from Mevagissey in the west to Rame Head in the east as somewhere in need of proper exploration, and yet so often in the past we have been on passage to somewhere like Plymouth or the Scillies, on a tight schedule with a tide to catch, and so many hidden delights have passed us by. For this is a coast with a port around almost every corner and surprises at every turn.

The gently curving coast is in fact a bay of bays. First there's Mevagissey Bay, divided by Black Head from St Austell Bay. Just east of the entrance to Fowey are Lantic Bay and Lantivet Bay, secluded coves ideal for a swim and a Sunday picnic. Sail east another three miles and beyond Polperro are Talland and Portnadler Bays, bordered with rocky islets including St George's Island. East and West Looe lie about a mile and a half further on in Looe Bay, and from then on Whitsand Bay, with its high rugged coast, sweeps southeast some twelve miles to Rame Head. Round the headland is Plymouth Sound. This time we had both the time and the

Mevagissey youngsters at the quayside in 1913.
Reg Watkiss Archive

inclination to loiter, and there were four ports on our itinerary, all different, all significant in their day.

Mevagissey

From Charlestown we back-tracked five miles southwest to Mevagissey, now a busy holiday village but once a major pilchard fishery and still a working harbour with several dozen small fishing boats making a living crabbing and long-lining.

The curious name is derived from the names of two saints, St Meva and St Issey, and there was a harbour on the site as early 1313. The first stone quay was built a century later but Mevagissey remained open to easterly gales until the outer harbour was completed in 1890. By the eighteenth century the place was Cornwall's fourth largest pilchard port: ten local businesses specialised in curing fish, mainly for the Italian market, and shipped out up to 35 million a year. The harbour was continually being enlarged to accommodate the growing pilchard fleet of over 100 luggers employing more than 300 men. Quayside cottages were adapted as curing cellars and storage rooms and many Mevagissey streets were found to be too narrow for loaded pack animals, hence the common sight of men walking in single file with barrels of pilchards slung from poles carried on their shoulders.

Like every Cornish port, Mevagissey built its own fishing boats, mainly open toshers of around 20 feet used to catch pilchards, mackerel, hake and whiting, but by the 1860s Mevagissey yards were also producing luggers and mackerel drivers of up to 40 feet, many sailing as far afield as the North Sea. The winter of 1863 found the Mevagissey lugger *Band of Hope* fishing off the Essex coast. She was completely open except for a tiny cuddy in the bows with 3ft 6in headroom, which was accommodation for four men.

An assortment of boats in Mevagissey harbour, 1909.
RIC / David B Clement collection

Mevagissey boats were claimed to be some of Cornwall's fastest – eight knots was common and many claimed to average ten and sail within five points of the wind with a jib set. Their best point of sailing was with the wind on the beam. The Mevagissey fishing year comprised seasons for crabs, mackerel, pilchard and herring. When catches were poor some of the smaller boats collected seaweed and sold it to farmers as manure.

Today, apart from fishing, Mevagissey's seaborne commerce has gone. The last

The busy harbour at Mevagissey today.

commercial coaster brought in a cargo of salt in 1950 and there was an unsuccessful attempt to introduce Spanish fishing methods a few years later. Nowadays Mevagissey lives on tourism. The cottages in its narrow streets are now gift shops, craft workshops, galleries, cafés and pubs. There are many fish restaurants and fish and chip shops. There is a folk museum, and an aquarium in the old lifeboat house displays locally caught fish. Wilberforce noticed an extraordinary number of shoe shops for such a small place but no one could tell him why.

Fowey

Fowey (locally pronounced Foy) is only some eight miles by sea from Mevagissey but, as we found with Padstow and Newquay on our north-coast trip, in terms of cultural and financial difference the distance was immeasurable. Mevagissey is still in essence a fishing village. Fowey has been a pukka seaport since 1300, when it sent nineteen ships and over 500 men to join the British fleet. A century later it had superseded its great rival Lostwithiel, six miles up-river, as the area's major maritime centre, trading with half-a-dozen European countries and even with Iceland despite a royal ban. There was regular import trade in soap, cloth, canvas, glass, timber, olive oil, raisins, cork, sugar and salt. The more exotic exports included wrought pewter, beeswax and 800 bullocks' horns.

Sail and steam in Fowey, 1914. The steamer *Tenbergen* is alongside an unidentified vessel.
RIC / David B Clement collection

Cook, Drake, Raleigh and Frobisher all sailed into Fowey, as did the celebrated local pirate Captain John Wilcock. Fowey merchants financed the building of his ship the *Barbara*, and it was a wise investment. During a fourteen-day cruise off southern Brittany Wilcock seized fifteen French ships and brought them into Fowey.

But the greatest change in Fowey's fortunes came in the 1870s, when the little ports of St Austell Bay could no longer handle the fast-growing output of the china clay industry and Fowey became for a while Cornwall's major clay port. New jetties were built on the river bank linked by a railway line to Par and soon Fowey was handling about half the output of the Cornish china clay industry, servicing ships of up to 10,000 tons and exporting as far afield as Tasmania, India, the USA, North Africa, Russia and the Baltic ports.

Enchanting Fowey from Hall Walk. A tug tows a three-masted schooner upstream. © RIC (FOWsh.22)

In recent years Fowey has lost some of its trade to Par, which has improved its berthing facilities to accommodate larger ships, but it is still the eleventh largest port in the UK, currently handling nearly 1.3 million tons of china clay a year, although the massive jetties are discreetly concealed from the town. Indeed, the 1,000-acre harbour is now designated as an area of outstanding natural beauty and has become a major yachting centre and tourist destination.

Across the river from Fowey is the village of Polruan, less touristy but full of character and with a very obliging shipwright and rigging repairer. Daphne du Maurier lived nearby for many years. It's believed by the locals that Kenneth Grahame wrote *Wind in the Willows* after sailing up the Fowey river, and that Toad Hall is based on Fowey Hall. It's worth making a trip up-river towards Lostwithiel if you have a shallow-draught boat, if only to see the sign at the village of Golant which reads 'If you cannot see this sign, the road is flooded.' Also at Golant is the Sawmill recording studio, where the pop group Oasis recorded their first album. Not many people know that.

Fowey today.

Fowey, an elegant village clinging to the steep hillside, has a seemingly superhuman population of 2,500 who stride up the near-vertical streets and daunting flights of steps. Wilberforce preferred to stay at sea level in the bar of the King of Prussia. He claimed any exertion was almost certain to loosen the suspect filling in a back tooth.

Polperro

Polperro is often regarded as the most beautiful fishing village in Cornwall. Sheltered in its cliff inlet, the white stone cottages wind up a jumble of steep narrow streets. Around the tiny harbour the houses crowd in so closely that their walls are sluiced by the tide. In my younger days I once took a girlfriend I wanted to impress to the poshest restaurant in Polperro. She ate so much and so expensively that the waiters gathered round to marvel at the size of the bill. Afterwards she said that she wouldn't be seeing me again because she was getting engaged to someone else. To be fair she did thank me for a delicious meal.

Although the distant memory still rankles, it's hard to be disgruntled for long in such an idyllic place. Polperro, like most small Cornish harbours, owed its initial prosperity to pilchards and mackerel and today remains a working fishing port. At high tide we watched local boats unloading their catch in the inner harbour and Wilberforce bought a dressed crab. What makes Polperro different is that it wasn't just another lugger port. It evolved its own distinctive fishing craft, quite unlike anything found in neighbouring harbours: first, small open sprit-rigged boats known as 'spreeties', then the celebrated Polperro 'gaffer'.

It was the violence of the Cornish storms which put paid to the 'spreeties' in two weekends of mayhem. In January 1866, the *West Briton* newspaper reported:

> At Polperro the ruin is dreadful. Out of 45 fishing boats belonging to the place 30 have been dashed to atoms and most of those remaining are incapable of being repaired. Upwards of 60 families are deprived of bread. The pier is nearly destroyed ... the entire damage to Polperro is upwards of £6,000.

When most of the fishing fleet was once more destroyed in 1891, Polperro fishermen decided to try a very different sort of boat. Talks with shipwrights at Looe and Fowey resulted in a carvel-hulled half-decker of around 25 feet with outside ballast and a pole mast setting a loose-footed gaff sail. Nothing like that had been seen at Polperro before and the first arrival, from Hugh Stephens' yard at Looe,

The impressive fishing fleet is seen in this scenic view of Polperro harbour, c.1888 .
© RIC (POPgv78)

was watched by a group of sceptical old-timers as it sailed in.

'Everyone in Polperro had been brought up on luggers and spreeties,' one fisherman remembered. 'Then this thing came in with a gaff sail and a main-sheet on a horse. We all expected it to miss stays in the harbour mouth but it didn't and it made a big impression. Soon people were going over to Looe and ordering their own. A 27-foot hull and spars cost not much more than £40 and would go out in any weather. No one wanted spreeties after that.'

The object of the Polperro gaffer was to get the greatest amount of sail on the shortest possible mast, which included setting a huge reaching jib and a topsail. They were super sea-boats but lively in a lop. Seine-netting for pilchards evolved into an almost surrealistic ritual: two gaffers carrying the nets were accompanied by a small boat known as 'the lurker' which scouted for pilchard shoals and alerted the gaffers by signs – fish were known to be alarmed by noise. Massive catches were left in nets anchored in shallow water for as long as a week and taken ashore each night by the boatload for salting and curing.

There was music on the sea in those distant days. On summer evenings when the Polperro fleet was seining in the darkness someone would start to sing a hymn and gradually the whole fleet would take it up. Sometimes an old fisherman, Tom Mark, would even preach an impromptu sermon, stopping abruptly in the middle of a sentence when his nets began to fill with fish deep in the black water, and beginning again once the nets were hauled. Fishing was a hard and often cruel life but there were moments like these that men would remember all their lives.

Polperro harbour in 1904.
RIC / David B Clement collection

Looe

Some five miles east of Polperro, the villages of East and West Looe stand either side of a tidal river, united by a fine seven-arched bridge. A sheltered land-locked harbour is protected by a distinctive banjo-shaped pier. The drying harbour primarily caters for a fishing fleet of around 35 but there are moorings and quayside berths up-river. For small shallow-draught craft, the river is navigable at high tide for a couple of miles of the nine-mile stretch towards Liskeard.

In fact Looe was once the seaport for Liskeard when it was a centre of Cornish tin-mining, and as early as the fourteenth century a fleet of twenty Looe ships was exporting tin to France and bringing back wine. By the nineteenth century the place was a busy general port dealing in pilchard oil, corn, tobacco, coal and iron. Granite was shipped out for building London's Westminster Bridge and the base of the Albert Memorial.

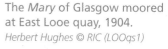

The *Mary* of Glasgow moored at East Looe quay, 1904.
Herbert Hughes © RIC (LOOqs1)

Schooners and ketches moored on Buller's Quay just inside the harbour entrance. Nearby is the yard of the legendary Tom Pearce, builder of some of the West Country's finest luggers and long-liners, including the 28-foot gaff-rigged *Dayspring* – later renamed *Certa* and owned by my friend, the marine artist Leslie Spence. In the 1980s, depressed by her deterioration, he reduced her to firewood with a chainsaw, and has regretted it ever since.

A visitor venturing onto the docks in 1851 left this description of Looe as a busy working port:

> Curious old quays project over the water at different points; coastal vessels are being loaded and unloaded. The inhabitants are as good-humoured and unsophisticated a set of people as you will meet any-where. The women take a very fair share of the hard work out of the men's hands. You see them carrying coal from the vessels to the quay in curious hand-barrows. They laugh, scream and run in each other's way. As to the men, the whole day long they are mending boats, cleaning boats, rowing boats, or standing with their hands in their pockets looking at boats.

A tranquil moment at
West Looe quay, 1888.
© *RIC (LOOhs13)*

Looe had a fishing industry, too. The traditional sprit rig gave way to the lugger in the 1870s, and although gaffers were built in Looe they never became as popular there as the big mackerel-drivers. Crabbing was the main occupation early in the year, using home-made pots made of local hazel and withies. Crabbers shot their pots in fleets, a dozen or more pots attached to ropes marked with buoys and weighted with stones. White stones were thought to bring bad luck and were never used. After crabbing came seining for mackerel, followed in June by drift-netting for pilchards. Looe boats went haking in October and a month later the larger boats would sail east for the herring-fishing off Plymouth or as far as Brixham and Torbay.

Luggers sailing out of Looe.
Stengel / David B Clement collection

Today Looe is an unashamed holiday resort, but we found West Looe the quieter side of town, with a few shops and a good bar in West Looe Square. East Looe sells everything from pasties to diamond-encrusted watches. There are good pubs with tempting menus. We found one on Fore Street which was once a pilchard store. Its floor still slopes to allow the rain to run through and the landlord advises wet-weather drinkers to bring their wellies. Another pub was once a coffin store and is claimed to be haunted. All in all, Looe still has a jaunty seafaring air, but there's no doubt about which way the wind is blowing. The once-busy quays are, slowly but surely, being turned into tourist car-parks.

26
Lethal secrets of the Tamar

Enough arsenic stored to kill half the world's population

To tell the truth, we almost gave Plymouth a miss on our sentimental journey. Our excuse was that the Pilgrim Fathers, Francis Drake, the arrival of Catherine of Aragon, the Civil War siege and four centuries of naval history was too rich a diet to digest in a short visit. And anyway, apart from the ferries in Millbay Dock, there's less merchant shipping in Plymouth nowadays. Instead, we sailed up the sound, past Drake's Island, turned left at the Royal Western Yacht Club and into the Hamoaze, a landlocked six-mile stretch of water which leads into the River Tamar, which was in any event our next destination and where people were waiting to give us tea.

The Hamoaze is lined with naval dockyards, mothballed dreadnoughts and the chilling black humps of nuclear submarines. They don't like amateurs in small boats on the Hamoaze. You get shouted at through loud-hailers if you sidle alongside warships or tack too close to quays piled with sinister-looking things in crates. You also have to watch out for ferries which cross the river on chains, seemingly oblivious to all other river traffic. The chains rise up out of the water in front of the ferries like enormous snakes. Wilberforce found the whole experience of navigating the Hamoaze most disturbing. He was also not convinced that Hamoaze was a real word. Later we discovered that it might have come from the Celtic *hamwose*, meaning the end of a tidal river. Another possible derivation is *hammoaz*, the Phoenician word for fortress. The Phoenicians are thought to have shipped tin down the Tamar some 3,000

Saltash railway bridge and the *Mount Edgcumbe* Industrial Training Ship for Homeless and Destitute Boys, previously the 56-gun HMS *Winchester*.
David B Clement collection

Saltash Bridge, Plymouth

years ago and built a fortress at the river mouth to protect their shipping. By this time Wilberforce couldn't have cared less whether it was a real word or not.

Whatever it was called, the Hamoaze became the heart of Plymouth. A town called Plymouth Dock grew up on its banks, and by the early eighteenth century it was half the size of Plymouth itself. By 1800 Plymouth Dock had grown to 35,000 inhabitants as against Plymouth's 21,000 and was looked on by the city folk as enemy territory and almost as foreign as Cornwall across the river. In 1824 the Dock was officially renamed Devonport, and it became the country's biggest naval base.

Once the only link across the river – the Torpoint ferry at Devonport at the beginning of the twentieth century.
Sarah Foot and Michael Bossiney

But to live up to its new status, Plymouth needed to be made safer. It was open to southwest storms, which made it a dangerous anchorage and which were the main reason why it had always lagged behind Southampton. The building of a massive breakwater three miles out in the Sound began in 1812 and was finally finished in 1841. It is a mile long and has a white granite lighthouse on the western end. Its builders claimed the breakwater made the harbour one of the safest in Europe.

———◆———

On this September Saturday there was little traffic on the Hamoaze. We passed under the road and railway bridges at Saltash and so entered the tidal Tamar, the river I have always regarded as perhaps the most interesting and evocative in the southwest.

The River Tamar at Morwellham.
Morwellham & Tamar Valley Trust

As the flood tide gathered strength, the curiously tinged yellow water looked like high-speed custard and the Tamar carried us on its broad back into the no man's land between Devon and Cornwall. We sailed up sixteen miles of steep valleys edged with oak and ash hanging so low that even our modest mast was garlanded with twigs.

We saw few boats apart from the odd moored dinghy and a few hauled-up salmon skiffs. No movement except the heavy departure of a heron and the splash of salmon riding the tide. Either side of the valley were cherry orchards and still-fruiting strawberry fields, because this strange and largely forgotten place has a microclimate all its own.

It was hard to believe that we were on passage to what within living memory had been Britain's busiest inland port – Morwellham Quay, 23 miles up the River Tamar on the Devon–Cornwall border. Once it served the richest copper mines in Europe and carried more shipping traffic than Liverpool and the Mersey. I had sailed up the Tamar several times in the past, both in the smack *Shamrock* and in my gaff-cutter *Swift*, but we still managed to put the flatner aground outside a pub at Cargreen, luckily on a rising tide.

Rising within two miles of the Bristol Channel and flowing 61 miles to meet the English Channel in Plymouth Sound, the Tamar is for most of its length the boundary between Devon and Cornwall. But only for its last twenty miles is the tidal stream navigable – up to Weirhead, below the village of Gunnislake. But by the middle years of the nineteenth century both banks of the tidal Tamar were dotted with quays, tucked away in lonely places, thick with foxgloves in summer – and today, amid the uneasy peace of industrial decline, a reminder that when Queen Victoria took a trip by steamer in 1856 the Tamar was a major social and commercial highway, and Morwellham was turning round up to a dozen 300-tonners a day.

As traffic increased, groundings and collisions were frequent. In 1841 a marine surveyor named P G Hearder engaged 'two watermen capable of enduring more than ordinary fatigue' to row him from Devonport to Weirhead to compile a pilotage guide which was to hold good for over sixty years.

Mining was responsible for most of the shipping on the river. On his journey upstream, Mr Hearder saw 'huge chimneys pouring forth volumes of smoke and heard the rush of waterwheels and the creaking of mining engines. At Weir Quay, I saw brigs and barges bringing up limestone, culm coal and other commodities and receiving in return freights of metal and metallic ores.' He also reported that 'the people of the Tamar live by its tides, battle with its currents, erratic winds and shoaling bends. The conditions they contend with are arduous to say the least.'

What Mr Hearder saw was the river booming in the wake of the industrial revolution and the great upsurge of mining along the banks of the Tamar, which by the

The *Garlandstone* and the *Lynher* moored at Morwellham.

mid nineteenth century was serviced by at least 300 sailing barges, mostly of 20–30 tons and 30–60 feet in length, one of Britain's largest estuarine fleets.

Barges of a sort had sailed the Tamar, based on the ports of Saltash and Morwellham, since the thirteenth century, and by the 1840s had evolved into bluff-bowed open boats with a single mast and sail. Known as market boats, they were unwieldy to handle and capsizes were not unknown – a market boat overturned in a gale at Bere Ferrers in 1834 drowning all the passengers.

As the carrying trade grew, so did the Tamar barges. A new generation appearing about 1900 carried up to 40 tons of cargo, double that of the market boats. A deck was added forrard plus a small cabin, and a ketch or smack rig was adopted. These were 'inside barges' or Tamar sloops, unregistered and discouraged from venturing outside Plymouth breakwater. Beamy and shallow draught with a hard turn of bilge, inside barges had a heavy transom-hung rudder, sometimes a running bowsprit on which a jib was set, a tanned smack mainsail set on a short mast in a tabernacle, and no topmast. The massive mooring and mainsheet horse on the stern was known as a Plymouth gallows. Wet sand was a perilous cargo, and an overfilled barge sitting on a bank would sometimes fail to rise with the tide. This fate befell the barge *Secret*, drowning the ship's boy, asleep in the cabin.

'Outside barges', registered merchant vessels, were only subtly different from the river-goers – bows sharper with more flair, more freeboard, sloping counters, slightly rounded athwartships and a more pronounced sheer. At a distance they were indistinguishable from West Country trading smacks. Outside barges had a tall fidded topmast on which was set a massive square-headed topsail above a gaff main. Secure with decks and hatches, they worked the Cornish coasts and even the Channel Islands.

It was often said that the coming of the railways killed the Tamar barge trade, but in fact barge traffic in the upper reaches of the river continued after the First World War, when about thirty barges, most fitted with paraffin auxiliaries, battled for dwindling cargoes of stone, sand, bricks and coal. A sought-after freight was dock-dung – the sweepings of the hundreds of horses used in Devonport dockyard and sold to market gardeners up the valley.

About seventeen miles from the sea, at the tiny Cornish port of Calstock, our journey ended for the day as the ebb quickened and we moored under the grandiose neo-Roman railway viaduct that spans the river and town. Only yards away on the Devon bank was the birthplace of some of the Tamar's most exquisite barges and ketches – the Bere Alston shipyard of the legendary James 'Daddy' Goss.

Only a few skeletal remnants of sheds remained among the alders and nettles but Daddy's reputation lived on in the *Lynher*, a beautifully restored Tamar sailing barge, and the classic ketch *Garland-stone*, now to be seen fully rebuilt at Morwellham. Born in 1848, James Goss's early years were turbulent. Sailing as carpenter in an Australian-bound barque, he thumped the captain, who unjustly accused him of theft. He was gaoled in Sydney, but escaped and joined a ship in the 'yellow bird' immigrant trade between China and Australia.

Returning to his native Appledore, Goss, impulsive and hot-tempered – it was

The Calstock viaduct under construction, *c.*1906. On the slipway below is the *Garlandstone*.
Morwellham & Tamar Valley Trust

claimed he could bend six inch nails with a finger and thumb – quickly fell out with his family and walked to Cornwall to build boats for his uncle in Gunnislake before taking over the Calstock shipyard in 1882.

Daddy Goss was an intuitive shipbuilder. He had no knowledge of marine geometry and could hardly read or write but soon he was the busiest boat-builder on the Tamar. The railway line alongside the Tamar was a grievous blow to the barge trade and Goss made the courageous decision to build the 100-ton *Garlandstone* on spec, a six-year project resulting in her sale for a reported £5,000 in 1909. She was the second-last wooden merchant ship built in the Southwest.

Daddy Goss's last barge was the 50-ton *William and Fred*, later used as an ammunition hulk. When he retired, his sons Lewis, Harry and Tom carried

The outside barge *Lillie* nearing completion in the Goss yard at Calstock, 1899 – James 'Daddy' Goss (third from left) with Lewis (holding the dog) and Harry (seated in the foreground. At the right are members of the Larson family – immigrants from Scandinavia.
Morwellham & Tamar Valley Trust

on the yard, building salmon boats and small admiralty vessels. They also repaired barges and made ladders for cherry-pickers. Daddy Goss still kept an eye on things. On one occasion when a barge came in for major repair it was done with such skill that the owner, Jack Crossley, remarked, 'Goss's is a shipbuilders true and proper, not simply a shipwrights or repairers.' Daddy Goss, who died in 1942 aged 94, could not have wished for a better epitaph.

The Cornish copper boom which made Morwellham into a major port was as brief and spectacular as its Klondike counterpart. In November 1844, Josiah Hitchins, a Tavistock mining prospector, digging in abandoned copper workings in a plantation overlooking the Tamar at Gunnislake, stumbled across a 30-foot-thick copper lode – the longest and richest ever found in western England.

Within weeks, £1 shares in Hitchins' mine were changing hands at £800 and prospectors and speculators thronged the Tamar valley. Eventually mines were to spread over 140 acres, with 40 miles of underground galleries, as over a thousand miners worked around the clock. A year later the tiny riverside village of Morwellham (pronounced Morwell-HAM), nearest to the discovery, had become the country's major copper outlet, eventually handling over 30,000 tons a year from its hurriedly constructed wharves. According to a contemporary account,

> So sudden and unexpected was the discovery and in such quantities was the ore being thrown up that the place was crammed with copper, much more resembling heaps of gold, the like of which will never be seen again.

Indeed, during the 1850s and '60s, when its quays were crammed with up to 4,000 tons of glittering ore waiting to be dispatched, Morwellham was the centre of the UK copper kingdom. Eventually congestion on the quays became so great that output had to be restricted until more ships could be handled. In 1859 a new 300-foot dock capable of taking 300-tonners was excavated from the mud at a cost of £5,000. Quays were paved with tiles, constantly washed and swept to prevent mineral ores being contaminated. In the next five years further quays were necessary to deal with the massive imports of timber used for shoring up mines, and the export of 72,000 tons of refined arsenic, worth more than £4 million and used in dyes, paints and glassmaking. It was said that there was enough arsenic stored at Morwellham at any time to kill half the world's population.

The Goss yard, with a schooner (probably the *Eleanor*) and an unknown ketch. The boat in frames is thought to be the *Garlandstone*.
Morwellham & Tamar Valley Trust

Morwellham was transformed from a sleepy backwater to a vibrant port. The Ship Inn, with its specialities of English roast beef and 'October' stout, was a favourite with skippers and crews. A local historian, Frank Booker, recreated the scene in his book *Morwellham in the Tamar Valley*:

> In the golden days of Morwellham's prosperity, masters and crews of Victorian ketches and schooners rounding the bend from Calstock for the first time stared in astonishment at the forest of masts and bustling quays where sailors and workmen chanted and hammered, windlasses creaked and great piles of glistening mineral ores waited for shipment.

The work was relentless. Day and night ore came down from the hills to the quays in carts, down slopes so precipitous that the heavy metal skids became hot enough for the carters to fry their breakfast bacon on them. On the docks, work was equally hard and dangerous: loading a 300-tonner could take two days, and quick turnarounds were rewarded by free beer and cider. There were accidents: a docker was cut in half by a hauling cable and several others crushed to death by falling ore.

A diary kept by 18-year-old Alfred Pengelly, a docker at Morwellham in 1870, records:

> The Ketch *Emma and Esther* berthed on Sunday and we started discharging on Monday. By Wednesday evening we had unloaded her cargo of 180 tons. It was all manhandled – there was no steam winch to haul it out. By Friday, she was ready to go downstream loaded with arsenic. We had worked almost non-stop since Monday. Our pay was a penny-half-penny per ton for each man.

A spot check in 1861 showed twelve vessels being worked on Morwellham quays and four more waiting in the river. Most had brought timber or coal for Tavistock and sailed with copper ore or arsenic. That year, 900 vessels were regularly sailing the Tamar, most Morwellham-bound.

It couldn't last, and it didn't. By the 1860s came the first signs that copper ore was running out, and production dropped to little more than 5,000 tons a year. The mines ceased to pay dividends. The miners moved away and by the 1890 the mines were derelict and flooded and Morwellham sank gently into decay. Over a million tons of copper ore had been removed from the Tamar valley and now all there was to show for it was a ravaged lunar landscape and a forgotten port.

Morwellham lay on history's mortuary slab for over seventy years before volunteers started the daunting task of bringing the place back to life, restoring its long-derelict buildings, including a pub, and making a start digging out its docks – the first stage in a long-term plan to make Morwellham a major maritime centre and encourage working craft to return.

The restoration work took over ten years. What once had been a lordly granite dock was now a huge blancmange-like acre of mud and silt up to ten feet deep on which alders and willows flourished undisturbed. Slowly and stealthily the Tamar had reclaimed its own until by the 1970s only a muddy ditch, hung with brambles, provided refuge for a very occasional intrepid pleasure craft.

James Goss in the 1920s with his sons Harry (to his left) and Lewis (to his right).
Morwellham & Tamar Valley Trust

Reclamation was just beginning when, on a cold September evening in 1975, Morwellham's then curator, George Garlick, could be seen on the river bank pointing to an apparently impenetrable thicket and shouting 'Turn in here!' – and *Shamrock* became the first working boat into Morwellham for at least fifty years. Crashing through the undergrowth, we found ourselves in a water-filled country lane hung with enough blackberries to make a creditable blackberry and apple crumble. If I remember, George opened the pub for us too.

Morwellham has changed a lot since then, and it is now a major tourist attraction and an impressive approximation of its copper-port days. Volunteers come from nearby Tavistock to dress up as Victorian stevedores and man the shops and car-parks. The pub is still operating and there's a museum and restaurant. Even a small mine has been reopened for tourists. Traditional craft are welcome and *Yankee Jack* rafted up comfortably against a Morecombe Bay prawner, which was also a long way from home. Wilberforce was, inevitably, one of the last out of the pub.

Returning down-river after visiting Morwellham, we paused briefly at the idyllic Cotehele Quay, not to inspect the other *Shamrock*, a 104-year-old Tamar ketch-rigged sailing barge saved from oblivion by a six-year National Trust renovation – that would have to wait for another time – but to make a long-arranged visit.

It was a short walk down a lane to a remote granite farm set in the shadows of its own tiny valley. In their vast library, converted from a derelict barn and crammed with exquisite boat models and rare photographs and pictures, Basil and Ann

Dr Basil Greenhill in his library.
© *John Nash*

Greenhill were busy with their latest book, a massive ten-year project on the history of the merchant steamship. Graciously, they stopped and offered us tea.

Dr Greenhill, former director of the Greenwich National Maritime Museum, was the country's most distinguished maritime historian. During his fifteen-year tenure the museum was transformed from a dusty shrine displaying Nelson's underwear into an institution of worldwide influence. His thirty books on maritime history and archaeology, many co-written with his wife, were seminal works. He knew all about flatners, but when I had tentatively contacted him for advice when building *Yankee Jack* I hardly expected that, nearing 80, the great man would jump in his car and drive to Somerset to see what we were up to. From then on, we kept in touch and it seemed unsociable not to visit when we were so near.

Basil Greenhill was a tall thin man with a penetrating look and there was something rather intimidating about him until he started talking about boats. Over tea he said that he still enjoyed what he called 'a gentle potter' with his wife on one of their three boats kept on the nearby river – a clinker-built salmon-boat, a local double-ender and a flat-bottomed Maine lobster skiff. 'I've always had small working boats,' he said, adding somewhat predictably, 'We've never been yachts-people.'

Afterwards, we walked in their huge organic garden, which apparently made the household self-sufficient in fruit, vegetables and eggs. 'Ann's in charge. I'm just the labourer,' Dr Greenhill explained. He said that he had described his hobby in *Who's Who* as 'coarse gardening'. But even in that secluded garden, a large anchor in the herbaceous border served as a reminder that in Basil Greenhill's life and work, the sea was never far away.

We sailed back to Plymouth and Dr Greenhill returned to his library and to the book he never finished. He died suddenly a few months later aged 83. Wilberforce and I were glad we had stopped off for tea on that September afternoon. Wilberforce said he particularly enjoyed the scones.

───◆───

The passage back to Plymouth was mercifully uneventful, but navigating an un-buoyed tidal river on the ebb is always a worry. On the Tamar the general rule is to keep to the outside of the bends but we still managed to scrape the gravel when approaching Weir Quay and were thankful for a boat with a flat bottom of two-inch planks. The channel buoys start on the long stretch of river approaching the elegant modern Saltash road bridge but that's no reason to get complacent. I once managed to put *Swift* aground actually under the massive bridge, and the boat lay on its side like a dog in a heatwave. When the tide eventually rose, water poured through the top seams of the hull and soaked a fruit cake we had bought for tea.

Nothing like that happened this time, and we sailed serenely through the Hamoaze, making such good time that it seem curmudgeonly not to call in on Plymouth now it was so near. We followed a small pleasure-steamer into Sutton Harbour, and this time no-one shouted at us from the dreadnoughts.

With its ferries and fishing fleet, Plymouth remains a salty city, despite the decline of its dockyards and maritime trade. Its magnificent harbour is still busy, but now largely with tourists and pleasure craft. There are half-a-dozen major marinas and plans for more. But happily the essential Plymouth remains. The Barbican, the original medieval seaport, with its maze of narrow streets and alleys, survived the Second World War bombing and is still a working harbour and fishing port.

Plymouth's bustling Barbican in the late nineteenth century.
Valentines /
David B Clement collection

On that sunny afternoon the streets and quay were busy with tourists, but the ancient place still has a maritime bustle and surprises are round every corner. The House That Jack Built is a parade of tiny and unusual shops. In New Street the beautifully restored Elizabethan House, a captain's dwelling dating from 1548, has a spiral staircase winding around an old ship's mast. Across the road, men carried live crabs ashore and fishermen drank tea in a dark shed and threw sandwich crusts to the gulls.

History is everywhere in the Barbican. The Pilgrim Fathers lodged here before leaving on the *Mayflower*. Raleigh, Drake, Hawkins and Cook strolled its quays. Scott of the Antarctic left the adjoining Sutton Harbour on his final fatal adventure. Wilberforce bought some postcards and a dressed crab. Whether that will also ultimately find its way into the history books of the future is not for us to say.

27
Taking an inch at Salcombe

The entrance should not on any account be attempted

When I sailed across Salcombe Bar for the first time, over thirty years ago, I began to wonder if it would be the last. We were surfing sideways in my Essex oyster smack *Shamrock* with half the crew urging the skipper to carry on and the rest telling him to try to turn the thing round and get the hell out of there.

Against the express instructions of the *Pilot's Guide to the English Channel*, we had sailed into Salcombe in a southerly gale and a spring tide and found ourselves in a maelstrom of foam from which rocks protruded like rotten teeth. On that occasion we got away with it, and were soon celebrating with double scotches in the Ferry Inn – but better sailors than us weren't so lucky, including, long ago, thirteen men of the Salcombe lifeboat *William and Emma* and the crews of at least four well-found sailing coasters.

Ironically, Salcombe is one of the most secure of West Country harbours – once you get beyond the bar and behind the ring of hills which protect the pretty, if yachtified, little town from virtually any weather. The entrance to the harbour is in a rocky bay midway between Prawle Point and Bolt Head and the bar stretches from shore to shore, shallowing to less than six feet at low water. The problems

A yawl and a cutter cruise past Salcombe Town.
A E Fairweather / David B Clement collection

come with southerly winds and strong ebb-tides when, according to the *Pilot's Guide*, 'The sea breaks over the bar with such violence that the entrance should not on any account be attempted, even by craft of the lightest draught.'

At first sight Salcombe may look like an estuary, but it isn't. There's no river, but an inland creek running up to Kingsbridge – which on the evening we arrived was as smooth as glass. The town moorings and pontoons were noisy and crowded so we motored slowly past and found a small deserted creek on the edge of a meadow near Scobie Point and sat on a bed of coltsfoot to eat the sandwiches we had saved for supper. It was so quiet we could hear the tide sucking at the stones.

The smack *Yealm* of Plymouth and the paddle-steamer *Salcombe Castle* in Salcombe harbour.
© Judges /
David B Clement collection

Salcombe would seem a strange place for a major West Country port, but when John Short brought in a cargo of timber and coal in the summer of 1900, he found that the town was enjoying unprecedented prosperity. Over 200 vessels employing 1,000 seamen were registered in the town, and some 200 shipwrights built ketches and schooners in four busy yards. That year nearly 17,000 tons of cargo were landed and over 7,000 tons dispatched, mainly local corn, flour, malt, potatoes, slate and cider.

There were six sail-lofts, three shipsmiths and a whole range of specialist craftsmen producing casks, masts, rope and chandlery. But despite the bustle and prosperity, adversity was never far away. In those days Salcombe had the doleful distinction of having more widows per head of population than any other UK seaport.

The reason was not hard to find. The out-of-the-way harbour with its treacherous bar and paucity of deep-water anchorages seemed an unlikely home for a legendary blue-water fleet, but by 1860 nearly 100 topsail schooners were registered there, ships that knowingly sacrificed safety to bring home foreign fruit at speeds which would not be bettered until the tea and grain races involving craft three times their size.

No one could argue that the Salcombe fruit schooners were some of the fastest and finest fore-and-aft traders of their generation, bringing citrus and dried fruit back from the Mediterranean, the Azores and the Bahamas in minimum time, at maximum speed, usually regardless of wind and weather. Regularly pressed to the limit, hatch-covers off in mid-ocean to ventilate the cargo, the safety record of the fruiterers was chilling. In 1851, seven Salcombe fruit schooners sank in a hurricane off the Azores and nearly every family in the town lost a relative.

The yards of Dartmouth, Brixham, Kingsbridge, Galmpton, and eastwards as far as Rye and Colchester all built classic fruit schooners, rarely more than 200 tons and deeply ballasted, but the Salcombe boats had the legs of them all. Their secret

was claimed to be the adoption of the raked clipper bow, said to reduce drag and give a finer entry – but whatever the reason, Salcome fruiterers like the 150-ton *Elinor*, skippered by the redoubtable George Dornom, continually outran the opposition on the 1,200-mile run from the Azores port of St Michael with cargoes of green oranges.

In 1856 her sister-ship, the *Bezaleel*, owner W Sladen, on her maiden voyage, was almost driven under on a record passage from St Michael to

The topsail schooner *Brooklands* (ex *Susan Vittery*), under full sail.
David B Clement collection

Liverpool in five days twelve hours, riding a westerly gale from the edge of the Gulf Stream. Later she was lengthened for the Newfoundland fish trade and was lost in 1884.

By 1850, 15 million lemons and 60 million oranges, each wrapped separately and packed in chests of 1,000, were arriving at London's Covent Garden market between December and May aboard a fleet of mainly Salcombe schooners on the London–Azores run. The West Indies pineapple trade, which began about 1840, rapidly increased to the point where over 200,000 pineapples a year were being shipped into London a decade later.

While London was the main fruit-importing centre, many schooners docked in Bristol, Southampton, Liverpool, Cardiff and Swansea. George Coley, a crewman of the fruiterer *Susan Vittery*, later the *Brooklands*, recalled shortly before his death in 1910:

> We lived like fighting cocks and got £4 a month, twice the usual coasting rates. The skipper kept the ship like the royal yacht. We had a new Ratsays mainsail every year and the very best manila cordage. We had a crew of eight, twice the usual number on a trading schooner, and we always got a bonus if we were first back with the fruit. It was usually a dead run back from the Azores with the prevailing southwesterlies and when we spread out royals, topgallants and studding-sails we could sail off the wind as well as any square-rigger. If we took more than six days from St Michael to the Pool, the skipper would be in a right temper.

The Salcombe fleet rarely visited its home port, but when it did it was a stirring sight, with ranks of bowsprits arching across the town's main street – and on at least one occasion poking accidentally through a pub window. As Salcombe's prosperity as a fruit-schooner port peaked, its top-earning skippers achieved pop-star status with exploits of almost masochistic daring. George Dornom's most legendary exploit was to leave London's St Catherine Docks in the *Elinor* in December 1869 on passage to the Azores in the teeth of a westerly gale which left 100 vessels windrode off the Downs. Undeterred, Dornom, in company with the Salcombe schooner *Emily*, clawed to windward for three days before the *Emily* gave up and put into Torbay. Dornom battled on, reached St Michael in nine days, changed ballast for oranges in 24 hours and was back in the Pool eight days later, passing the same windrode ships on both outward and homeward passages. A renowned speed merchant, Captain Dornom left the *Elinor* the following year for the 170-ton *Rebecca* in the Newfoundland fish trade. She was lost with all hands in 1889.

The crew of the *Susan Vittery*.
David B Clement collection

A typical West Country fruiterer was the 126-ton *Via*, built in 1864 as a heavily rigged double tops'l schooner with royals and stun's'ls. Her flush deck was broken with three small cargo hatches, deckhouse galley and whaleback wheel shelter. *Via* had the characteristic fruiterer's sheer, high flaring bows, sharply raked wide transom stern, and a teak companionway leading down semicircular stairs to a surprisingly elegant saloon with maple and teak panelling, crimson plush settee – the skipper's pride and joy – and a tiled fireplace with a brass mantelpiece.

But, sadly, the *Via* went the way of most fruiterers – she fell out of Lloyds classification and into general home trade. Throughout the 1920s she carried coal

On *Brooklands*'s topsail yard.
Douglas Bennett / David B Clement collection

at rock-bottom rates from Liverpool to Ireland, but just enough to keep her sailing. She was lost on a reef in thick fog while on passage to Kilkeel in 1931. The crew escaped in the ship's punt.

The heyday of the fruit boats was to be less than twenty years, their decline hastened by the steamships now tramping from one fruit port to another snapping up partial cargoes which would have been uneconomic for schooners. Eventually only the Salcombe-registered *Spring* was scratching a living in the

The approach to Salcombe today.

fruit trade before ending her days as a hulk at Gravesend, while *Brooklands*, the last engineless merchant schooner in home waters, became a coal coaster. 'She was a sad sight, with her rig cut down and filthy with coal,' George Coley remembered in a letter to his daughter. 'It is hard to imagine her with all square canvas set, romping up the Channel. It was a hard life on a fruit boat but a true sailor wouldn't have swapped it for any other.'

Today Salcombe has no deep-sea trade and even the fishing isn't what it was. Once the brown crabs caught in the rocky bays around nearby Bolt Head and Bolt Tail were some of the biggest and best in the West Country, but EU regulations governing boats and catches have changed all that, according to veteran Salcombe fisherman Fred Inch. He hadn't a good word to say for Brussels. 'If it was up to them, I wouldn't even be called Fred Inch any more,' he said. 'I'd be Fred Two-Point-Five-Centimetres.'

As we left Salcombe next morning I was thinking about Alfred Lord Tennyson, who had anchored in Salcombe in a friend's yacht in 1889. Sitting on deck on a Sunday evening as the bells rang out for evensong over the water, Tennyson heard how the 'waves gave forth a surfy slow deep mellow voice and with a hollow moan, crossed the bar on their way to the harbour.' A few months later he wrote the poem that was read at John Short's funeral: *Crossing the Bar*.

Wilberforce, too, seemed deep in thought, but not, it transpired, about *Crossing the Bar*. 'Fred Two-Point-Five-Centimetres,' he muttered. 'I must write that down before I forget ...'

28
Dartmouth and the dancing beggars

By midnight we were fending off the rocks with brooms

John Short visited Dartmouth for the last time in *Annie Christian* in the autumn of 1903 with a cargo of steam-coal. On the last of the flood tide she sailed through the narrow entrance, between the high cliffs topped by two Wagnerian-style castles, and picked up a buoy off the town.

The entrance to the River Dart, on which the towns of Dartmouth and Kingswear lie, is some fourteen miles northeast of Salcombe, around Start Point and across Start Bay. One of the most beautiful of West Country rivers, it affords good shelter behind a range of hills and is navigable, with care, as far as Totnes ten miles to the north. Steep wooded banks rising from the river's edge give the winding estuary a sepulchral mystery. I have in the past anchored in a gale among the trees beyond the village of Dittisham, and three miles up-river at water level it has been as calm and peaceful as the grave.

But despite being a popular port of refuge for over 1,000 years (the Pilgrim Fathers put in for repairs on their way to America in 1620) Dartmouth can be

An early view from Dartmouth, looking across the river to Kingswear.
Dartmouth Museum

A panoramic view of the Dart on Regatta Day.
Dartmouth Museum

difficult, or even impossible, to enter under sail when the wind and water funnel between the castles, regardless of conditions elsewhere in the bay.

A variety of hazards on the approach, including a nasty ledge of rocks known as the Dancing Beggars, makes it essential to keep to the narrow fairway. The *English Channel Pilot* warned that 'sudden gusts descending from the high lands surrounding the entrance can blow up squalls of considerable strength in the Narrows, especially if the wind is west or northwest. This makes it unwise or even dangerous to consider proceeding under sail alone and those navigating sailing craft against adverse winds are advised to employ a pilot.'

But to John Short, his skipper Isaac Allen and seafarers like them still coasting under sail, it was all pretty routine stuff, once again emphasising the gulf between those who sailed for a living and those who nowadays do it for what can be loosely called pleasure. I once made an almost identical landfall at Dartmouth to *Annie Christian*'s a century earlier, and a right pig's ear I made of it.

When preparing to leave Exmouth in *Shamrock* for a classic boat race in Dartmouth one summer afternoon we found that the engine had seized solid. The sun was out and spirits were high. It was only 25 miles and wind and tide were fair. Who needed an engine? Seven hours later there was a foul wind and tide and darkness and everything the *Pilot* had warned about entering Dartmouth under sail was fast becoming reality. By midnight we had drifted perilously close to the castles and were fending off the rocks with brooms. Eventually the twentieth century fortuitously arrived in the form of a crabber back from a night's pot-hauling, with diesels roaring and lights blazing, which towed us up-river and put us on a mooring off the town quay.

There was a southeasterly gale the next day and the race was cancelled but we got a trophy for making the most seaman-like passage to the race. I would like to report that honesty compelled us to refuse it, but sadly I can't.

From then on Dartmouth, through no fault of its own, has continued to cause me problems. In wellies and oilskins, one cold spring day, I was swept over the side of a yacht which gybed all standing in that fluky wind between the castles and was chased and hauled aboard by a young crewman who luckily had just boned up on man-overboard procedure for his yachtmaster's exam. On another occasion, again while approaching the castles, I was led, temporarily blinded, to Dartmouth Hospital after a violent gust had torn a staysail from my grasp and lashed a shackle into my eye. Wilberforce, too, had a harrowing tale to tell of having his stomach pumped at the same hospital after an unwise visit to a restaurant known locally as Botulism Joe's.

But on this visit little harm could surely befall us – because *Yankee Jack* was safely away from the sea and on its trailer en route to an open-boat race as part of the Brixham Heritage Week (more of this in the next chapter) and the Dancing Beggars could do their worst as far as we were concerned. Relieved for the moment of any maritime responsibility, Wilberforce and I had a nice time in Dartmouth.

A striking interpretation of Dartmouth Castle by the nineteenth-century artist Thomas Allom.

With a permanent population of around 7,000, which can double in the summer, the pretty town is now a yachting centre, rather than a port, with narrow streets, overhanging medieval houses and restaurants, galleries and antique shops. We met friends for a drink in the Cherub pub and ate elegantly and expensively in the New Angel restaurant, once the Carved Angel, on the South Embankment. Afterwards we strolled gently to Bayard's Cove at the seaward end of the town, a cobbled quay little changed for a thousand years and once featured regularly in *The Onedin Line*. Richard the Lionheart and 146 boatloads of Crusaders had sailed from Bayard's Cove a little earlier, but without the television coverage.

The castles, shorn of their marine malevolence, glowed gently in the late-evening sun. Dartmouth Castle, built in 1481, was the first to be built specifically for artillery and by Victorian times had guns said to fire a distance of two miles. Further protection for the merchant community was provided by heavy chains strung between Dartmouth and Kingswear castles in time of war – and that was pretty often. Dartmouth was involved in more or less every maritime conflict

from the Crusades to the Second World War. The town developed as a port in the twelfth century, when wine and wool were traded, but piracy was soon found to be more profitable, and in 1340 Dartmouth seamen were accused of 'plundering the sea in contempt of the King and to the shame and scandal of the whole kingdom and the delay of important business'.

Geoffrey Chaucer, who had a day job as a customs official, was later sent to investigate Dartmouth piracy, and thus in the *Canterbury Tales* we have the

The brig *Harrier* passing Dartmouth Castle.
David B Clement collection

Dartmouth Shipman, a skilled sailor but also a pirate, and probably based on the town's fourteen-times mayor John Hawley, who built Dartmouth Castle and first slung chains across the river mouth. To avoid these defences, a Breton fleet landed at night on Slapton Sands in Start Bay (it's a nudist beach nowadays). Hawley's ships were away at sea so he gathered a force mainly of women and children, who sent the invaders packing with sticks and stones. Wilberforce said he'd heard that the women of Dartmouth haven't changed a lot since then.

When under threat from the Spanish Armada in 1588, Dartmouth sent eleven ships to join the English fleet and captured the Spanish flagship *Nuestra Señora del Rosario*, which was subsequently anchored in Dartmouth for over a year while the crew worked as servants at nearby Greenway House for Sir Humphrey Gilbert and his half-brother Sir Walter Raleigh. A subsequent owner of the house was the author Agatha Christie. While searching for the Northwest Passage in 1583, Gilbert claimed Newfoundland for England, resulting in Dartmouth becoming pivotal in the colony's cod trade.

The town's Newman family were soon shipping French salt to Newfoundland and then taking the resulting salt cod and meat to Spain and Portugal, bringing back wine to Dartmouth to complete the triangle. To prevent the wine deteriorating on the voyage, it was fortified with spirit, creating sherry and port, whose national distribution was largely controlled from Dartmouth.

Each spring Newmans would recruit what were called 'pauper-apprentices' to be shipped to Newfoundland for an eighteen-month apprenticeship in the fishing trade. Known as 'green-men', they were given the option of returning to England at the end of their indentures but most of them stayed in the colony and a large percentage of the present Newfoundland population can trace their ancestry back to Devon. Newmans stayed in business in Newfoundland until 1907.

But long before then Dartmouth had gone into serious economic decline, ironically caused in part by its most famous son, Thomas Newcomen, inventor of the first practical steam engine. As a result hand-weavers lost their jobs and steamers replaced the sailing ships traditionally built in the town. The economy gradually recovered in the second half of the nineteenth century, mainly because the Royal Navy moved in, training cadets on ships moored in the Dart from 1863 and building the present Naval College in 1905.

In the mid nineteenth century there were still three shipyards in Dartmouth – Moore's, Kelly's and Simpson Strickland – making a tenuous living building smacks and small ketches despite the competition from such classic trawler-builders as W A Gibbs, Sanders and Co. and Calley in the creek at Galmpton four miles up-river. Kelly's had operated the Sandquay shipyard since 1800 and was reckoned to be pretty set in its ways until a young Scotsman, George Philip, arrived with his wife and son to become manager – and turned the place round in pretty dramatic style. Four years later, Philip took over Kelly's and changed the name to George Philip and Son. A few years later he bought out Moore's and subsequently Simpson Strickland.

From 1858 until production finally ended in the last shipbuilding yard in south Devon in 1963, Philip and Son launched nearly 1,500 vessels, from schooners and brigantines to trawlers and classic cruising yachts. Production was at its highest in the Second World War when a workforce of 800 built 230 Royal Navy and RAF

Dartmouth, as seen from Mount Boone, 1889.
© *Francis Frith Collection*

corvettes, minesweepers, minelayers, tugs and air–sea rescue launches. In September 1942 three German bombers attacked the Philip yard, killing twenty workers, including two women, and injuring forty others. But if the purpose of the raid was to put Philip and Son out of business it failed. Production was resumed within 48 hours.

The first commercial vessel built by Philip was the schooner *Mary & Elizabeth* and the last the Brixham trawler *Ocean Spirit* in 1963, but repair work continued until 1999, when the firm converted both Sandquay and the yard they owned at Noss, on the opposite bank, into marinas. I had once owned a pretty little Philip yacht, and after supper on a warm evening walked with Wilberforce to see where *Swift* had been built. We found the site was now occupied by the Dart Marina Hotel. This large and luxurious establishment has a health spa, gourmet restaurants and binoculars in every room for guests to keep tabs on what's happening on the river. It was hard to visualise men in caps and aprons bending planks in steam-boxes in dark workshops and stopping for a smoke.

They had built *Swift* in 1932. She was one of many 30-foot gaff cutters designed by Philip and Son for what they called 'discerning gentleman yachtsmen'. She was a typical West Country long-keeled coasting yacht of the period with a fine entrance, easy turn of bilge and a transom buoyant enough to keep her stern up in a sea-way. She had a coal-stove on which to dry your socks, a wash-basin with brass taps, a tie-rack and some very nice *art nouveau* berth covers. There was nothing fancy or particularly stylish about her fitting-out: just high-quality austere joinery in teak and mahogany, dovetailed drawers, high fiddles, sturdy hand-rails, a spacious chart-table and a galley easily worked at sea. I had *Swift* for five years until eventually selling her to a bookseller in Looe.

The Dartmouth to Kingswear ferry slipway today – the ferry is still the only way across the river.

Eventually Philip went into glass-fibre, producing over fifty 36-foot Atlantic Clippers before venturing into major production with the Philip 43, a cruiser-racer designed by Holman & Pye, to be built at the rate of two a month. Six had been completed when calamity struck. VAT on pleasure craft was increased from 10 per cent to 25 per cent and no yard of any size sold a boat in the UK for six months. Firms like Camper & Nicholson managed to survive on foreign sales, but for Philip, who were still organising overseas markets, it was the end. They built their last Philip 43 in 1975.

During the Second World War American troops took over the Naval College, which became a major base for D-Day rehearsals. The countryside inland from Slapton Sands was evacuated for practice attacks and a fleet of 480 landing craft, carrying nearly half a million men, left the Dart for Normandy's Utah Beach on 4 June 1944.

Today the shipyards have gone, there is little commercial shipping and, although crab-fishing still flourishes, Dartmouth has found true prosperity from yachting and pleasure-boating. On that sunny summer evening as we towed *Yankee Jack* behind the car to Brixham, the castles guarding that unpredictable narrow entrance and the gloomy warnings in Wilberforce's battered *Channel Pilot* were the only visible reminders of how things used to be.

29
Brixham – the best plaice in England

We had to be content with a small brass badge

When I last saw Ken Harris he was leaning over the stern of his beloved Brixham trawler *Vigilance* moored on the town buoys at Dartmouth on a summer evening 25 years ago. Ken was wearing a suit of black leathers and lowering a motorcycle onto his large wooden dinghy with the aid of an iron davit. Balanced on the stern rail was a cardboard box. Ken took the box, climbed down into the dinghy and cast off. He put the box on the stern thwart and at the last moment a black cat jumped down from *Vigilance* and sat beside it. 'Joe's ashes,' said Ken, pointing to the box. 'We're taking them to Compass Cove to throw them in the sea. That's what he wanted.' He rowed away towards the town. The evening sun glinted on the fuel tank of the motorbike and the black cat looked straight ahead.

One-Armed Joe had sailed with Ken for as long as any of us could remember and was one of the few people he allowed into his largely solitary life. In fact there had been little room in Ken Harris's life for much else than *Vigilance*. For 42 years

One of the earliest photographs of the Brixham fishing fleet, taken in 1868.
David B Clement collection

Two trading ketches in the harbour at the beginning of the twentieth century – the fishing fleet beyond.
David James collection

she had occupied pretty well his every waking hour. She was a burned-out hulk when he bought her for £80 when he was in his twenties and by the time he had finished he was drawing his pension. He rebuilt her from the waterline almost single-handed, moving around the country wherever there were cheap moorings, and financed the work with jobbing boat-building, deliveries and eventually chartering. It was an extraordinary feat but then Ken Harris was an extraordinary man. Tall and bearded, he looked like a genial giant in a Grimms' fairy tale and no job was beyond him. He told me once that he had single-handedly taken an ex-army tank engine out of *Vigilance* and installed a replica over one weekend. He had also, on occasion, pulled out his teeth with a pair of pliers to save time going to the

Vigilance (foreground) – home at last.

dentist. He felt that both incidents were hardly worthy of comment. He could also sail the 78-foot trawler on his own at a pinch, using a deck-mounted donkey-engine to haul up the mainsail – but invariably One-Armed Joe was at the helm for races, cruises and charters.

Vigilance, BM76, completed for £1,000 at J W & A Uphams' yard in 1926, was believed to be the final sailing trawler built at Brixham, last of a fleet of classic ketches which had made Brixham the West Country's most successful fishing port. Realistically, *Vigilance* was an anachronism even before she was built. No other major British fishing port still trawled under sail, but Brixham lacked the capital to build steam trawlers and in any event there were no local supplies of coal. In fact *Vigilance* fished out of Brixham until 1937, when she was finally laid up in Uphams' yard for the next twelve years.

Six years later, after the ketch was converted to a yacht, her new owner was drowned and *Vigilance* was virtually destroyed by fire on the day of his cremation. Ken once told me that it was believed the man's widow had started the fire to prevent her son taking over what she believed was a jinxed boat, but the story was never confirmed. In any event, Ken didn't believe in jinxes and he had already decided to undertake the massive restoration, which quickly turned from a hobby into a way of life.

Shortly after Joe was consigned to Davy Jones's locker, Ken sailed away from Datmouth and we lost touch. There were reports of mishaps in south Wales, a trip to the Arctic Circle with a school expedition and a Tall Ships race crewed entirely by women. Then, in 1997, Ken sold the trawler to a group of enthusiasts calling themselves the Brixham Preservation Company and *Vigilance* finally returned to the place where she was built. Today the trawler is moored only yards away from what was once Uphams' yard but is now holiday flats. Slowly, other Brixham

The *Kenya Jacaranda* (formerly *Torbay Lass*) returns for a trawler race.
The Mayflower Sail Training Society

trawlers, most of which had left the port half-a-century earlier, began to come home. *Pilgrim*, built by Uphams in 1895, and long since made into a motor-boat, was brought back to Brixham for conversion back to sail.

Others have returned for the town's revived trawler races in Torbay, and in the summer of 2003 these included *Leader*, *Keewaydin*, *Kenya Jacaranda* (formerly *Torbay Lass*), *Provident*, the mule *Regard*, the mumble-bee class *Golden Vanity* and the lugger *Our Daddy*. They were a fine sight back on the water for which they had been built. Representing the Bristol Channel was *Yankee Jack*, entered in a race for small open fishing boats and looking little and vulnerable among the massive relics of another age. The weather on race day was appalling – heavy rain and a strong easterly which turned Torbay into a lee shore of breaking sea and thick spray.

A young sailor swabs the decks of the *Kenya Jacaranda*.
The Mayflower Sail Training Society

As the smallest boat in the race we were assured that there would be nothing dishonourable in withdrawing before the start, particularly as the weather appeared to be getting even worse. Wilberforce had overslept and was not present for the decision, but our two other crew, Bob Eaglesfield and Rick Pook, said it was up to me and I said I wasn't sure. Three negatives mysteriously made a positive and we found ourselves in the middle of Torbay surfing down ten-foot waves and losing sight of the rest of the fleet as we disappeared into the troughs. The boat was soon half-full of water and we were left far behind but we completed two lengths of the course before we decided that both boat and crew had had enough and made a course for the harbour without rounding the last buoy.

The return was almost a dead run so we dropped the jib and continued on mainsail, rolling and pitching so violently that the spectators watching from the breakwater, especially Wilberforce, were certain that every moment was our last. In one particularly violent gust the boat gybed and with no jib, shrouds or forestay to restrict it the sprit-sail swung round and round the mast and rolled itself up neatly like an umbrella. We baled out over thirty buckets of water when we eventually reached the shelter of the quay.

Swamped but unbowed, Tony, Bob Eaglesfield (left) and Rick Pook return from the Brixham trawler race.

As the wind increased to almost gale force the trawlers ploughed on. We later learned that the open-boat race had been stopped on our last leg and that with our generous handicap, had we rounded the last buoy we would probably have come first and won a large cup. As it was, we had to be content with a small brass badge. The King George V Trophy for trawlers was won by *Vigilance*, sailing serenely round the course without putting in a reef.

Vigilance is the last of a line stretching back to the middle of the eighteenth century, when Brixham boats began catching prime turbot, hake and sole in hitherto unfished grounds up to twenty miles south of Start Point. By 1800 the town had a fleet of 100 trawlers and the harbour, previously a small natural cove on the south side of Torbay, was extended to accommodate them. Some historians believe that Brixham fishermen actually invented modern beam-trawling – certainly they introduced the technique to Dover and Ramsgate in 1815, from where it quickly spread to Great Yarmouth, Hull, Lowestoft and Grimsby.

By 1850, Brixham had the largest fishery in England, with almost 300 vessels totalling 20,000 tons and employing over 1,500 men and women. Most of the fleet consisted of gaff cutters of under 60 feet, known as mules or mumble bees, but by the 1880s these had evolved into the classic Brixham trawlers, known in Torbay as dandies or big sloops, but which were in fact powerful gaff ketches of around 80 feet, capable of hauling trawls over 30 feet wide. By now the harbour was so busy and crowded that many trawlers had to anchor out in the bay, resulting in a catastrophic night in 1866 when 60 anchored craft were driven ashore in a gale, resulting in the loss of 100 lives. The lighthouse was demolished, a dozen wrecked vessels blocked harbour-side streets, and the coast was strewn with wreckage for miles around. A new breakwater was built and from then on up to 300 vessels could lie in safety.

A typical big sloop was around 78 feet overall, 60 feet on the keel and drawing 11 feet. It's generally reckoned that *Ibex*, built and owned by Uphams in 1896 and winner of 29 of her 33 races, was the fastest and most sea-kindly of all the Brixham trawlers. She was skippered by Jack Widger for eighteen years. He loved his ship. 'She goes over the sea like a lifeboat,' he once remarked. 'She's so dry you can walk about the deck in your carpet-slippers. She rises to the sea instead of crashing through it.' He attributed this to the fact that *Ibex* had nearly 40 tons of iron ballast under the fishroom and plenty of air in the hold for buoyancy. 'She handles like a yacht and Mr Upham always makes sure we have the very best sails and manila cordage. He takes it very personal if anyone goes past us.'

That didn't happen very often. The speed of *Ibex* was legendary. Jack Widger remembered leaving Trevose Head on the north Cornish shore against the tide at five one evening and arriving at Plymouth in south Devon, 140 miles away, at 8 am, an average of ten knots – which he regarded as pretty ordinary. Not surprisingly, *Ibex* was virtually unbeatable in regattas and eventually no one would race against her until Uphams agreed to reduce her sail-plan by shortening the boom

A classic picture of Brixham trawlers as a pleasure-steamer approaches the harbour.
David James collection

and taking a cloth off the leech of the mainsail. Paradoxically, the changes only made her faster. She won her first race by 15 minutes and was banned from all future Devon and Cornwall regattas.

But *Ibex* was more than just a racer; she could take care of herself in virtually any weather. Caught in a northeast gale west of Lundy island on a winter's night, Jack Widger was taking a rest below when 'there was an almighty crack. It was three o'clock and the night was as dark as a bag. I ran on deck but I knew the mast had gone. We cut away to make her head come up into the wind and she lay there quite happily like a duck. I got out my accordion and played "A little ship lay on the sea". At daylight we hoisted a jury rig and arrived at Padstow just as a tug came out to tow us in. You could always rely on *Ibex* to look after you.'

The heyday of Brixham trawler-building was the last decade of the nineteenth century, with yards like Uphams, Dewdney, Gibbs and Jackman producing vessels which have never been bettered for power and safety. To cope with demand, Uphams were building three big sloops at a time. The price, including trawling gear, was under £1,000 and there was no shortage of finance. Householders sold their homes to buy into the burgeoning fish trade and by 1900 Brixham claimed to be the wealthiest town of its size in the Southwest. Comic postcards announced 'Brixham is the best plaice in England!'

Brixham remained one of the last strongholds of British working sail, but steam trawlers were taking over the best fishing grounds and when the decline came it was swift and spectacular. In 1914 the Brixham fleet of sailing trawlers suddenly became a target for German U-boats. Six were sunk in one week despite the efforts of an armed steam trawler sent to protect them.

Brixham's fishing fleet today.

Nearly fifty Brixham boats were lost in the next three years and the war had only a few months to go when *Ibex* finally joined them. In January 1918 she was fishing with other trawlers off Berry Head when a submarine surfaced and shelled them. Within minutes, *Ibex*, *General Leman*, *Addax* and *Perseverence* had sunk. Jack Widger, fishing that day in the Uphams trawler *Gazelle*, watched *Ibex* go down. 'It's always tragic to see a ship sink,' he said. 'But she was something special.'

By 1939, fewer than ten sailing trawlers were fishing out of Brixham. Dr Basil Greenhill once told me that he regarded the big sloops as the finest sailing trawlers ever developed in the British Isles and it was a tragedy that fewer than twenty had survived. The town still has a fishing fleet, of course, mainly beam-trawlers and scallopers, bringing in catches which are sold in the busy market in the early hours – but nowadays Brixham is primarily a yachting and holiday town with a huge marina and a large and hospitable sailing club hanging vertiginously from the cliffs. Pubs, shops and art galleries fill the narrow lanes which wind up both sides of the harbour.

At the landward end of the inner harbour a statue marks the spot where William of Orange landed in 1688 to take the crown of England from James II, and nearby Wilberforce witnessed a fight in a fish and chip shop – but fortunately he had already collected our chips. Eating them on the cliffs, we had a wonderful view of Torbay in the evening sunlight. It was while looking across the bay at sunset in 1847, not long before his death from tuberculosis, that Henry Francis Lyte, Vicar of All Saints, Brixham, wrote the hymn *Praise My Soul the King of Heaven*. Wilberforce seemed somewhat depressed by this story. He gave some of his chips to the seagulls and said that watching the race in the wind and rain had given him a cold. Or perhaps even tuberculosis. It certainly didn't seem the time or place to mention that the unfortunate Reverend Lyte had in his final hours also written the funeral hymn *Abide With Me*.

30
A whale of a time on the Exe

We could have been stuck on the sand for a fortnight

The harbours of the Exe estuary in the northwest corner of Lyme Bay were our last ports of call and a logical conclusion to *Yankee Jack*'s sentimental journey. This is another drowned river, stretching some eight miles long and two miles wide, to the south of Exeter. It is a remote and lonely place which dries out almost completely at low tide, leaving a meandering channel through vast mud-flats, the home of waterfowl and flocks of wading birds.

No commercial traffic uses the estuary now. The channel is sparsely buoyed and constantly changing but once it was busy with shipping en route to Exeter, via the six miles of England's oldest canal, and vessels of the Exeter Whale Fishery Company set off each spring for Greenland.

On both sides of the estuary are villages, now quaint and immaculate dormitories of Exeter, which once made a living from the sea. On the eastern shore are Topsham, Exton, Lympstone and the seaside resort of Exmouth, a noisome commercial port until 1991 when it succumbed to marina development. To the

Exmouth docks – centre right is *Kiwi*, next to a gentleman's yacht.
David B Clement collection

west are Starcross and Cockwood and the medieval grandeur of Powderham Castle. Brunel's experimental Atmospheric Railway, running from Exeter to Plymouth and working literally on hot air, ran briefly alongside the Exe before it was abandoned as impractical in 1848.

The evening sun was tipping the top of Haldon Hill and the sandbanks were in deep shadow. The massive body of water, for once almost stationary as the tide turned, was the colour of translucent tomato sauce. The scene had all the makings of a greetings card entitled 'Happy Birthday To A Dear Nephew' and I felt I was home again.

I had taught myself the rudiments of sailing on the Exe many years earlier in an old wooden Enterprise dinghy. Sometimes I would take the dinghy out alone on moonlit nights from the silent villages of Lympstone or Topsham and sail the silver channels between the dark mud. I would have the vast estuary to myself. The tide hit the hull with a strange chopping sound and the wind funnelled up from the unseen sea.

The learning curve was so steep as to be almost vertical. Once I got the tide wrong and had to drag the boat through half a mile of mud. When I forgot to tighten the rigging screws the mast fell down. These simple rules of cause and effect were strangely comforting. Sailing, I decided, was pretty basic and maybe wasn't beyond me after all. Later I had several largish boats on moorings in the river and had many adventures which we can go into another time. Now, years later, I was back among the sandbanks in another little boat, this time one I had built myself.

The *Pilot's Guide to the English Channel* was at pains to point out something I had personally learned the hard way: that the Exe is no place for the faint-hearted.

> Entrance at night or in bad weather should not be attempted by strangers. The channel changes frequently and buoy positions can be misleading. The estuary should not be depended upon as a refuge, particularly in southerly winds. For yachts a reliable engine is essential. The fairway has strong tides with numerous rocky dangers and unmarked ledges over which the tide runs at great strength.

Problems start at the beginning of the Exe fairway, a narrow channel in places less than a cable wide, separated from the sea by Pole Sands and running parallel to the beach for some two miles. At the western edge of Exmouth, where current and sea-tide meet and mingle, a current of up to five knots at spring tides sluices over the sandbanks like a rapid. It was here, in 1865, that some lunatic decided to build Exmouth docks.

Sailing up the channel on a fine summer morning there is little hint of what can be in store. You see golden sands backed by dunes and trees, and then elegant hotel frontages leading back to a gentle hill crowned by Georgian and Victorian terraces. The neglected Lady Nelson lived in one of those high white houses, looking sadly to seaward for the sight of a husband whose ship never came in. Even the few amusements allowed on the beach are fossils of another genteel age: hand-pulled swing-boats and a sedate carousel. From the sea Exmouth, east Devon's largest and most prosperous resort, has the timeless complacency of a Victorian water-colour.

There were commercial ports on the Exe since Roman times, but by the early 1990s Exmouth was the only one left – and was busier than at any time in its 125-year history. The port handled 500 freighters a year, contributing about £4 million to the local economy, and at least 200 people relied on the docks for a living. Bustling, noisy and enveloped in cumulous clouds of hen-food dust, the docks had the boisterous squalor of a busy port, handling five or six freighters on its three quays. Skippers called it the Felixstowe of the south coast. Then in 1991 it was abruptly closed down, to be turned into a £63-million marina village after a bitter two-year battle which divided the town.

Part of the massive re-development of Exmouth docks.

The anti-dock lobby claimed that most Exmothians were fed up with the noise, inconvenience and smell, and that a dock was out of place in an up-market holiday town. 'In fact it was a thriving and successful port and could have remained so, but the owners wanted a lucrative change of use and there was a £13-million marina development deal on the table,' remembered Captain Nigel Stokes, a long-time sailing friend and chief pilot at Exmouth until it closed. 'How many local people could afford what is in effect a luxury housing estate with a few private moorings? The only people to benefit were the developers and wealthy outsiders.'

Nigel had been a pilot at five ports, including Watchet (he is now a senior pilot at Dover), and was in no doubt that Exmouth was the most challenging. 'Before I arrived I heard that if you could be a pilot at Exmouth you could pilot anywhere, and I soon found it was true.' The fairway channel is so shallow that Nigel remembered looking down from the bridge of a freighter he was piloting and seeing shells and sand on the bottom. Ships had to be warped at right-angles into the narrow dock entrance without any assistance from tugs.

'How the old sailing pilots did this if there was the slightest tide running, I honestly don't know,' Nigel said. But he did begin to get some idea after bringing the 100-year-old Dutch steel ketch *Albatros*, Europe's last commercial sailing vessel, into Exmouth on five occasions with cargoes of soya-bean meal. 'She had an engine but it was only an auxiliary, and there were some anxious moments.

Europe's last commercial sailing vessel, the Dutch steel ketch *Albatros* – a frequent visitor to Exmouth.
Capt. Ton Brouwer collection

A barquentine and a three-masted Western Ocean schooner at Topsham quay in 1910.
Topsham Museum / P C Osborne series

The tides were falling. If we had missed the entrance we could have been stuck on the sand for a fortnight!'

The port of Exeter had closed in 1972, and after Exmouth docks shut up shop the only commercial vessel still using the Exe was the South West Water Company's sludge tanker *Countess Wear*, and this finally sailed away in 1997. For the first time since the thirteenth century, when the river was blocked by a weir, there was no commercial navigation on the Exe estuary.

A sedate Edwardian scene as members of the Holman family row on the canal, 1906.
Topsham Museum

It's been said that historically the closure of Exmouth docks was no great loss. 'Topsham and Exeter were the traditional Exe ports,' I was once told by Bill Sleeman, a local historian and author of a definitive book on the area. 'Exmouth was little more than a pilot station.' On the other hand, Topsham, an elegant riverside town four miles from Exeter at the extreme northern end of the navigable Exe estuary, was once regarded as a serious rival to London as a port and shipbuilding centre. A total of 27 warships were built by Topsham yards, including those of Bowdon, Ayles and Davy, for the navy in the Napoleonic Wars. One, HMS *Terror*, built by Robert Davy, was later lost near Baffin Bay on a disastrous expedition attempting to discover the Northwest Passage from the Atlantic to the Pacific in 1845. The crew of the *Terror* died of starvation after being trapped in the ice for twenty months.

Robert Davy lived a few weeks short of his hundredth birthday. He retired after going blind at 84 in 1846 and sold his yard to John Holman, a Topsham master mariner, who built up a fleet of schooners and barques which traded with the West Indies, South America, Japan and Australia. Sadly the shallow estuary, combined with the demand for large iron-built vessels, spelled the end of Topsham's wooden shipbuilding. The Holman family moved their shipping and insurance business to London and their Topsham yard finally closed in 1898 after running at a loss for several years. The imposing dry dock and slipway were demolished just before the First World War.

Today Topsham, with its Georgian and Dutch architecture, is a fashionable Exeter suburb with expensive shops and restaurants. Most of the population of 5,000 seem to own either a Mercedes or a BMW, or both, and park them all in the narrow streets.

(Above left) In 1924 father and son Dick and Jim Voysey pose with their catch – the largest salmon ever caught on the Exe. It weighed over 61 pounds and was presented to Exeter Museum.
Topsham Museum / Underway

(Above right) Tony finds that the occcasion has been charmingly re-created on the wall of a cottage in Topsham's main street.

There are marina berths and moorings for yachts but we had difficulty finding anywhere to buy a loaf of bread. There's little of the seaport about Topsham nowadays. Nigel Stokes took one of the last small freighters up to Topsham Quay in 1990. 'Buoyage ended at the entrance to the Exeter Canal some two miles downstream and from then on the channel, such as it was, was marked by a few posts and withies. It's not an experience I would care to repeat.' It's not likely that anyone will have to.

Some three miles down-river, the pretty village of Lympstone huddles in a small sandstone bay, its tiny streets of white cottages strangely empty and silent on a sunny Saturday afternoon. Some of the houses facing the river seem to use the narrow beach as a front garden, and we walked among lines of washing and a

Topsham's pretty river at low water.

dining table laid for tea. A dog lay asleep on the tide-line. The clock on the elegant red-brick structure known as Peter's Tower at the edge of the sand can be seen only by those with business on the water. You get the feeling that Lympstone is a place which would prefer to keep its secrets and history to itself. Now largely a quiescent dormitory, things were different 150 years ago when *White's Devonshire Directory* described Lympstone as

> A parish of 999 inhabitants and a very considerable fishing station, having about 60 small fishing boats and large beds of oysters in the estuary brought there to fatten from the sea-coast. There are commodious lodgings for the accommodation of visitors who throng there in the proper season.

Lympstone can trace its history back to the Romans, but is more proud of its sailors. Ralph Lane went on Raleigh's second expedition to the New World in 1585 and was later present at the Armada. A descendant was the musical comedy star Lupino Lane, who died in 1959 and whom Wilberforce claimed to have once seen on the London stage but didn't find very funny. John Nutt of Lympstone was a celebrated seventeenth-century pirate. Around the same time, two Lympstone ships, the *Speedwell* and the *Lark*, were captured by Turkish pirates, the dreaded Sallee Rovers. After having their tongues removed, the crews were sold at auction as slaves. Back in Lympstone their families never knew of their eventual fate.

Lympstone – once a major fishing station but always picturesque.
David B Clement collection

But perhaps the most remarkable period of Lympstone's history came in the eighteenth century, when it became the unlikely home of the Exeter Whale Fishery Company. Formed in 1754, the company prospered for thirty years, paying dividends as high as 25 per cent to its local shareholders. The ships left Lympstone for Greenland each spring, returning in July or August with blubber, fins and whalebone. The company's first ship, the 346-ton *Exeter*, sailed annually until 1780 but a second ship, the *Worthy Shepherd*, was lost in the ice in 1759.

A good season's catch was ten whales and 400 seals. The whales were harpooned from small boats and the blubber stowed in casks and boiled ashore when the ships came home. The blubber would then be reduced to about 40 tons of oil. The fins and whalebone were sold through newspaper advertisements. The ships wintered in Parsonage Style, a cove to the south of the village. Much of the profit from whaling came from government bounties, and when these were suddenly decreased the company's remaining ships, *Lympstone* and *Alcyone*, made their last Greenland voyage in 1787 and were sold by auction on their return. Shipbuilding at Worthington Brice's yard continued at Lympstone into the nineteenth century but today, apart from a few small fishing boats, dinghies and yachts, there is little sign of any nautical heritage.

The same certainly can't be said of a house in the neighbouring village of Exton a couple of miles up the road, where nautical heritage is positively bursting with vigorous health to the point where the spacious premises can hardly contain it. One could hardly call a man as outgoing and energetic as David Clement an *eminence grise*, but no one I know has more interest in, and more influence on, the Southwest's historic boat scene – and certainly no one gives more generously of his time and knowledge.

A family man and busy legal consultant, David appears to have found some alchemy which allows him to do twice as much in half the time as normal mortals. Apart from his business, which keeps him constantly on the move, he researches and writes books, chairs the South West Maritime History Society, lectures abroad for the Society for Nautical Research, is Chairman of the Topsham Museum Society, is involved in marina management, and until recently sailed a 52-foot ketch.

Peter's Tower – still telling the time, but for sailors only!

That didn't prevent him taking almost a day out of his relentless schedule to guide us through a dozen huge photograph albums (part of his collection of over 30,000 archive pictures) and offering us anything we wanted for this book. He refused any recognition or payment and he had to be virtually frog-marched to the nearest pub for the meal which was the only form of thanks he would accept. Some of his super pictures grace this book and, whether he likes it or not, our thanks for his kindness and generosity are recorded here.

The Exeter Ship Canal

The last leg of our voyage, the six miles up the Exeter Ship Canal to the basin in the heart of Exeter, was undertaken in heavy rain and took considerably longer than we had planned, mainly because Wilberforce insisted on visiting every public house en route to rearrange his waterproofs and dry his shoes. In each of them he said that while we were there it seemed churlish not to take a small glass of something.

It was in the twelfth century that the Earls of Devon built the first weirs across the tidal Exe, blocking the navigable route to Exeter and forcing boats to unload at Topsham – and charging heavy tolls for transhipment into Exeter, a situation

Mary Eliezer of Hull on the Exeter Ship Canal.
David B Clement collection

which was allowed to remain, despite constant complaints, for the next 300 years. Finally a group of Exeter businessman commissioned John Trew of Glamorgan to engineer an artificial cut which would follow the course of the river, bypass the weirs and rejoin the Exe in the centre of the city.

The finished canal, completed in 1563 and hailed as Britain's first ship canal, was a sad disappointment. True it contained the first-ever locks with vertical gates, but it stretched only two miles from Exeter, was only three feet deep and 16 feet wide, and couldn't be used on low tides. Improvements were made, and over the next 150 years the canal was gradually extended to Topsham, where a lock was built opposite the town. But the canal was still unable to handle large sailing ships. Finally in 1820 a local contractor named James Green was commissioned to reconstruct the entire canal, making it six miles long, 50 feet wide and 15 feet deep, and extending it to emerge into the tidal Exe at Turf, on the opposite bank from Topsham and two miles downstream. But sadly the canal was a marine anachronism. Even before it was finished it was already too small to accommodate the new generation of steamships, and the wool export trade, which it had largely been built to serve, was in terminal decline.

The derelict locks at Topsham on the Exeter Ship Canal, 1978.
© *Clive Ponsford*

Things were no better in Exeter Basin, a 900-foot-long dock excavated alongside the river in 1830 and surrounded by impressive warehouses. Goods were shipped in but couldn't be efficiently removed because Exeter Corporation inexplicably refused to allow a railway line to be built to the dock. It took the South Devon Railway thirty years to persuade the Corporation to change its mind, but by the time it was completed in 1867 the Exeter Ship Canal was so deeply in debt that it couldn't even pay interest on the loans taken out to finance James Green's improvements. Eventually the major creditors took over the canal and its basin for the next sixteen years, and from then on commercial decline was inexorable.

In 1972 the small tanker *Esso Jersey* was the last commercial ship to leave Exeter Basin, and the life of what was once Britain's fourth most important port seemed over. But in fact, in the derelict warehouses on either side of the river, it was already coming back to life in an unexpected form. A retired army officer, Major David Goddard, persuaded the city council to lease the buildings for a maritime museum, which was opened by round-the-world sailor Sir Alec Rose in 1969 with an exhibition of 23 boats. A few years later it had become one of the biggest in the world, with over 100 major static and floating exhibits, and was a major West Country tourist attraction.

David Goddard appeared to run the museum as something of a benign dictatorship, filling it with an eclectic array of craft which took his fancy, ranging from a Bristol Channel pilot cutter, a Venetian gondola, a Bahraini pearling dhow and a Hong Kong sampan to a steam tug and a rowing boat in the shape of a white swan. This eccentric approach had made him enemies among the city councillors, who constantly urged him to organise the sort of themed collection which was currently fashionable.

I had wintered my Essex smack *Shamrock* in the canal basin for several years, and the museum kindly allowed us to use their workshops for fitting out. In 1980, hearing that I was looking for something smaller which could be handled by a smaller crew, David Goddard remarked, 'I think we'd better have her for the museum. Come and have a cup of tea tomorrow and we'll sort out the money.' Next day he was waiting with tea and cakes and a signed cheque for my asking price. 'I know she's got nothing to do with the West Country,' he said. 'But she's a pretty boat and I know you've looked after her.'

Turf Lock and the adjoining hotel today.

So *Shamrock* was moored alongside a Corfu reed-boat and a Portuguese xavega and was regularly used for sail-training over the next seventeen years. Meanwhile, the museum battled through financial heavy weather until it was finally sunk in 1997 and its exhibits dispersed to other collections. *Shamrock* was taken over by a committee of well-wishers and was last reported to be lying ashore in Lowestoft in a piteous state. I was sad to hear it but I wasn't tempted to do anything about it. I felt I had done my bit for old-boat preservation – and so did my bank manager.

Back to the canal. The lock at Topsham no longer exists but you can enter the sea-lock at Turf at half-flood and half-ebb and the slate-hung Turf Hotel, built in 1820, stands alone on a narrow spit of land, protected by windblown yews. There is no public road to pub or lock. Apart from Topsham on the opposite bank of the river, there's virtually no modern civilisation in sight, apart from the London–

Cornwall main railway line, and that's largely hidden by willows. From the lock basin the canal runs north, often only a few yards from the river, through reedy wetlands in a shallow valley. Only pleasure craft and canoeists use the canal now, but fishermen and birdwatchers lurk on its banks and dogs run along the towpath and bark into the wind.

An assortment of craft in Exeter Basin today.

The bridge carrying the unseen M5 spans river and canal above Topsham and is surprisingly low. Even with her topmast reefed, *Shamrock*'s mast would graze the arch when the canal was full – and even in *Yankee Jack* we almost felt we had to duck. A mile further on is Double Locks (actually a single lock), which, at 312 feet long, was once the largest manually operated lock in Britain. Nearby is the Double Locks pub, a CAMRA pub of the year. Wilberforce had a pint of Old Bastard and said he felt all the better for it.

Just before the Exeter Basin, the Welcome Inn sat invitingly on the towpath. They supplied shillings and pence for the juke-box. The basin was full of an assortment of craft, from trawlers and yachts to Dutch barges and cabin-cruisers in various stages of restoration and disintegration. On the land around the basin there had been massive redevelopment, and the place had changed out of all recognition since the days when we wintered *Shamrock* there. Warehouses and dock buildings were replaced by unlikely-looking Italianate piazzas and rows of bijou dwellings. It was hard to believe it had once been a busy thriving port. The riverside warehouses, now apartments and shops, had been skilfully enhanced with *Onedin Line* nostalgia. But on the new developments around the basin, weathered concrete was already starting to give the place a bleak look.

It was raining hard and all the cafés in the Piazza Terracina were closed. I could have killed for a cup of tea. Eventually a friend arrived with the trailer and *Yankee Jack* was hauled out and loaded up for the 50-mile trip to Watchet which would finally complete our West Country circumnavigation. It had taken three weeks longer than Joshua Slocum had spent sailing the equivalent of nearly twice around the world, but then we had stopped off more often for refreshments.

The squares between the new buildings were silent and empty and no one saw us drive away. Neither Wilberforce nor I had thought much about how our sentimental journey would actually end, but we didn't imagine it would be quite as anticlimactic as it was. Wilberforce said it just showed that sailing was always full of surprises. He presumed that no one would object to stopping at the nearest motorway services for a pork pie.

31
Journey's end

I want my tin back

After the voyage, *Yankee Jack* needed a breather. It went into temporary retirement as an exhibit in the Watchet Boat Museum, surrounded by its press-cuttings, and I bought myself a plastic yacht, the first sensible boat I had had for 30 years. It took some getting used to.

The museum is housed in a former Great Western Railway broad-gauge goods shed next to Watchet station on the West Somerset Railway, the longest preserved steam line in Britain. The shed, claimed to have been designed by Brunel, had lain derelict since the demise of the docks three years earlier in 1993 and had seemed the ideal place in which to build *Yankee Jack*. When people started wandering in, usually to pass the time while waiting for a train or to shelter from the rain, it seemed sociable to provide a few small diversions.

Calmer waters for *Yankee Jack*, Tony and his partner Vivienne.

It was the Somerset county museums officer David Dawson who first suggested we organise a small collection of Bristol Channel coastal craft run by volunteers under museum service patronage, and we thought it might be worth a try so long as it didn't cause too much personal inconvenience. The Harold Kimber boat was draped with borrowed spratting nets, and two more flatners, once used for carrying reeds and peat on the Somerset Levels, arrived from the County Museum store-rooms.

A couple of other boats were found locally, one on a town rubbish tip, and were brought in to swell the numbers. The museum service provided green baize boards for photographs and a notice reading 'Museum – Admission Free' and the Friends of the Flattie Association was in business. Bruce Scott, a local boat-owner, was treasurer, John Nash, a former soldier, was curator, and I, for a while, was chairman. On weekend afternoons we put out our sign and sat with our modest collection in the gloom of the huge windowless building wondering if we were wasting our time. None of us really wanted to run a museum. It just happened that way.

Ten years on, the Watchet Boat Museum has assumed a life of its own and has metamorphosed into something that has taken us all by surprise. Today it is actually referred to with a straight face as the World Flatner Centre and is regarded as a leading authority on flat-bottomed boats. Its collection of flatners is the largest and most comprehensive in the country and its historical information on boats and fishing is regularly consulted by researchers and academics. Schoolchildren come on educational visits and old men appear with ancient artefacts in supermarket carrier-bags and tales of lifestyles which have disappeared into history.

One old man had saved some of his pension for two weeks to afford to visit us by bus from Bridgwater to tell his story. He said he had spent his life on the Somerset Levels. Flatners, he said, were farmers' boats. They were rough and ready but could take any punishment. 'When I was a lad I once got lost in the fog and drifted down the Parrett into Bridgwater Bay. They found me two days later run aground off Steart Island. The boat looked after me. I didn't come to no harm. At least not until my dad got me home.'

Tony lets *Yankee Jack* take a well-earned rest in Watchet Boat Museum.
© *George Ody*

In 2001, Dr Basil Greenhill became the museum patron until his death two years later, and extensive alterations and improvements were opened by the local MP Tom (now Lord) King. Bob Thorne, the River Parrett salmon-fisherman, became, whether he liked it or not, our consultant guru – although he made it plain that he couldn't imagine why anyone should want to conserve flatners, which to him were merely expendable tools of the fishing trade.

He had no intention of visiting Watchet, some twenty miles from his cottage, to see what we were up to, saying that car travel made him sick, 'and anyway, no one wants to see all that old stuff.' Only when he had assured himself that we were thoroughly discouraged did Bob lead the way into his maze of sheds, where he gave us a beautifully built oak flatner he had bought in 1948, his grandfather's and uncle's nets, and enough exquisite marine artefacts to fill a small lorry. 'It's nobbut rubbish,' Bob said. 'It's time I had a clear-out.'

Still astonishingly active in his eighties, Bob continues to provide the museum with information, gifts and advice, albeit with all the apparent reluctance of a man extracting his own teeth, but friends have told us that he is secretly pleased to share a life spent in a skilled, hard and largely solitary trade which today no longer exists outside his own memory. On a recent visit, John Nash was presented with a rusting pre-war biscuit tin. Inside, were bills and receipts from long-extinct fishmongers and a meticulous record of every salmon Bob had caught since 1935. 'You can have all this stuff if you like,' Bob said. 'But I want my tin back.'

———◆———

We had returned from our sentimental journey with some doleful statistics. Of the forty Southwest harbours we visited which were busy and prosperous in John Short's time, only a handful were still trading as commercial docks, although fifteen did have fishing fleets of varying viability and a couple were busy clay ports. Some, like Devoran, Lilstock, Hartland, Wadebridge and Highbridge, had been destroyed by natural causes and others, like Exmouth and Bridgwater, had succumbed to lucrative housing development.

It also became apparent that the success of the Watchet Boat Museum was nothing out of the ordinary. In nearly every Southwest harbour which, like Watchet, had closed as a cargo port, nostalgia was alive and well. In museums and marine archives, invariably manned by elderly volunteers, photographs, documents and artefacts of the golden years of coastal trade were being carefully filed and docketed in the hope that someone in the future would be interested to know what life had been like for their forebears who made a living from the sea.

We lost count of the times we heard the lament, 'Nothing's been the same since the big ships left', as we were shown faded photographs of busy port scenes and lists of vessels long since gone under the ship-breaker's torch. In many places the closure of the docks to commercial shipping brought real hardship to the community and was only achieved in the face of determined and even bitter opposition. For instance, in Watchet, Ben Norman has never forgiven his local council for making what he considers only half-hearted efforts to find more business after the resident shipping company pulled out.

There were similar complaints in other ports, including Exmouth, Appledore, Bideford, Bude and Hayle, where the belief remains today that properly organised, small coastal shipping could still be a viable proposition. Sadly, the small British coasters once found in every Southwest port have largely gone, either for scrap or to places like East Africa, the Greek islands and the West Indies, where they are ideal for servicing small island communities.

Tourism and pleasure-boating have brought a new prosperity to many of the more picturesque ports, but it has come at a cost. House prices in previously unfashionable towns have more than doubled in the past five years, often unravelling the tight social structure built up over centuries. There are middle-class accents in the shops and pubs. A typical example is a small Bristol Channel port where locals can no longer find jobs or afford houses. The electrical shop is an estate agent, the butchers a boutique, the shoe shop a restaurant, the bank a centre of Celtic crafts, the greengrocers a charity shop and the bicycle shop an up-market coffee house. Most people now go to a supermarket six miles away for their basic shopping. There are nearly 200 boats in the new marina, mainly owned by outsiders – few local boatmen or fishermen can afford marina prices and many have given up their boats. Ironically, with the increase in pleasure-boating, the harbour is now busier than it has been for years.

It's also ironic that as the days of coasting under sail recede, interest in the preservation of memories of those distant times inexorably grows. The seventieth anniversary of the death of John Short went largely unnoticed but only three years later there are the first stirrings of recognition that this son of Watchet was maybe something special. Recently there were shanty concerts featuring his songs. There is now a small slate plaque on his cottage. It wrongly calls him a master mariner, but it's the thought that counts. Currently there is the possibility of a life-sized statue of John Short overlooking the harbour. The English Folk Dance and Song

Old salts contemplate the Mevagissey harbour scene in 1909. Today the village lives mainly on tourism but is still an active fishing port .
Herbert Hughes © RIC (MEVhs13)

Society now include his picture on their website. Wherever we took the flatner on our travels people asked about its name and we were pleased to explain. Wilberforce on several occasions had to be forcibly restrained from singing all six verses of *The Watchet Sailor*.

On an autumn evening soon after returning to Watchet, Wilberforce and I walk up a steep lane past the paper-mill and its lunar landscape of discarded cardboard, to where St Decuman's church stands alone on a hill above the town, surrounded by a windy graveyard and trees bent by centuries of Bristol Channel gales. This is the kirk on the hill above the lighthouse where Coleridge's *Ancient Mariner* told his story to the wedding guest. Somewhere among the leaning headstones John Short lies buried, but no one knows where. A pity. It would have rounded things off nicely. We could have left a few flowers and maybe taken a photograph, but that isn't why we have come. Our sentimental journey starts and ends here.

It's getting dark. To the north the coast of Wales lies across the grey water like a line of type. To the west the lighthouse on Nash Point on the corner of Swansea

Bay begins to flash. The night wind is rising from the sea and the trees around the church begin to whisper. It's getting cold. Wilberforce puts up his collar. We leave the churchyard in silence, shut the gate and walk down the steep path back into the town.

Wilberforce speaks first. 'It was a great trip, wasn't it?' he says, out of character.

He is right. Yankee Jack had sailed again and we got the briefest of glimpses of what life must have been like under sail before the reassuring presence of engines and electronics. We searched for Highbridge in the mud, surfed into Porlock Weir, fled from the grim rocks of Hartland, sidled past the Doom Bar at Padstow, drifted up the Fal on a still evening, raced with the trawlers at Brixham and were the first boat for decades to sail up the deserted creeks of the Torridge, where the skeletons of stone-barges lay.

We met old friends and made many new ones, and received kindness and hospitality which our largely self-indulgent trip scarcely justified. And everywhere people produced pictures and told stories and even sang songs, anything to confirm that the past had actually happened and wouldn't be forgotten. This book is our small contribution to their efforts.

Tony James

Tony James is a freelance journalist and writer. Before moving to the West Country twenty years ago he was a newspaper and news-agency reporter and Fleet Street editor. The author of over twenty books, he still writes regularly for magazines and newspapers worldwide, specialising in nautical subjects.

He lives with his partner Vivienne on the edge of Exmoor and has two children and three grandsons. When not at sea he plays jazz trombone and double-bass, makes model boats and, under strict supervision from his partner, potters in the garden.

Tony has sailed the equivalent of twice round the world, in a variety of craft, in waters as varied as the Caribbean, the Persian Gulf, the Mediterranean and the River Trent. He now sails a four-berth fin-keeler in the Bristol Channel, but still hopes he is not too old and sensible to take *Yankee Jack* sailing again one day.

Acknowledgements

This book would not have been possible without the help of many people, but I feel I must single out a few for special mention.

My warmest thanks to my good friend Stephen Swann, Editor of *Traditional Boats & Tall Ships*, for detecting the bones of a book in the series of articles I wrote for his magazine and for permission to reproduce some of that material. I also thank him for his constant encouragement at times when it was tempting to scurry back to port and write a book on snooker.

Special thanks are also due to

- David B Clement, the doyen of Southwest maritime research, who threw open his vast archive and gave freely of his time and expertise;

- Martin Hesp, my old mate, for his support and generous foreword;

- John Nash, my friend and colleague (and computer-wizard) for his unfailing help, support and patience as we assembled a vast jigsaw of archive material;

- Ben Norman, author of *Tales of Watchet Harbour*, for giving us the freedom of his picture collection and for sharing his personal recollections of John Short; and

- my partner Vivienne, who has put her own busy life on hold for months to mastermind the project down to the very last detail. I send my love and heartfelt thanks. As usual, I couldn't have done it without you.

Thanks and appreciation go to Patricia Eve and her production team at Seafarer Books, particularly Hugh Brazier and Louis Mackay.

Every effort has been made to ensure accuracy of the facts in this book. Similarly, much research was carried out to ensure the archive photographs have been correctly credited. Apologies for any unintentional mistakes.

Very many thanks, for their contributions, to all those listed below: the trustees, curators and volunteers of museums, other public and private photographic collectors, photographers, interviewees, authors, historians and maritime enthusiasts throughout the West Country. Sincere apologies to anyone inadvertently omitted.

Gerald Ambler, Pawlett, Somerset: archive photographs • Apex News and Pictures (www.apexnewspix.com) • Ralph Bird, Devoran, Cornwall: President of the Cornish Pilot Gig Association • Blake Museum, Bridgwater, Somerset: Jessica Vale, Carolyn Cudbill and David Sebborn • Roy Bolitho, Porthleven, Cornwall • The late Frank Booker: author of *Morwellham in the Tamar Valley* • Cliff Bowden,

Bude, Cornwall • Captain Ton Brouwer, Master of the *Albatros* • Bude Museum, Cornwall: Anne Longley • Charles Cooper, Bridgwater, Somerset • Dartmouth Museum, Devon: Walter Fleet • Alun Davies, Falmouth, Cornwall: author of *The History of the Falmouth Working Boat*: archive photographs • Robin Davies and the Square Sail Company, Charlestown, Cornwall • Pat Dennis, Watchet, Somerset: illustration of Cruel Coppinger • Dovery Manor Museum, Porlock, Somerset: Dennis Corner, historian • Ron Eglinton, Newquay, Cornwall • Sheila Ellis, Clovelly, Devon: author of *Down a Cobbled Street*: photographs by Paul Ashton Ellis • English Folk Dance & Song Society, London: Malcolm Taylor OBE, librarian • Paul Fennel, Wadebridge, Cornwall • Rod Fitzhugh: author of *Bridgwater and the River Parrett* • Sarah Foot and Michael Bossiney: author and publisher of *Views of Old Cornwall* • Alan Francis, Highbridge, Somerset • Francis Frith Collection, Teffont, Salisbury, Wiltshire (www.francisfrith.com) • George Garlick, former curator, Morwellham, Devon • Captain Malcolm Gater, Newquay, Cornwall • John Gilman: author of books including *Exmoor's Maritime Heritage* and *Legacy of Smoke* • Major David Goddard, Exton, Devon • Ted Gosling: author of *Brixham Revisited* (Images of England series) • The late Dr Basil Greenhill • Steve Guscott, Minehead: photographer • Jim Harding, Ilfracombe, Devon • Ken Harris: former owner of *Vigilance* • Hartland Quay Museum, Devon: Mark Myers RSMA, F/ASMA • Graham Haw, Horner Mill Services, nr Porlock, Somerset: archive photographs • Alex Hollweg, Nettlecombe, Somerset • Dr Mike Hope and the Mounts Bay Lugger Association, Cornwall • Ilfracombe Museum, Devon: Sue Pullen • Fred Inch, Salcombe, Devon • David James, Brixham, Devon: archive photographs • Judges Postcards Ltd, Hastings, East Sussex (www.judges.co.uk) • The *Kathleen & May* Trust, Bideford, Devon: Steve Clarke • Peter Lucas, Dartmouth • Lyndale Photo Graphic Ltd, Lynmouth, Devon • The Mayflower Sail Training Society, Maidstone, Kent • The Morrab Library, Penzance, Cornwall: Jan Ruhrmund, photographic archivist • The Morwellham & Tamar Valley Trust: Clive Grenfell, archivist • Captain Chris Muller, Minehead, Somerset • Mark Myers and Michael Nix: authors of *Hartland Quay: the Story of a Vanishing Port* • Harry Nancarrow, Padstow, Cornwall • National Centre for Traditional Folk Music, Dance & Song, Halsway Manor, Crowcombe, Somerset: Cynthia Sartin, librarian • Russell and Susie Needham, Milverton, Somerset • North Devon Maritime Trust, Appledore, Devon: Mrs Pat Wiggett, administrator • George Ody, Minehead: photographer • Terry Orchard, Brix-Boox, Brixham, Devon • John Owen, Stawley, Somerset • Leon Pezzack, Mousehole, Cornwall • Trevor Platt, Padstow, Cornwall • Clive Ponsford: author of *Topsham and the Exe Estuary*: archive photograph • Sue Pullen & Jane Harding: authors of *Ilfracombe* (Images of England series) • Stan Rawle, Minehead, Somerset • The Royal Institution of Cornwall (RIC), Truro, Cornwall: Robert Cook, photographic librarian • Bruce Scott, Watchet, Somerset: photographer • Brendon Sellick, Stolford, Somerset • Robert Simper, Woodbridge, Suffolk: use of photographs from *The Lugger Coast* (The Coast in the Past series) • Somerset Studies Library:

David Bromwich, librarian • Brian South, Roadwater, Somerset: photographer • Leslie Spence, Saltash, Cornwall • Alan Spencer, Porthleven, Cornwall • St Ives Museum, Wheal Dream, St Ives, Cornwall: Brian Stevens, honorary curator • Captain Nigel Stokes, Deal, Kent • Vernon Stone, Watchet, Somerset • Bob Thorne, Pawlett, Somerset • Topsham Museum, Devon: Catriona Batty, documentation officer • Phil Trebilcock and the Newquay Rowing Club, Cornwall • Peter Tutthill: author of *Wadebridge: a Brief History*: archive photographs • Derek Vivian, Crowcombe, Somerset • Watchet Boat Museum, Somerset: John Nash • Watchet Market House Museum, Somerset: Roger Wedlake • Reg Watkiss, Penzance, Cornwall: author of *Lost Cornwall* and *Reflections of Old Cornwall*: archive photographs • Colin Wilkins photographic collection • Bill Young and Dudley Stamp, Bude, Cornwall: authors of *Bude's Maritime Heritage* • Bill Young, Bude, Cornwall: archive photographs • Wilberforce, my stalwart sailing companion.

Index

Page numbers in **bold** refer to photographs

Also from **SEAFARER BOOKS** *www.seafarerbooks.com*

UP THE CREEK
A lifetime spent trying to be a sailor

TONY JAMES

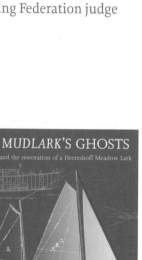

Up the Creek charts Tony James's unintentional voyage from his father's broad bean bed, in landlocked Derbyshire, to a marina in Somerset via the Caribbean, the Persian Gulf and the bottom of a swimming pool in Ottery St Mary. On the way Tony gathers a motley crew of unfogettable eccentrics and maritime misfits, brought to hilarious life by his acute observation of the ridiculous and by his wry acceptance that, whatever happens at sea, things can only get worse. The funniest and most original sailing book for years.

'Laugh-out-loud funny ... unlike any other sailing memoir ... destined to become a classic'
    STEPHEN SWANN – Editor, *Traditional Boats and Tall Ships*

'Waves of humour in a sea of sailing experiences ... will delight sailors and landlubbers alike'
    DON SUTHERLAND – Royal Yachting Association, International Sailing Federation judge

'A comic masterpiece'
    MARTIN HESP – Western Morning News

With a foreword by Stephen Swann • Illustrated • ISBN 0-9547062-7-7 • £9.95

MUDLARK'S GHOSTS
And the restoration of a Herreshoff Meadow Lark

IAN SCOTT

Mudlark, built in 1953, is a modified version of the iconic Meadow Lark, a shallow-draft leeboard sharpie ketch designed by L Francis Herreshoff. But she is about to sink. Ian Scott decides to save her, and to do the work himself. This is the story of why and how he devoted many years to the restoration, and of what he learned in the process – about wooden boats, the timbers they are made of, the designers and craftsmen who make and repair them, the tools they use and, not least, about himself.

'Most how-I-restored-an-old-wooden-boat books will make your eyes bleed. Not this one. Ian Scott's *Mudlark's Ghosts* is literate, intelligent, and informative – an inspiration'
    PETER H SPECTRE – Editor, *The Mariner's Book of Days*

'Into this world of mass production comes a one-off book by a one-off author about a one-off boat ... required reading for anyone contemplating doing up an old wooden boat'
    PETE GREENFIELD

Illustrated • ISBN 0-9550243-1-5 • £14.95

JOSEPH CONRAD: MASTER MARINER

PETER VILLIERS

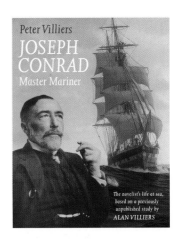

Before he published his first novel in 1895, Joseph Conrad spent 20 years in the merchant navy, eventually obtaining his master's ticket and commanding the barque

Otago. This book, superbly illustrated with paintings by Mark Myers, traces his sea-career and shows how Konrad Korzeniowski, master mariner, became Joseph Conrad, master novelist. Alan Villiers, world-renowned author and master mariner under sail, was uniquely qualified to comment on Conrad's life at sea, and the study he began has been completed by his son, Peter Villiers.

'A book that finally does justice to Conrad's time at sea'
Traditional Boats and Tall Ships

Illustrated with 12 paintings in full colour by Mark Myers RSMA F/ASMA

ISBN 0-9547062-9-3 • £14.95

CRUISE OF THE CONRAD

A Journal of a Voyage round the World, undertaken and carried out in the Ship JOSEPH CONRAD, 212 Tons, in the Years 1934, 1935, and 1936 by way of Good Hope, the South Seas, the East Indies, and Cape Horn

ALAN VILLIERS

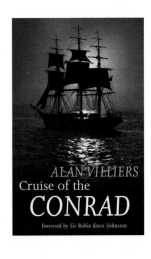

In 1934 the Australian sailor and writer Alan Villiers set out to fulfil his life's ambition – to obtain, equip and sail a full-rigged ship around the world, and enthuse others with his own love of sail before the opportunity was lost for ever. He was successful. His record of that extraordinary journey, more odyssey than voyage, was first published in 1937. In this new edition, complete with a short biography of Alan Villiers and richly illustrated with his own photographs, it will inspire a new generation of sailors and sea-enthusiasts.

'No other book like this will ever be written'
The Sunday Times

With a foreword by Sir Robin Knox-Johnston • Illustrated with photographs

ISBN 0-9547062-8-5 • £12.95

THE LONE RANGER STORY
From salvage tug to super yacht
JON JULIAN

Lone Ranger worked as a salvage tug (then named *Simson*) and towed some of the largest oil installations ever built during twenty of the most challenging years in the history of the business. During the mid-1990s she embarked on a second career and has become the world's pre-eminent exploration yacht. As befits her name she goes to the cold extremes of latitude where few other ships are found, but is also seen in the warm seas of the Caribbean and Mediterranean. Here, her proud and purposeful lines stand out among pleasure craft that have never battled through a storm to take a distressed ship in tow or stood by a bulk carrier threatened with destruction on a lee shore. She begins her fourth decade as supremely seaworthy as ever with more long voyages in prospect, thanks to the vision and commitment of her owner and crew.

ISBN 0-9550243-0-7 · £19.95

ROUGH PASSAGE
COMMANDER R D GRAHAM

In 1934, Commander R D Graham (of Bridgwater) sailed alone in his 30-foot yacht *Emanuel* from England to Newfoundland, cruised on the coast of Labrador, fell ill, sailed to Bermuda in November ('twenty-three days of uninterrupted misery'), wintered there, and finally brought his little vessel back across the Atlantic to her old moorings in Poole Harbour.

Also included is *The Adventure of the Faeroe Islands*, an account of *Emanuel's* 1929 voyage by R D Graham's daughter Helen (later Helen Tew).

Illustrated with original photographs, this new edition of the seafaring classic is brought up to date by Robert Holden's account of the recent restoration of *Emanuel*, allowing R D Graham's 'little yacht' to take her rightful place as part of Britain's maritime heritage.

A must-read for anyone with the slightest interest in the sea, or in human nature.

'One of the most remarkable small-boat adventures of this or any other time'
> *Arthur Ransome*

One of the 'great cruising accounts' listed in Peter Spectre's *A Mariner's Miscellany*

Illustrated · ISBN 0-9547062-4-2 · £9.95

THE WAPPING GROUP OF ARTISTS
Sixty years of painting by the Thames

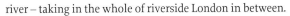

For sixty years, members of the Wapping Group have met to paint by the River Thames en plein air. Outdoors and undaunted in all weathers, come rain or shine, they have set up their easels from the broad tideways of the estuary to the willow-fringed backwaters up-river – taking in the whole of riverside London in between.

With 200 illustrations, the story of the group since 1946, a meditation on the pleasures and pains of painting outdoors, and personal accounts by all the current members, this book captures the essence of the Wapping Group, "the last proper artists' society left in England".

'... a delight to the senses and an essential new addition for any bookshelf'
E14 Magazine

'Sixty years after it was created, the Wapping Group is still flourishing and has won itself a secure niche in the artistic life of the capital ...'
Classic Boat

ISBN 0-9547062-5-0 • £19.95

WITH A PINCH OF SALT
A collection of nautical expressions and other stories
as interpreted by
CAPTAIN NICK BATES

Are you **clewed-up** about all those expressions that so enrich the language of sailors – not to mention the landlubbers who have **Shanghaied** their vocabulary? Do you know **Captain Setab's Second Law of Dynamics**, or why **timbers shiver**, even in **horse latitudes**, where a **brass monkey** has nothing to fear? This little book, **chock-a-block** with the wit and wisdom of a Captain who **came up through the hawse pipe** to command one of the most famous vessels afloat, gives you **the whole nine yards**.

'... a nice piece of work ... remember it when Christmas comes'
Telegraph [NUMAST magazine]

ISBN 0-9547062-3-4 • £7.95

SMEATON'S TOWER

CHRISTOPHER SEVERN

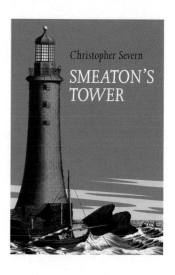

In 1755 the Eddystone Lighthouse was consumed by fire, but still the general opinion was that Nothing but WOOD will last upon the Eddystone. Nonetheless, John Smeaton, the world's first civil engineer, was determined to build a lighthouse of stone on the infamous reef of red rocks fourteen miles out from Plymouth in the English channel. It was a revolutionary design and it became the prototype for other wave-washed lighthouses. Based on Smeaton's own account, and illustrated with Smeaton's engravings and the author's dramatic drawings, *Smeaton's Tower* tells the true story of how the third Eddystone Lighthouse was built, and describes in detail the scale of the achievement. Interwoven with the historical story is a fictional tale of mystery, revenge and love.

'... a throughly researched and refreshingly imaginative read which engages the reader in a way that a dry history could never achieve'

> *Western Morning News*

'... a really gripping read'

> *The Lifeboat*

Illustrated • ISBN 0-9542750-9-8 • £13.95

EDDYSTONE
The finger of light

MIKE PALMER

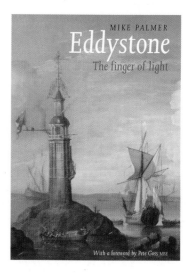

An authoritative and well-researched account of the construction of lighthouses on the savage Eddystone Rocks, this book is a salute to the heroes who struggled to put a lighthouse on the most notorious maritime blackspot of its day – a struggle illuminated by ten years of research, excerpts from the lighthouse builder's diaries and letters, some previously unpublished pictures and a passion for the subject which shines through Mike Palmer's writing. Film maker and author Mike Palmer has been attracted to the sea and in particular to the study of pharology. Indeed with the help of Trinity House he has visited many rock lighthouses. Mike joined the Royal Navy at 15 years of age and has since had a variety of jobs, including baboon and lion keeper, prison officer and ferryman. He won an award for MGM showman of the year.

'A very fine book'

> *The Nautical Magazine*

Illustrated • ISBN 0-9547062-0-x • £13.95